Sports Illustrated

BLOOD, SWEAT AND CHALK

The Ultimate Football Playbook:
How The Great Coaches Built Today's Game

TIM LAYDEN

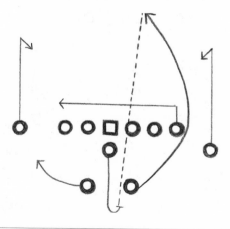

BLOOD, SWEAT AND CHALK

TIM LAYDEN

For Janet, Kristen and Kevin. The home team.

CONTENTS

"Aww, hell, that's the great thing about football coaches. They'll kick your ass on Saturday afternoon and then tell you how they did it."
—BARRY SWITZER

PROLOGUE

I N THE fall of 1997 I spent a week with the Michigan State football team. The coach of the Spartans at the time was Nick Saban, who would later go on to LSU, the Miami Dolphins and Alabama. I spent more time in meeting rooms that week than in any week of my life, watching film with Saban and his coaching staff. Aside from being fodder for a story in SPORTS ILLUSTRATED—and despite the fact that the Spartans would lose that weekend to eventual national champion Michigan—my week in East Lansing opened a window, allowing me to see into the work that goes into planning every snap in a football game, work that's extraordinary in both its volume and detail. Saban's days began in predawn darkness and ended late at night, an effort that foretold championships that would come later at LSU and Alabama. Saban treated every second of videotape as if it might unlock an opponent.

I'd been in meetings before. I'd spent a week at Tennessee with Peyton Manning in 1995, when he was a sophomore, and doubled my previous football knowledge in those seven days. But my week at Michigan State was the first time I had watched an entire staff conceive on paper what they expected to take place on the field. This is what coaches do. Their work is equal parts science and art—the science of outmaneuvering an opponent like a military field commander and the art of understanding the subtleties of players' abilities. Just because you diagram a 24-yard comeback pass to the wide side of the field, that doesn't mean your quarterback can complete it.

In the business of coaching, the word "genius" is tossed around casually. I have used it myself over the years, and more often than I care to remember. Yet whether or not there are true football geniuses, there is, no doubt, plenty of genius in football. In researching this book, I saw it at work many times. I also found that there are a few key principles that help define the way football is coached and played.

• Almost no coach will lay claim to inventing anything. Early in my reporting I had a long conversation with Joe Gibbs, who guided the Washington Redskins to three Super Bowl titles and is regarded as one of the most gifted strategists of modern football. During the interview I twice tried to credit Gibbs with being the "first coach" to run a particular scheme. Both times Gibbs stopped me in my tracks. "You'll never hear me say I was the first to do anything," he said, "because there's a pretty good chance somebody did it before me, but nobody knows about it."

• Occasionally an offense or defense is created out of pure inspirational lightning. But usually not. Most of the time, change grows from weakness or desperation. In 1968, Darrell Royal at Texas was "fixin' to get fired," as they say in Austin, when he let his assistant Emory Bellard install the wishbone (Chapter 4). Fearful opportunism is evident in almost every innovation in the game's history.

• Stealing is an integral, and acceptable, part of the game. If a team does something with success, other teams will copy it. Guaranteed.

• Chalk work is all about concepts. But the game isn't played by concepts; it's played by human athletes. Boomer Esiason was a smart quarterback who executed Sam Wyche's no-huddle offense (Chapter 21) with precision. But when Wyche tried the same offense in Tampa with other quarterbacks, things didn't go so well. An often repeated locker room scenario looks something like this: A coach diagrams a system with X's and O's that shows how it works, let's say a seven-step drop-back pass to complete a post pattern to a wideout. But at the end of his spiel, the coach circles one of the defensive X's and says, "This play should work, but if that X is Dick Butkus, it's a different story. Dick Butkus is too good an X."

ON A cold, foggy morning at Duke University, an hour before sunrise on an early spring weekday in 2008, dormitory windows are dark, office parking lots are empty. In the southwest corner of the campus, adjacent to iconic Cameron Indoor Stadium, shadowy figures begin to appear in the courtyard outside the Yoh Football Center. They shuffle into view like zombies from the mist, wearing blue hoodies and fleece jackets, hands stuffed deep into their pockets, heads dropped low as if they're still beating back exhaustion. Football players start work early.

In a fourth-floor conference room inside the Yoh, quarterbacks convene with Duke offensive coordinator Kurt Roper. The lights are dimmed, but there is no possibility of surreptitious sleep, because Roper, the 35-year-old son of a football coach, plunges into his work with relentless energy. He narrates the day's lesson while using a laser pointer on a video screen and peppers the QBs with terms from the Duke offense. *Shack package; 500 protection; shallow cross.* Roper punctuates his every explanation with the phrase, "Does that make sense?" But it's really not a question, and he doesn't wait for an answer. Because it damn well better make sense to the three quarterbacks sitting at the table.

It is the 10th day of spring practice for Duke in preparation for the opening of the 2008 season in five months. The Blue Devils program is starting over—and not for the first time—after winning just four out of 46 games in the previous four years under coach Ted Roof. In December 2007 Duke hired former Mississippi coach David Cutcliffe. Coaches generally grow from one side of the football or the other; Cutcliffe is an offense guy, having guided the college careers of both Peyton Manning (while the offensive coordinator at Tennessee) and Eli Manning (while the head coach at Mississippi). He can recite pass protections the way an actuary can reel off mortality rates. His friends all call him Cut, which is easy enough to remember.

Cutcliffe was raised in Birmingham, and he has never left what could loosely be called the Football South. He coached at his high school alma mater, at Tennessee and at Ole Miss. And now, Duke. The 53-year-old Cutcliffe speaks in a baritone that has deepened with age and employs the kind of metaphors that younger coaches seldom use.

Like this one, to describe his offense: "My first year at Tennessee as an assistant coach in 1982, the offensive coordinator was [future NFL coach] Al Saunders," says Cut. "He brought some West Coast offense with him. When Al left, Walt Harris came in and we dipped that offense in the Tennessee River and got some of that Pacific Ocean saltwater off it. And we became pretty dominant. Then we went to Mississippi, and we dunked that offense into the Mississippi River. Now we're in North Carolina, just a couple hours from the Atlantic Ocean, and back to the saltwater."

That's a colorful way of expressing what is true of almost every offense (and defense): It is the product of everyone who has touched it.

This book is about the language and the complexity of football. It is about the game that is planned long before it is played, about those hours spent by coaches in darkened rooms conjuring novel schemes to deploy 11 people on a field. It is about a game contested in the mind, about being smarter than the guy wearing the headset on the other side of the field.

On this day in North Carolina, Cutcliffe and his offensive staff are engaged in the process of "installation," the means by which a system is taught to players. Before the start of spring practice Duke players are given two binders. One is the playbook. The other is the "install book," which is broken down by calendar days, with a detailed description of which schemes and plays will be installed on each day, long before the season starts. "The playbook at first is pretty general," says Cutcliffe. "The install book"—Cutcliffe puts his emphasis on the first syllable—"has more specifics to everything they might see in a particular play. Fewer plays, more details."

The install book teaches the language and method of the game, the tools players will use to play football with their brains. One of Roper's fundamental jobs is teaching the new offense to the quarterbacks.

"Learning a new offense is like learning a new language," says Roper. "The players understand football, and they understand plays. But it's like they're thinking in English, and we're teaching them in a foreign language. At this point we tell them something and they translate it back to the other language. Our job is to get them to think in our language."

At this stage, juniors Thaddeus Lewis and Zack Asack are competing for the starting QB position. After practice that day, Lewis describes a play from the Cutcliffe system, freshly dipped in the Atlantic Ocean: Flip Right Don 668 B Shack. It's a play designed to work against a quick blitz and get the ball to the tight end on a short drag route. Lewis is asked to recall what a similar play would have been called a year earlier under the previous staff. He pauses and rubs his chin. "You know what?" he says. "They make you forget it."

Half an hour later Cutcliffe is back in his office. It's a long way from four wins in four seasons to anything resembling success. There are photos of both Manning brothers on Cutcliffe's office wall, a reminder of where he has been and also of the distance left to travel now. "This team is pretty long on want-to at this point," Cutcliffe is saying to a couple of friends in town from Knoxville. "But we're a little short on know-how."

(They will get better: With Lewis throwing for more than 5,500 yards over two seasons, the Blue Devils will win a total of nine games in 2008 and 2009.)

Like any coach, Cutcliffe draws upon the methods and terminology of an earlier era. In coaching parlance the term *cut-ups* is used to describe pieces of video arranged to address a particular aspect of the game—red zone offense, third-and-long defense, or any other scenario. When game film was actually film, cut-ups were made by cutting the film with scissors (thus the name) and splicing together the sections needed for study. Cutcliffe has been coaching long enough that in his early years he actually cut up film. "You had to remember, 'Shiny side up, shiny side up,'" he says. "Because if you didn't, it would come out backward, and you'd have a lefthanded quarterback and a lot of other problems."

He asks about the book, and what systems will be covered. Names are exchanged: West Coast offense, zone blitz, wishbone and many others. From a small notepad of Duke football stationery, he snatches three pages and begins drawing up zone blitzes, having seized on that scheme. He scribbles furiously, narrating. This is something all coaches are inclined to do. Then he stops suddenly. "You know what?" he says in that deep voice, straight out of Birmingham. "Here's what a system does: It tries to put players in a position to succeed. That's what it is."

SINCE MODERN football first began taking shape not long after the turn of the 20th century, hundreds of offenses and defenses have been tried. Fourteen of them, some with variations, are examined in this book. It's not a comprehensive selection but a representative one, exalting those systems that have either endured or profoundly impacted the game. Beyond the X's and O's, though, these pages tell the stories of the men who held the chalk.

It all starts—as does nearly everything in football—with Pop Warner.

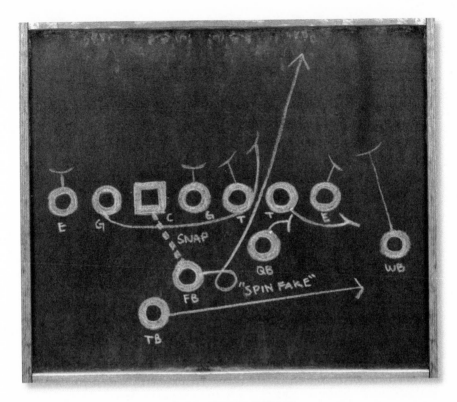

A-9—THE SPIN

From Glenn Scobey (Pop) Warner's 1908 single wing playbook, this play is a classic combo of power and deception. From an "A formation," with an unbalanced line (two tackles on the right side), the ball is snapped to the "up" back (FB), who then spins clockwise a full 360 degrees, faking the handoff to the tailback, who carries out his fake around right end. The outside tackle pulls to the right, enticing the defensive lineman to charge into the backfield, where he is blocked by the "quarterback" (essentially a blocking back in the single wing). The left guard pulls to the right and runs through the hole vacated by the pulling tackle, then seals off the middle linebacker. The right guard and inside tackle execute a double-team block on the defensive tackle. After executing his spin fake, the fullback follows the pulling guard through the hole.

CHAPTER 1

THE SINGLE WING

It's more than 100 years old, the offense of Pop Warner, but it's still out on the field today—you can ask Bill Belichick

September 21, 2008

O N THIS Sunday after-noon, a high school foot-ball player named Jeremy Gallon was at home in Apopka, Fla., doing what America does every Sunday afternoon in the fall: watching the NFL on television. Right there on Jeremy's screen, the Miami Dolphins dismantled the New England Patriots 38–13, ending the Patriots' 21-game regular-season winning streak. Six times during the game the Dolphins lined up with running back Ronnie Brown in the position normally occupied by a shotgun quarterback. Brown ran, passed and handed off to fellow running back Ricky Williams. The Patriots played as if they had never seen such football, and in fact, most of them had not. But Jeremy Gallon had.

Eighteen months earlier, just before the start of spring football practice at Apopka High, a large suburban school 15 miles northwest of Orlando, head coach Rick Darlington had laid out the offense that the Blue Darters would be running in the coming season. There would be no quarterback. There would be a running back who would receive shotgun snaps and just take off with the ball. Another running back would be lined up right next to him, and sometimes he would get the snap. There would be end-less play-fakes and many different ballcarriers, but few passes. It was like nothing any of the Apopka players had ever seen before. "I didn't get it," recalls Gallon, who would be inserted into the starting backfield and receive most of the center snaps. "I didn't get it at all. It was just weird."

Darlington is a football coach to his bones. If you cut into him with a sharp knife, you'd hit a thick layer of pigskin. His first job was working with the Lakeland (Fla.) High junior varsity team when he was still in high school, and he has coached every autumn since. He won the Florida 6A (largest) state title at Apopka in 2001, later coached three years at perennial national power Valdosta High in southern Georgia, then returned to Apopka in '06. Darlington's teams have run offenses ranging from the triple option to the shotgun spread passing game. Yet here in the spring of '07, at the age of 43, he found himself without the type of accurate passer who would play quarterback in most systems. What he did have was a bunch of very good running backs, like Gallon. So Darlington decided to dig up a dinosaur.

The coach told his players they were climbing into a time machine; the offense he was giving them was called the single wing, and its roots were at least a century deep, reaching all the way back to the legendary Glenn Scobey (Pop) Warner. The great Jim Thorpe had once played the same position for Warner at the Carlisle Indian School in 1911 and '12 that Gallon would play for Apopka: single wing "tailback." Darlington showed films of teams running the single wing. "He showed us guys wearing leather helmets," says Gallon. ("It was some old stuff," admits Darlington, "but I don't know about leather helmets. They probably *looked* like leather helmets to these kids.") On most plays the ball was snapped, shotgun-style, to a tailback. Multiple fakes and complex line blocking ensued. It looked nothing like the football the young Blue Darters of Apopka had seen—or played. But in the 2007 season Apopka went 12–2 running the single wing, averaged nearly 40 points a game and reached the Florida 6A semifinals before losing. Gallon rushed for more than 1,600 yards. Coach Darlington and his Blue Darters stayed with their new-old offense the following season.

It is a Friday night in November 2008. The Blue Darters enter a game against West Orange with a 7–2 record and bound for the state playoffs. Apopka's squad has breathtakingly fast, young athletes. They wear the best in modern football equipment and are supported by a precision squad of cheerleaders and a massive marching band. It is 2008 by every measure. Yet at the moment Apopka's offense cranks up, it is as if the team is performing an ancient football ritual: Nearly every play includes a direct snap to a tailback who runs or sprints out and passes.

In combination with Apopka's speed, the single wing is lethal. The Blue Darters win 49–7, and after the game Darlington is surrounded by his wife, Shelly, and the couple's seven children. "You don't see anybody unhappy about running an old leather-helmet offense out here," says Darlington, surveying the celebration. "You look at this offense, it gives so many kids a chance to run the ball. It was hard for a lot of the kids at first, but now we've got our whole feeder program running it. Our freshman team is undefeated."

The Blue Darters are not alone in their discovery. On the following Saturday afternoon, 1,000 miles to the north, in Windsor Locks, Conn., the high school team of Housatonic-Wamogo takes the field as a cold rain falls from low, dark clouds. It is a decidedly more spartan atmosphere than that of the previous night in central Florida, yet the methods—and outcome—are very much the same. Housatonic-Wamogo rolls to an easy victory on the shoulders of the old single wing.

Early in the game on a slow, muddy field, sophomore tailback Tanner Brissett takes a direct snap, fakes to senior Will Kennedy as Kennedy runs into the middle of the line. Almost simultaneously, senior Sam Schwartz scoots past from his wingback position as if running a reverse around the left edge. Brissett fakes to him as well, then turns back to the line of scrimmage and runs off tackle, untouched, 70 yards for a touchdown. "The defense can't figure out who has the ball," says Kennedy. "There have been times when I've run straight into the line with the ball and the whole defense is running away from me to tackle somebody who doesn't even have the ball."

The coach at Housatonic-Wamogo (a cooperative of two high schools, serving seven small towns in the northwest corner of Connecticut) is 44-year-old Deron Bayer. When he was hired as an assistant in 1997 to help coach a program that annually dresses fewer than 35 players, he promptly logged into his school's fledgling Internet system in search of an offense that might work with so few athletes. "The search engine was Hotbot, that's how long ago it was," says Bayer. His search led him to the single wing and eventually to a conclave of single wing coaches in 2001. There were 11 in attendance; at the conclusion they took a group photo posed in an unbalanced-right single wing formation, straight from Pop Warner's playbook. Bayer installed his offense two years ago and, like Darlington, showed his players vintage films. "We watched video tapes," says running back Kennedy, "but in the audio you could hear a film projector whirring in the background."

It was the sound of time standing still.

The single wing, hatched more than 100 years ago, is experiencing a rebirth on every level from youth and high school football to the NFL, where during the 2008 season at least seven teams used some variation of the old-school package, all the while calling it the Wildcat. College football is on board as well. The University of Florida offense that '07 Heisman Trophy winner Tim Tebow operated for head coach Urban Meyer is, in the words of Patriots coach and football history aficionado Bill Belichick, "the perfect blend of single wing running and spread passing. Call it what you want, but it's single wing football." And simply by speaking those words—"single wing"—Belichick dismisses a taboo. Modern coaches have long concocted aliases for the old offense, like *quarterback run game*, to avoid a name that might make them seem out of touch. In fact, they are on the cutting edge.

Brewster, Mass.
November 2008

THE SINGLE wing's serpentine road through the 20th century and into the 21st is clearly viewed from an 800-square-foot office above the garage of Ed Racely's stately home on a waterfront bluff in Brewster, Mass., on the inside elbow of Cape Cod. Racely, born in 1928, worked a long and profitable career as the co-owner of a road-building business in Northern California, but long before that, as a young boy in Walthill, Neb., he had a passion for the history and traditions of football. He wrote letters to famous football coaches like Wallace Wade at Duke and Gen. Robert Neyland at Tennessee, requesting copies of game programs. Through high school, college (University of Nebraska), the Marines, seven years working back home in the family businesses, graduate school (USC) and his entire business career, Racely kept indulging his football hobby, gathering the game's arcana wherever he could find it, with a particular emphasis on the single wing offense.

The result is a sprawling treasure trove of football history that fills the office—and this doesn't include the nearby storage shed that houses even more material. Racely owns thousands of DVDs, VHS tapes and even 16-millimeter films, all documenting the evolution of the single wing. He has cabinets full of playbooks and personal correspondence from the likes of legendary turn-of-the-century coach Amos Alonzo Stagg. There are eight windows in the office looking out on a beautiful New England world, but there is a mighty temptation to simply sit instead in front of the 48-inch flat screen, with Racely's corded coach's remote in hand, and let history unfold.

Racely is the go-to guy on single wing history, the unpretentious, unofficial curator who speaks of football's past with pride and sincerity, as if he had been there on the turf with the men he has researched. If you make a phone call or send an e-mail to any of the many coaches who have adopted the single wing in some form, you will almost always hear in return, *Have you talked to Ed Racely?*

"People ask me all the time who started the single wing," says Racely. "I tell them it was President Theodore Roosevelt." The line is delivered as if it's a joke, but a visitor is unsure whether to laugh or not because Racely's one-liner is based on a popular mythology: that early in the 20th century Roosevelt intervened in football when he felt the game had become too violent, and that he changed the rules. This much is generally accurate: In 1905 Roosevelt was a participant in a process that pushed college football toward rules changes designed to make the game safer, outlawing dangerous mass-momentum, closed-formation plays like the flying wedge. These rules changes gave rise to the game of modern football, including the forward pass and the single wing. As for Roosevelt's fanhood, author John Sayle Watterson, in his exhaustive history of college football published in 2000, writes, "Despite Roosevelt's concern about brutality and unsportsmanlike play, he came to believe that the growing public clamor against football had gone too far. He had always favored a middle-of-the-road approach, and football was no exception." Meaning that if someone tells you that Teddy Roosevelt tried to outlaw football—a not uncommon claim—you can tell him that he's wrong.

POP WARNER has been immortalized as the namesake of football's most well-known youth organization. Long before he became a brand name, Glenn Scobey Warner was one of two coaches—the other was Stagg—who built the foundation of the modern game. Warner had been a two-way guard at Cornell from 1892 to '94; a year after his graduation, at the age of 24, he was the head coach at the University of Georgia. From 1897 to 1914 Warner coached, in two stints each, at his alma mater, Cornell, and at the Carlisle Indian School in Pennsylvania; during this time, most football historians agree, Warner created the single wing offense.

In 1908 Warner wrote and distributed a correspondence course for coaches; copies of the course quickly sold out. In '12 and '27 Warner wrote expansive books outlining his football philosophies in terms that would influence the game for nearly half a century. In the preface to the taut, 205-page 1927 edition, Warner began, "In 1908 I published a correspondence course for football coaches and players. At that time the game was in the process of being revamped from the old push-and-pull, close-formation game into the more open game of today. . . ."

If modern fans were to watch Warner's early-20th-century teams, they would find his description perplexing; the game would look primitive. But the single wing was, in fact, a far more open and complex system than football had previously seen. In his book Warner earmarks the likely creation date for the single wing. Under the chapter heading "Formation A," Warner wrote, "This offensive formation has often been referred to as the 'Carlisle formation,' because it was first used by the Indians. . . . I have used this formation or variations of it ever since pushing and pulling the runner was prohibited in 1906." The birth date of the single wing has been frequently debated (Racely wonders if Stagg might have tinkered with it first), but Warner's writing strongly suggests it was born in '06 at Carlisle.

His 1927 book includes diagrams of the Carlisle formation that clearly show what came to be known as the single wing: An unbalanced line (a guard, two tackles and an end on one side; a guard and an end on the other); a tailback lined up in a shotgun position, and next to him a full-back; at the line of scrimmage behind the guard, a blocking back; and outside the strongside end, a single wingback, later to be the source of the formation's name. Warner's explanation for the creation of Formation A is a marvel of utilitarian economy, both in concept and description. It encapsulates the birth of modern football, yet Warner makes its invention seem obvious.

> Before [1906] it was customary to mass the backs behind the line and even bring one or two heavy linemen back, so as to be able to hurl a mass of men at any spot in the defensive line. The idea was to get behind the man with the ball and shove and jam him through the line, or let him jump in the air feet first while the other men shoved him over the line and helped him by dragging him along. . . .
>
> When the rules changed to prevent pushing the runner, there was no more reason for the backs being massed. Those behind the runner were of no use, and in line-bucking plays only two men, the ballcarrier and a man to precede him or lead him through the hole, were needed.

THE SINGLE wing relied on slick backfield ball handling (including 360-degree spins and fakes by the backs) and precise pulling and blocking on the offensive line, with crushing double teams and traps that used small, nimble linemen. Warner described all of this in his 1927 writings. His offense would be the dominant formation in football for nearly half a century, employed by coaches like Knute Rockne of Notre Dame (who ran it from his famous "box" formation), Fritz Crisler of Michigan and Carl Snavely of North Carolina.

Single wing tailbacks would be the glamour players of the sport. Because of strict substitution rules and conservative strategy, teams often punted before fourth down. (When this notion was related to Belichick, a football historian to his marrow, he fairly shouted back, "Fourth down? They would punt on first down if the field position was bad enough!" It's true. Time and again Racely's tapes show single wing teams pinned deep in their own territory, only to punt immediately, hoping for a better outcome on the next exchange). As a result of this quick-kick strategy, single wing tailbacks were much more valuable if they could punt effectively. Those that flourished were true triple threats: runner, punter, passer. Jim Thorpe was a single wing tailback under Warner at Carlisle. So were George Gipp of Notre Dame, Ernie Nevers of Stanford, Nile Kinnick of Iowa, Tom Harmon of Michigan and Doak Walker of TCU, among many others.

Belichick's father, Steve, was a single wing fullback at Western Reserve University, and Belichick played in the single wing in junior high and against it in prep school. "You found a guy back then who could do all three things and stay on the field," says Belichick. "And the guys who could do those things became your All-America, Heisman Trophy single wing tailbacks."

The last of them was Princeton's Dick Kazmaier in 1951. Four years earlier Michigan had won the national championship with an extraordinary single wing backfield nicknamed the "Mad Magicians"; Princeton's version was nearly as dazzling. On Ed Racely's big screen Kazmaier comes to life in a 13–7 victory over Penn at Franklin Field in Philadelphia, the Tigers' 16th consecutive victory in a streak that would reach 24 games a year later. The cameraman often lost sight of the ball, and the camera would swing left and right, searching. One can only imagine a defense's confusion without benefit of the camera's stadium-top perch. The architect of Princeton's single wing was head coach Charlie Caldwell, who at the conclusion of Kazmaier's career wrote a thick handbook on the offense, so detailed in its descriptions that even modern single wing experts find it occasionally impenetrable.

Even in the pretelevision NFL, the single wing had its moment. Jock Sutherland, an All-America in Pop Warner's single wing at the University of Pittsburgh in 1916, brought the single wing to the Pittsburgh Steelers as head coach in '47. The Steelers, who had never won more than seven games in a season, went 8–4 and lost to the Philadelphia Eagles in an Eastern Division playoff game that season. Sutherland died of a brain tumor before the '48 season and is remembered as the last coach to run the single wing in the NFL.

It wasn't long before the T formation took over football, followed by the I formation and the various two-back pro-style offenses. The passing game matured. Substitution rules were altered. Two-platoon football and more wide-open attacks made the triple-threat tailback unnecessary. By the mid-1950s the single wing had become a relic. Tommy Prothro, who learned the offense under Red Sanders while coaching at both Vanderbilt and UCLA from '46 to '54, installed the single wing when he became head coach at Oregon State in '55 but ditched it in '61 when Terry Baker, a tall, graceful, lefthanded quarterback became the Beavers' starter. Passing out of the wing-T, Baker won the Heisman Trophy in '62.

That left only Princeton, where Dick Colman had replaced Caldwell as head coach in 1956 and changed nothing about the Tigers' offense; Princeton continued running the single wing through the '60s and in '64 won the Ivy League championship with a 9–0 record. "It was so different by then, it gave us an edge," says Cosmo Iacavazzi, a fullback on that unbeaten team, voicing a theme that would be echoed much later. "We were the only team running it, and that made it really tough for teams to get ready to play us."

The last outpost of the college single wing—old school version—was Denison University in Granville, Ohio, under coach Keith Piper from 1977 through '92. Journalists would occasionally pass through Piper's domain to chronicle the antique, as if witnessing living history. One was SPORTS ILLUSTRATED's Rick Telander, to whom Piper said in 1982, "The thing that people don't understand about the single wing is that it was never caught up with or overrun. It works. But football is like men's fashions. Coaches don't run the single wing because they don't want to be out of fashion."

Piper was a native Ohioan who was raised in Niles, rival to legendary Massillon High. He became Denison's head coach, his first job in the business, in 1954, six years after Woody Hayes left there. For 23 seasons Piper ran the popular T formation before converting to the single wing for the fall of '77. Telander wrote, "It took [Piper] that long, he says, to realize the advantages of a forgotten system in a follow-the-leader world. 'When you're at a school like this,' Piper said, 'where you don't have great talent, the single wing is ideal. It's good for utilizing slower, smaller players, and because opponents only see it once a year, you take them by surprise.' "

Piper retired from coaching after the 1992 season and died five years later at the age of 76. His career record was 200-142-9, and just before his death the stadium at Denison was named in his honor. Yet if Piper is remembered by many for turning to a nearly forgotten system—in desperation? in madness?—his reasoning has been borne out dozens of times since.

The single wing disappeared, in steady order, from the professional game, major colleges, then small colleges. But it never completely died at the high school level, and in some places it proved dominant. Apopka, with its speed and talent, is a glaring exception. More commonly, the single wing has served as an equalizer, the province of the disciplined and the dedicated.

From the time Kazmaier left Princeton through the late '90s, the single wing had been kept on life support by a small cadre of devotees like Ken Hofer of Menominee High in the Upper Peninsula of Michigan, who won three state championships, the most recent in 2007; George Rykovich of Manitou Springs High in Colorado, who won two state championships; and Mark Bliss, who has run the offense at four high schools since 1997 and won four state titles at Conway Springs High in Kansas. They all had their bibles, most notably Dr. Ken Keuffel's *Winning Single Wing Football*.

IF THE single wing was barely breathing through much of the '70s, '80s and '90s, the offense seems to have suddenly sprouted a second life in the most recent decade, enabled by Internet message boards on which coaches exchange ideas and tales from the trenches. The Single Wing Conclave, which had begun in 2001 with a gathering of 11 high school coaches at Kings College in Wilkes-Barre, Pa., had mushroomed; by the spring of 2008 there were 138 coaches at the annual event, replete with a preconclave mixer. A summer symposium organized by the National Single Wing Coaches' Association started in 1996 with four coaches and now annually draws more than 100.

There are four primary reasons for the single wing's resurgence at the high school level:
• It does not require a skilled quarterback, which is the toughest position to fill on any team.
• Its complex double teams, trap blocks and backfield deceptions allow teams that would otherwise be overmatched physically to be competitive.
• The offense, by snapping to a player who can run with the ball, forces the defense to account for an extra running threat (instead of dismissing the traditional quarterback as a handoff machine).

• It is still, even with its growing popularity, relatively rare, so it complicates an opponent's preparation. Defenses simply don't see the single wing often enough to defend it comfortably, so it becomes an annoying disruption to the fastidiously organized practice and video regimen that dominates every week in a football season at every level of the game.

While these same axioms appeal to teams at the higher levels of football, the single wing fits most comfortably in the high school game, in which coaches still preach the values of teamwork, selflessness and preparation as the foundations of success. Linemen working as one unit, backs carrying out fakes and a center making accurate snaps—all facets of the single wing—combine to give an undermanned team the possibility of victory.

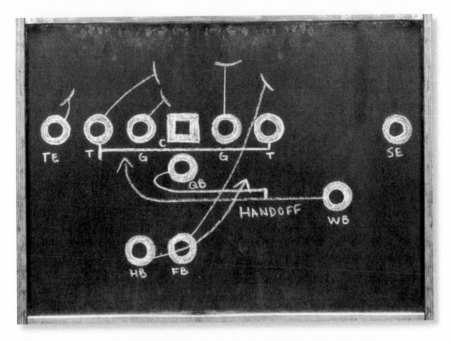

WINGBACK COUNTER

Popularized as a staple of the Delaware wing T of coach Tubby Raymond, the counter augmented Pop Warner's single wing principles of power and deception with modern speed. The quarterback, under center, takes the snap and does a reverse pivot, turning left to get to his right. The right tackle pulls left, while the fullback attacks the spot vacated by the tackle, followed by the halfback, which gives the impression that the play will be a simple off-tackle plunge. The QB fakes to the HB, then hands off to the wingback crossing the formation right to left ("counter"). The WB follows the block of the pulling tackle, either inside or outside. The faster the play hits, the more the defense is challenged to find the football and make a tackle.

CHAPTER 2

THE WING T

The offense of the '50s was curated by a legend named
Tubby and elevated by a team of Fightin' Blue Hens

I N THE fall of 1940 a strapping guard named Mike Lude traveled 60 miles from his home in Vicksburg, Mich., to Hillsdale College, a tiny school about 100 miles west of Detroit, where he would be a two-way lineman in the last decade of single wing dominance in college football. An hour to the east, in Ann Arbor, the University of Michigan was turning Tom Harmon into a Heisman Trophy winner in a single wing backfield that included future Iowa coach Forest Evashevski and a 5' 7", 155-pound halfback named Dave Nelson.

Football innovation repeatedly proves itself the product of coincidence, of personalities thrown together and forced to improvise strategy for the sake of survival. In the fall of 1940, while Lude was playing college football in a tiny backwater and Nelson was playing before 100,000 spectators in the same backfield as one of the great tailbacks in the game's history, they could never have known that a decade later they would together change the course of offensive football.

Lude played three seasons at Hillsdale before spending three years in the U.S. Marines. Nelson enlisted in the Naval Air Corps. Both were discharged in the summer of 1946. Lude returned to Hillsdale for his delayed senior year, where Nelson, still just 26 years old, with his Michigan pedigree, had been named the head coach. Nelson installed the single wing, and Hillsdale went 7–1 in Lude's final college season. For Nelson's second year at Hillsdale he made Lude, 25, his line coach. They coached the single wing again, and the Chargers went 7-0-2, giving Nelson a two-year record of 14-1-2.

(Back down the road in Ann Arbor, meanwhile, coach Fritz Crisler and Michigan's single wing Mad Magicians, so named for their deft backfield ball handling, went 9–0 in the regular season and crushed USC 49–0 in the Rose Bowl. It was the convention of the time to crown national champions before bowl games. Notre Dame was voted No. 1 by the Associated Press, but Michigan was given the title in a postseason poll conducted by the AP. The Mad Magicians are revered by single wing devotees as one of the most skilled faking teams in the history of the offense. And they were the last major-college team to win a national title running Pop Warner's offense).

In the wake of his success at Hillsdale, Nelson was hired as an assistant coach at Harvard in 1948 and a year later as the head coach at the University of Maine. He brought Lude with him to Maine as his line coach and installed the single wing. The Black Bears went 2-4-1 in that first year, and though they won the Yankee Conference with a 2-0-1 record, Nelson, Lude and backfield coach Harold Westerman were unsure that they should stay with the single wing.

"The biggest problem we had," says Lude, "is that we kept going through tailbacks. They were getting banged up. That's what happens with the single wing—the tailback is going to get hit frequently." There were other issues, as well, which would ultimately spell the demise of the single wing at the upper levels of football. Maine did not have a do-everything athlete like Harmon to play single wing tailback, and it did not have the backfield depth to distribute carries in the buzz-saw method of truly effective single wing teams. Nelson, Lude and the Black Bears needed another attack.

Throughout the 1940s the two dominant teams in college football had been Army under head coach Earl (Red) Blaik and Notre Dame under Frank Leahy. Each was running the full-house T formation, which was inexorably replacing the single wing as the dominant formation in all higher levels of football. (Famously, or notoriously, the Chicago Bears had run from the T formation in their 73–0 NFL championship-game rout of the Washington Redskins in 1940, still the most lopsided title game in the history of the league.)

The T, which in its original form is largely regarded as the work of 19th century football architect Walter Camp, put a quarterback under center, from where he would distribute the ball to any one of three running backs. It wasn't as tricky and deceptive as the single wing, but it put less pressure on a single back. Its linemen were principally straight-ahead blockers, with little of the complex double-teaming and trapping that made the single wing effective. But it eliminated the need for a superathlete at tailback, and it was working at Notre Dame and Army. So in the spring of 1950, as Lude recalls, "Coach Nelson sent me and Harold Westerman out on the road to learn from Leahy."

Come the summer of 1950, Nelson and Lude were convinced that they would put a quarterback under center. "Although," says Lude, "none of us even knew how to teach a center-quarterback exchange because all we had ever coached was single wing." And they were loath to give up the diabolical blocking schemes so effective in the single wing and afraid to let go of the intricate backfield play fakes. They needed some sort of hybrid.

They stayed up late every night, tinkering with plays, trying to marry single wing blocking and faking principles to an offense with the quarterback under center. "It was 3 a.m. on the night before the players reported for practice before Dave finally made his decision," says Lude. "He just all of sudden said, 'To heck with it; let's just go with it. He took all our blocking rules from the unbalanced single wing and converted them to a balanced line." It was a mix of the single wing and T formations, but it was the first step in bridging the dominant offense of the first half of the 20th century—Pop Warner's single wing—with what would become one of the most important offenses of the ensuing 30 years.

It would eventually be called the wing T, because—simply enough—it looked like the T formation with a single wing wingback, and it appeared to have elements of both offenses. There was a quarterback under center and a balanced line (T formation), and here were two backs in the backfield and a wing flanked to the strong side of the formation (single wing). The name was intuitive and practical.

Nelson's Maine Black Bears went 5-1-1 with their crude, improvised wing T. In 1952 Nelson became the head coach at the University of Delaware and again took Lude with him. It was there that the wing T really took flight. Nelson coached the Blue Hens for 15 years and won more than 66% of his games. Three years into his tenure at Delaware he hired Harold (Tubby) Raymond as an assistant, and it was Raymond who became the true curator of the wing T. A former single wing quarterback and linebacker under Crisler at Michigan, Raymond—this can get confusing—joined the Maine staff under Westerman in 1951 when Nelson and Lude went to Delaware. The two staffs, Nelson's and Lude's at Delaware and Westerman's and Raymond's at Maine, wore out clipboards refining the wing T from its rough beginnings the previous year.

"We took what Nelson started at Maine and worked with it," says Raymond. "The biggest differences between the wing T and everything that came before it was that the offensive skill requirements were shared more equally. You didn't need a Jack Armstrong at quarterback to do everything. You had a balanced line, so the positions were symmetrical, instead of asymmetrical. Now you could threaten several points of attack on the line of scrimmage on every snap."

Twelve years after arriving at Delaware, Tubby Raymond took over as head coach, a position he held for 36 years and 300 victories. His teams won three national titles and 14 Lambert Cups, emblematic of Eastern small-college supremacy. Raymond's success was sweeping and his offense so ingrained in his program that the wing T became known as the Delaware Wing T.

The wing T was one of the first offensive systems built on the idea of forcing the defense to make decisions in response to what it expects the offense to run and then having the offense attack with something slightly different. Raymond once told a coaching convention, "It is designed to create defensive player reacts [sic] to stop a particular play, placing himself in jeopardy for a related play."

It was Raymond's staff at Delaware that evolved the wing T into a truly modern offense, spreading the field, adding straight drop-back passing and, eventually, an option game. In a 1998 interview Raymond said, "Prior to 1966, all of the formations [in the wing T] were tight [similar to the single wing].... Our passing game was made up exclusively of play-action passes. We didn't have any three-step or five-step drops. [But] when we started in 1966, we incorporated the wideout and the various drops.... Our [other] contribution [was] running the triple option from a wing formation, as opposed to the wishbone formation."

The success of the wing T was not limited to Delaware and Maine. Even as Nelson and Raymond developed the offense, others followed and sought their advice. It became part of historic programs at the highest levels of the game. The first of those programs was Iowa, which adopted the wing T under Evashevski and won the Rose Bowl following the 1956 season. Next came LSU.

Paul Dietzel had played on the line at Miami University in Oxford, Ohio, in the late 1940s on a post–World War II team that included future coaching giants Bill Arnsparger, Ara Parseghian and Bo Schembechler. He worked under Red Blaik at Army and Paul (Bear) Bryant at Kentucky before being named head coach at LSU in 1955. The Bayou Bengals hadn't won a Southeastern Conference title since winning back-to-back SEC— and national—championships in 1935 and '36. And the Dietzel Era did not start with promise: LSU went 11-17-2 in Dietzel's first three years, running principally the T formation.

There was no groundswell of anticipation for the 1958 season. "University authorities expected no surge in fan interest. They ordered 30,000 tickets per game for a stadium that seated 67,510," according to a 2008 article in the Baton Rouge *Advocate* recalling that era. "There were a little more than 9,000 season-ticket holders. The LSU student body numbered less than 10,000."

Dietzel, however, saw promise: Junior running backs Billy Cannon (who would go on to win the Heisman Trophy in 1959), Johnny Robinson and junior quarterback Warren Rabb were all talented. "Splendid players," says Dietzel. "I knew that Davey Nelson and Mike Lude were running the wing T up north, and when I had a chance to see it, I thought, That's a nice-looking offense. The deception is good. With the T formation, the defense always knows where the ball is going. I also liked that the wing T always had a double team on the line of scrimmage at the point of attack and usually a lead blocker. It was physical. It was a *tough* offense."

Dietzel brought Lude to Baton Rouge in the spring and asked him to teach the offense to his staff. "They showed us the blocking and the ball handling, everything," says Dietzel. "But then the real payoff was that Cannon, Rabb and Robinson all were working summer jobs in Baton Rouge that summer. They got fascinated with the wing T. They worked on the ball handling every day, and when fall practice started, they actually taught the offense to the rest of the team. When the season started, it didn't look like we were running an offense that we'd never used before."

The Tigers opened the season with a 26–6 victory at Rice and then, in Bear Bryant's first season at Alabama, beat the Crimson Tide in Mobile 13–3. After the game Dietzel recalled that Bryant was asked if the wing T helped Cannon. "Coach Bryant said, 'I don't know about that, but I'll tell you one thing: Billy Cannon sure helped the wing T.' I guess that would be true too."

LSU won the national title in '58, going 11–0. Dietzel's Tigers won another SEC title in 1961 and another the year after that, when Dietzel had gone to Army to replace Blaik and Charlie McClendon had taken over in Baton Rouge. "The wing T was good for us," says Dietzel. "The best thing was the toughness. The second-best thing was the misdirection. And it was not without passing. You run, run, run, and your receivers get lost out there. We had a play where we would fake to the halfback on a cross buck and then dump it off to the fullback in the flat, and I'll tell you, that was one of the best plays we ever ran."

This was all in keeping with the flexibility of the offense. As the passing game developed through the 1970s, the wing T evolved with it. Raymond says, "When I came to Delaware in 1954, if you ran into a quarterback who could beat you with the pass once every other year, that was really something. But I always maintained, 'There is no defense for a well-thrown ball that's caught.' We had some great passers at Delaware—Jeff Komlo, Scott Brunner, Rich Gannon. And when we had those great passers, we used them in the offense accordingly."

Of course, not every team that turned to the wing T immediately won a national championship or a major bowl. In the same spring that Lude visited Baton Rouge, he also went to Fayetteville, Ark., where 33-year-old Frank Broyles had just been hired as head coach. Broyles installed the wing T and ran it in the season opener, a 12–0 loss to Baylor. The following week Broyles scrapped the wing T and never ran it again. "There was no problem with Davey Nelson's offense," Broyles recalled recently. "We had a very inexperienced team, and we just didn't have the backs to properly run the offense. We didn't have Billy Cannon."

In the spring of 1973 Raymond got a call from Ara Parseghian, who was looking to retool his Notre Dame offense. The Irish had gone 8–3 in the '72 season, which may not sound disastrous, but it was the first time in nine years that a Parseghian-coached Irish team had lost three games in a season. Two of those came at the end of the season with a 45–23 loss at USC and a 40–6 thrashing by Nebraska in the Orange Bowl. Parseghian was looking for a change.

"He flew me into South Bend, and we met up in a room at the airport," recalls Raymond. "I showed him the offense and then we talked every week afterwards, sometimes a couple times a week." Notre Dame went 11–0 in 1973 and won the national championship. The title was iced when Notre Dame quarterback Tom Clements faked a cross-buck handoff on third down from his own two-yard line and completed a 35-yard pass to tight end Robin Weber, giving the Irish a first down and allowing them to run out the clock against Alabama.

Parseghian invited Raymond back to South Bend in the spring of 1974 to watch film and evaluate Notre Dame's use of the wing T throughout the previous season. Raymond had always put great stock in the sequencing of plays, using certain formations and plays to set up others. He felt that Notre Dame, despite its success, had been too random in its use of the offense. "Your quarterback doesn't understand play-calling," Raymond told Parseghian as they sat in a darkened film room.

Parseghian recoiled. "I call the plays!" he shouted.

Thirty-four years later, in the winter of 2008, seven years after his retirement, Tubby Raymond, at age 81, was invited to speak at a national wing T clinic in Pittsburgh. More than 700 coaches—most of them from high schools and small colleges—attended, enthralled listening to the original master of a still-vibrant attack.

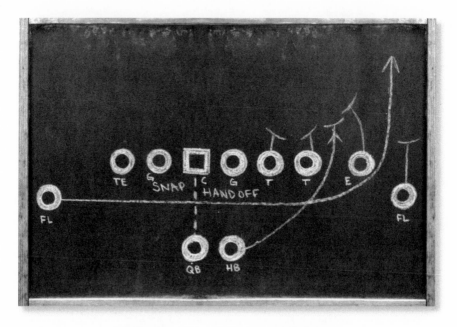

WILDCAT SPEED SWEEP

It is the simplest of plays but ruthlessly efficient. From an unbalanced line to the right, the "quarterback," usually a single wing tailback–type player (like Ronnie Brown of the 2009 Dolphins), takes a shotgun snap. The flanker (on those Dolphins, usually Ricky Williams) runs hard across the formation in front of the QB. The QB can either fake the ball to the flanker or, in the speed sweep, give it to him; the flanker then runs behind the blocking of the heavy side of the formation, in this case the right. The play, of course, can be run exactly the same way to the left.

CHAPTER 3

THE WILDCAT

The recent resurgence of an old idea has intriguing portent—the end of the quarterback as we know him

Simsbury, Conn.
Saturday, Nov. 1, 2008

TWO SMALL, Connecticut private schools are playing a football game on a clear fall evening. The matchup embraces the essence of the game: size, speed and power versus tactical strategy. Visiting Cheshire Academy is wearing white; home team Westminster School is in black. Neither school benefits from the population that would buttress a powerful football program; Cheshire has 324 students in four high school grades, Westminster 385. But on this night, in this season, Cheshire has bigger, faster athletes and would appear to be the stronger team. Yet football is always a game in which there are two ways to win—be better or be smarter.

Cheshire runs the popular spread offense, with a talented quarterback throwing darts to tall, fast wide receivers in the middle of the Westminster defense. Westminster is running something from the Dark Ages of football: a tight formation with a direct snap to a small, nimble senior quarterback named Calvin Brownridge, who executes an array of rollout passes, keepers and quarterback dives. Execution keeps Westminster close, and only a fourth-quarter pass interference call gives Cheshire the opportunity to score a late touchdown and win a tight game, 19–14.

In the aftermath, as parents mingle on the field, Westminster head coach

Dennis Daly, who has coached football at the college and high school levels for more than three decades, shouts at a writer covering the game, "Tell Coach Hugh Wyatt you saw his offense in action. And it worked."

SEVERAL WEEKS earlier, at Gillette Stadium in Foxborough, Mass., the New England Patriots, who the previous season had won 18 consecutive games before losing to the New York Giants in the Super Bowl, hosted the Miami Dolphins, 0–2 and on the cusp of panic in a league where 0–3 nearly guarantees missing the playoffs. (It's the same game Jeremy Gallon was watching in Chapter 1.)

The Dolphins beat the Patriots 38–13, largely on the success of an offensive attack they had never used before: running back Ronnie Brown as a shotgun quarterback, with quarterback Chad Pennington shifted to a wide receiver position and running back Ricky Williams as a wingback. They lined up in the formation six times and scored four touchdowns—three on runs by Brown, one on a pass from Brown to tight end Anthony Fasano.

After the game Dolphins offensive coordinator Dan Henning called the offense the David Lee Special, after his quarterbacks coach, but some media members recognized it as the same package that Lee had run at Arkansas in the previous two seasons, where it was called the Wildcat, or the Wild Hog, the latter in deference to the Arkansas nickname. Lee had pitched the offense to Henning on the flight home from the Dolphins' 31–10 loss at Arizona the previous weekend. "It had never come up before that week," Pennington would say later in that season. "I wasn't shocked, because I had been following some of the things that college teams were doing. But at the same time a lot of things don't carry over [to the NFL]. The fact is, we needed some offensive energy, and that gave it to us."

Patriots veteran safety Rodney Harrison told reporters after the game, "It's something we hadn't seen. We tried to make adjustments. We still didn't stop it."

Patriots coach Bill Belichick knew exactly what he was watching. And he knew that colleges were experimenting with it. "We knew this stuff was out there. We knew somebody was going to try it. But you've got limited practice time, and you just can't waste any of it preparing for something that a team hasn't shown yet."

NFL coaches—coaches at any level, in fact—are fond of the expression, *It's a copycat league.* It is their default response in explaining any trend. And it's generally true. Within hours of the Dolphins' victory over the Patriots, at least half a dozen teams were exploring the use of some sort of Wildcat-style package in their offenses.

And the concept was not entirely new to the league. Other NFL teams had dabbled with it in recent years, which made the Dolphins' all-in more of a culmination than a founding. NFL teams had been selectively direct-snapping to an alternate back for the better part of a decade. LaDainian Tomlinson, a future Hall of Fame running back, had taken direct snaps, and thrown touchdown passes, for the Chargers. The Patriots had used running back Kevin Faulk in the shotgun. Belichick recalled that Pittsburgh quarterback Ben Roethlisberger ran off-tackle from a shotgun formation in his rookie season, in 2004. Hines Ward, a former high school quarterback, had also taken snaps for the Steelers. But it was the Dolphins who took the last step and truly committed to the system, using the Wildcat on almost one out of ten snaps in 2008—and scoring 20% of their touchdowns with it. And many teams immediately followed.

The Baltimore Ravens put in plays for then-second-year quarterback Troy Smith, the 2006 Heisman Trophy winner as a run-pass threat at Ohio State. "We were trying to tap into what Troy has done well in the past," said Ravens offensive coordinator Cam Cameron. The Kansas City Chiefs scored a touchdown on a Wildcat-based play when tailback Jamaal Charles took a direct snap and pitched on a reverse to wideout Mark Bradley, who then threw a 37-yard touchdown pass to quarterback Tyler Thigpen, who was flanked wide right. "Pretty exciting," says Thigpen. "When I got deep, I looked back and I was thinking, is he throwing the ball to me?" The Atlanta Falcons ran several direct snap plays to running back Jerious Norwood, a high school quarterback in Mississippi. "You can hear the defenses just checking off like crazy, getting ready for the run," Norwood says. "But I can throw it."

The philosophy of the Wildcat is based on simple math. Defenses traditionally try to account for every possible ballcarrier and every gap. In doing so, they disregard a quarterback under center (except in an option system). "When you put a quarterback under center, you lose a blocker, you lose a gap, offensively," says Belichick. "You basically play with 10 men on offense. But when the quarterback is one of the runners, whether it's single wing or veer or wishbone, the defense runs out of people to defend you."

The ancient roots of the system are obvious, as Belichick indicated: the single wing. Snap the ball to a runner and let him carry it. The recent renaissance is trickier to pinpoint. In the days following the Dolphins' unveiling of their Wildcat, attention was quickly focused on Lee, the team's first-year quarterbacks coach. From Lee, the etymology of the offense was traced back to Gus Malzahn, who was by then working as the offensive coordinator at the University of Tulsa.

The desk in Malzahn's office at Tulsa is absolutely clean. It is clean because Malzahn spends almost no time in this room, but rather in the meeting room next door, scrawling offensive sets on a white board and studying tape in the darkness. Malzahn, 43 on this day in 2008, is a football lifer. He was a high school wide receiver in Fort Smith, Ark., and walked on at the University of Arkansas in 1984. "I tried, but I wasn't good enough," he says. He transferred to Henderson State College in Arkadelphia, Ark., and graduated in '90.

Malzahn went straight into high school coaching. "Always wanted to be a coach," he says. "Never wanted to do anything else." He coached for five years—the last four as head coach—at Hughes High in the northeast Arkansas delta. In 1996 he started a five-year run at Shiloh Christian High in Springdale, Ark.; his teams won two state titles and roasted defenses with a spread passing game. In 2001 he took his offense to Springdale High, a national power.

Among Malzahn's players at Springdale was a fast flanker named Dusty Johnson, who had also been a junior high quarterback. Malzahn ruminated on creative ways to get Johnson the football and attack the defense. Eventually Malzahn put Johnson in the shotgun and a ran variety of plays: a quarterback power series, a reverse and a speed sweep to a wingback cutting across the formation—exactly as the Dolphins would run seven years later with Ronnie Brown handing off to Ricky Williams. "We had pretty good success with it," says Malzhan. "People started asking me if I had any background in the single wing. I didn't know what they meant."

Malzhan was named offensive coordinator at the University of Arkansas in 2005 and began effectively using the formation with Darren McFadden (who would land in the NFL with the Oakland Raiders) in the tailback position and Felix Jones (who would go to the Dallas Cowboys) as a wingback running the speed sweep. "I brought the quarterback power [run] and speed sweep with me to Arkansas," says Malzahn. "One of my good friends coached McFadden and told me that McFadden had some experience playing quarterback when he was younger. Well, that's just the kind of guy you want back there because he's a threat to throw it too. Felix Jones could fly, so he was the perfect speed sweep guy. In a key '06 game, McFadden rushed for 181 yards and two touchdowns and threw for a third in a win over Tennessee. ESPN's GameDay crew was in attendance. "My phone started ringing pretty good after that game," says Malzahn.

The name Wildcat first popularly surfaced in that same 2006 season. Malzahn's explanation for the name is circuitous: "I didn't call it the Wildcat when I was at Springdale. I think we called it Heavy. When I got to Arkansas, they already had an unbalanced formation that they called Wildcat. I think they got that from Kansas State." (Kansas State's nickname is the Wildcats.) "I think we just kept that name," says Malzahn.

In a faraway corner of America, Hugh Wyatt vigorously disputes Malzahn's ownership of the Wildcat, classic evidence of the liquid nature of football innovation. Wyatt, born in 1938, is an energetic, entrepreneurial—and just slightly eccentric—Yale graduate who has coached high school football for 32 years and, in the summer of 2009, was preparing to begin his second season as coach of the North Beach Hyaks in Ocean Shores, Wash. "I believe Gus Malzahn has a selective memory," he says.

Wyatt played on the freshman football team at Yale in the 1950s and then served as practice fodder for the varsity for three years. Upon graduation he worked a decade in the business world before yielding to his passion and returning to football in 1970. First he coached and operated a semipro team in Maryland, and that earned him two years in front-office positions with teams in the soon-to-be-defunct World Football League. In 1976, at age 38, he started teaching and coaching at a small high school in Oregon. In the ensuing 32 years—in addition to jobs in Louisiana, Oregon and, of all places, Finland (where he coached football for seven years and got his first look at the double wing offense that he would refine and market)—he was a head coach at six high schools and an assistant at four.

Wyatt has been a highly successful coach, often taking teams with minimal resources and talent and using his tight-split, double wing offense to maximize his team's chances. When he first began coaching, he ran the Delaware wing T but gradually began molding the double wing that became his signature offense. "What I espouse is a derivation of the single wing," says Wyatt. "The blocking all comes from the single wing."

In addition to his coaching success Wyatt sells DVDs that instruct coaches on the process of installing the offense and conducts instructional clinics that are extremely popular among high school coaches. Dennis Daly, the aforementioned Westminster School coach, faced precisely the type of manpower deficit that Wyatt's double wing has often overcome. In the fall of 2008 Westminster started the season with five consecutive victories despite playing teams with a decided size and speed advantage. "The offense gives us a chance to get double teams at the point of attack," Daly says. "It's our best way to equalize the game."

Yet for all the popularity of the double wing among high school coaches, it is the direct snap Wildcat series that has made Wyatt a true pioneer. He says he first ran—and named—the package in the fall of 1997. He was at the time the head coach at La Center High in Washington state, and La Center's school mascot was the Wildcat.

In a magazine article in '98 Wyatt wrote,

> Whenever you've thought about throwing a curve at an opponent, the idea of running the Single Wing may have crossed your mind. Perhaps you've actually seen it in action—after all, a handful of schools still run it. Or maybe you've heard the old-timers talk about its legendary power and deception. You just know that its uniqueness alone would drive defenses crazy. You'd like to look at it, but you just don't know how to start.
>
> In that case, you might want to take a look at our "Wildcat" package. Nicknamed for our school's mascot, it's our direct-snap package—and an adjunct to the Double Wing system that we've been running since 1990.

WYATT GOES on to describe an offensive package that includes a series in which one of his two wingbacks—who line up facing inward at a
45-degree angle, rather than directly facing the defense—runs across the
formation and takes a handoff before continuing on around the opposite
end. It is almost identical to Malzahn's Shiloh/Springdale/Arkansas speed
sweep. In the winter of 2009 Wyatt wrote on his website: "Over the years
I've explained and shown the Wildcat to hundreds of coaches at clinics
and camps, and sold numerous playbooks and videos. I haven't the slight-
est idea how many teams have actually run my Wildcat at one time or
another, but there's a lot of them, and they know how it got its name."

When Malzahn was asked if he had, indeed, picked up the Wildcat
from Hugh Wyatt, he said, "Hugh Wyatt. I've heard that name. Well, I'm
sure I got it from somewhere. I just couldn't tell you where."

If the name and creator of the Wildcat is in dispute, its place in football is not. "The single wing type stuff is going to become more the norm
in the future," says veteran NFL coach and offensive coordinator Chan
Gailey. "Over the next 10 or 15 years it's going to evolve because the
runner-thrower is the kind of quarterback that the college game is produc-
ing now. You don't find a ton of the six-three, six-four, drop-back, stand-
up passer. They're not in college, so we're not getting them up here."

When Cam Cameron was head coach of the Dolphins in 2006, he no-
ticed a sea change in the quarterback position at all levels of the sport.
"I saw little kids playing Pop Warner—seven, eight, nine years old, doing
the belly-read option from a shotgun," says Cameron. "I was absolutely
floored by the stuff they were doing so young."

But wait: Isn't there madness in exposing a $10-million-a-year quarter-
back to a succession of crushing hits at the NFL level. "The hitting really
is at a much higher level than college," says quarterback Pennington. "I
don't think you would last very long."

Says Cameron, "It's one thing to have Darren McFadden back there,
but your quarterback? I don't know about that. Maybe [Florida's Tim]
Tebow can do it in this league."

The voices of the NFL cannot speak quickly or loudly enough in swat-
ting aside the concept of running from the quarterback position. Yet
coaches keep trying, whether in Lou Holtz's failed attempt to run the
outside veer option with the New York Jets three decades ago or the Ten-

nessee Titans' halfhearted attempt to incorporate Vince Young's feet into their offense, along with his arm. And many in between. There is clearly value, and seduction, in the idea of a pro quarterback who can throw and run and also survive. The question is, can it be done, and with whom?

As he began his pursuit of a second Heisman Trophy at Florida in the fall of 2009, the player who magnified this debate was Tim Tebow. Florida won the national championship with Tebow as a freshman in '06. Media fell over themselves in proclaiming coach Urban Meyer's offense the ultimate modern "spread" game (Chapter 15), but the quarterback running game was pure throwback. Tebow took direct snaps and ran off-tackle, just like George Gipp. Single wing groupies everywhere went wild when Tebow threw a jump pass—running toward the line of scrimmage as if to carry off-tackle, then jumping and throwing—for a touchdown against LSU. Dick Kazmaier used to throw jump passes at Princeton; you can see them right there in Ed Racely's Cape Cod garage. And here was Tebow doing the same thing.

Tebow won the Heisman Trophy in '07, passing for 32 touchdowns and running for 23, a true double threat, and at 6' 2½", 238 pounds, a durable one. The professional game has evolved significantly in many ways, but the quarterback position really has not. The ideal NFL quarterback remains an accurate thrower who can make decisions under pressure and, if rushed, buy time in the pocket. For all its growth, the league has not yet produced a player who is equally dangerous as a runner and a passer. (Michael Vick? Vince Young? Please.) With the influx of single wing–based offensive packages, the door is open. And at lower levels of the game the position has continued to move closer to the Tebow model than the statuesque Tom Brady version.

"There aren't many players who can run and throw," says Belichick. "Tebow, obviously, is a special one. But you've got major questions, because if you're going to run him 15 times a game, how long will he last before they break him in half? But he is obviously special, and it's going to be very interesting to see what happens when he comes into this league. Do you just run your regular offense and let him scramble when he scrambles? Do you put in a few plays just for him? Or do you really build an entire new offense around him?"

Tebow (who, to the surprise of many, was taken in the first round of the 2010 draft by the Denver Broncos) may or may not be the player who bridges the college game to the NFL. Kansas State's Michael Bishop, a dynamic college player, couldn't do it because he lacked the passing skills. Vick was even more dynamic, but ultimately—thus far—has failed for the same reason, caught between his spellbinding running skills and his limited passing accuracy. He was a running back playing quarterback, and that simply can't be anything more than a novelty.

Yet there are those who see the transition to a different kind of player, and a different kind of offense, as inevitable. "There are only so many plays in football; all we're doing is finding different ways to run them all," says Gailey. "But there's no escaping the fact that high school and college football are developing a different type of athlete. Pretty soon—I don't know how long, but pretty soon—somebody is going to find an athlete who can run and throw and just take the conventional quarterback off the field."

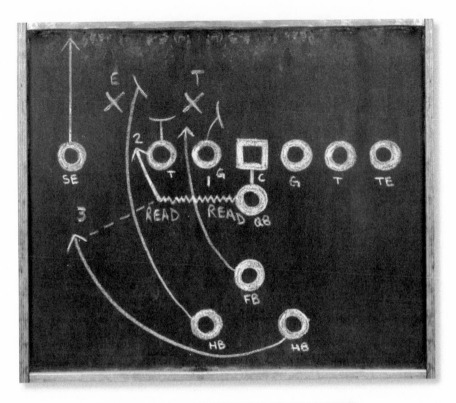

TEXAS LONGHORNS 53 VEER

This was the bread-and-butter of the wishbone, the triple-option play that stampeded football. The quarterback takes the snap and puts the ball in the belly of the fullback, who is attacking the hole of the offensive guard. The guard, however, does not block the defensive tackle. Instead, the QB "reads" the defensive tackle; if the DT goes for the fullback, the quarterback keeps the ball; if he goes for the quarterback, the QB leaves the ball in the arms of the fullback who bursts through the open hole. If the QB keeps the ball, he moves down the line of scrimmage. The offensive tackle does not block the defensive end, who is also read by the quarterback. If the DE goes after the quarterback, the QB pitches out to the trailing halfback. If the DE instead goes after the halfback deep in the backfield, the QB keeps the ball and runs up inside.

CHAPTER 4

THE WISHBONE

A good ol' Texas coach had a crazy idea, his boss said O.K.,
and the damn thing tore through football like a tornado

South Bend, Ind.
October 1996

THEY CAME bearing a relic. On a splendid college football fall weekend the Air Force Academy arrived in South Bend to play Notre Dame. The Fighting Irish were three seasons removed from their last serious national title run, but they still represented a formidable program, stocked with prized recruits. Notre Dame was 4–1, having lost only to a powerful Ohio State team. Air Force was 3–2, having been beaten in September at Wyoming and by Navy on the weekend before flying in to face Notre Dame. The Falcons were overmatched and, remarkably, were still using a piece of college football memorabilia that was seemingly the province of only the stubborn and the desperate.

College football fans of a certain age would recognize the formation and its basic plays: A quarterback under center with three running backs behind him in a Y shape, a fake (or handoff) to the fullback and then a classic keep-or-pitch option to the outside. It was a part of history. At its birth in 1968 Texas sprung the wishbone on an unsuspecting Southwest Conference and tore through 30 consecutive victories. The Longhorns' formation begat Oklahoma's wildfire 'bone that ripped up the sport for a decade and a half and spawned hundreds of imitators at all levels of the game. "That offense, it changed the game of football for 20 years," says Bill Bradley, a veteran NFL assistant coach who also happened to be the first wishbone quarterback in history while a senior at Texas.

The wishbone had even carried into the NFL. In 1981 Archie Manning was in his 11th year as quarterback with the New Orleans Saints. Bum Phillips was in his first season as the team's head coach, and he thought it might be useful to install an option play, recalling Manning as a scrambling folk hero from Ole Miss. In the third game of the season the Saints played the Giants in New Jersey, and Phillips called the option. Manning was ever the good soldier but, at age 32, he'd been battered by years of pounding on poor teams and long ago had been robbed of his quickness. He wobbled down the line of scrimmage with the ball and at the corner found himself face-to-face with Giants rookie linebacker Lawrence Taylor, a 22-year-old, 6' 3", 237-pound force of nature. Taylor exploded into Manning and deposited him on the concrete-hard artificial turf. "I knew I was done right there," said Manning. "And that was the last time we ran the option with the Saints."

Yet it was instructive that they tried. At the college level Texas (1969), Oklahoma ('74 and '75) and Alabama ('78 and '79) won national titles with the pure wishbone not long after its inception. Oklahoma (again, in '85), Notre Dame ('88) and Colorado ('90) did likewise with offenses based largely on triple-option principles. Yet by that day in South Bend in '96 it had become almost invisible on Saturday afternoons. Nebraska alone among major powers swam upstream against the trend, winning national titles in '94, '95 and '97 with an I formation–based option game. The wishbone was used almost exclusively by the service academies and dismissed by many as a crutch for the undermanned.

Reasons for the wishbone's decline were unclear. "I think it's one word: recruiting," says Lou Holtz, who ran option football at five stops in his college coaching career, including with his Notre Dame national champion in 1988. "Once alumni started treating recruiting like it was a season in itself, it became very difficult to run the option. All of a sudden, [if you were an option team,] you couldn't get the dominant quarterback, because you weren't going to throw the football and get him ready for the NFL. You couldn't get the dominant left tackle, because you weren't going to teach him to pass-block. You couldn't get the dominant running back, because he wasn't going to be featured enough. Now, you can still win with the option even if you don't get those people, but if you're not getting those top recruits, the alumni start to think you're losing and you're not exciting enough."

It was within this atmosphere, though, that the 1996 Air Force team and its 13th-year head coach, Fisher DeBerry, remained scrupulously committed to wishbone and flexbone hybrids. A year earlier in Colorado Springs, Notre Dame had pounded Air Force 44–14, racing to an early lead and shutting down the 'bone with a physical front. In '96 the Irish were physical again.

Air Force was led by senior quarterback Beau Morgan, a rugged Texan who would leave the academy as the first college quarterback in history to pass and run for 1,000 yards in each of two consecutive seasons. But Morgan had serious doubts about this game. In midweek, after watching film of the Fighting Irish, he called his father, Barry, who had coached him at Trinity Christian Academy in Texas. "These guys are so good up front," Beau told his dad, "I don't know if we'll gain a yard."

As it turned out, they gained lots of yards—304 on the ground and 355 overall. Morgan rushed for 183 yards on 23 carries, repeatedly attacking the middle of the Notre Dame defense with a wishbone variation called the midline option, in which Morgan often carried behind a blocking back nearly straight up the middle of Notre Dame's defense. They did it with a makeshift offensive line—sophomore Zach Jordan, a 240-pound guard, replaced injured Shawn Tellers after just three plays, and sophomore tackle Frank Mindrup started the game for the injured Chuck Parks. Most of all, they did it with superb wishbone execution, leaving Notre Dame in befuddled frustration. It was a classic predicament: Notre Dame, with superior talent, faced a seldom-seen offense with just a week to prepare. The Irish knew it too. Before the game, according to a story published in USA Today three days later, Notre Dame defensive coordinator Bob Davie, who would become head coach the following season, said he'd told Holtz before the game, "Coach, I am just amazed that more people in college football don't run the wishbone." Davie added, "I was always afraid to say that publicly because I'm a defensive coach. I don't want more guys going to it. It really is an amazing offense." (As for Holtz, his appreciation of the offense has never wavered. "If I was hired again somewhere," Holtz says, "and they told me they wanted to win the national championship, I would immediately put in the option. The dumbest thing I ever did in my career was get away from it. To this day, it is an offense that cannot be defended.")

The game's critical call came with just over seven minutes to play, when

Air Force faced fourth-and-one at the Notre Dame 26-yard line, trailing 17–10. The Falcons ran their basic triple option, Right 35—"It took me two seconds to call the play," says Morgan—and Notre Dame attacked Morgan on the corner with two tacklers, trying to force a rushed decision and an errant pitch or fumble. Typical of good wishbone teams, however, Air Force had spent 15 minutes every day on a drill called Ride and Decide, in which scout-team players would attack Morgan even more aggressively than the Irish defenders did, making him pitch with urgency under heavy pressure. "What Notre Dame did to me," Morgan said, "I had seen every day for three years."

Morgan kicked the ball outside in the instant the pressure reached him, sending halfback Tobin Ruff to the outside—and all the way into the end zone for the tying score. Air Force won with a field goal in overtime. In the locker room after the game, Notre Dame freshman free safety Deke Cooper put words to the helplessness felt by so many teams beaten by wishbone football. "I was just confused," said Cooper. "I didn't know what was going on. In practice I was picking it up. But on the field it was totally different."

Today Beau Morgan understands even better what took place on that afternoon and many others like it. "Notre Dame was a step behind all day," he says. "They had a defense that was very skilled, very tough, very fast, but they were unable to play the way they played against Ohio State or some other team with similar talent, because against us, they didn't know who had the ball."

Austin, Texas
Summer 1968

THESE WERE restless times for Longhorns football. A decade earlier coach Darrell Royal, a native Oklahoman who once played postwar defensive back and quarterback for Bud Wilkinson's powerhouse Sooners, had crossed the Red River to restore Texas to its burnt-orange glory. He took over in 1957 and had it rolling by '59, when the Horns went 9–2. They lost only eight games, with two ties, in a six-season stretch that included a national title in the 1963 season, when they beat Roger Staubach and Navy in the Cotton Bowl. But by '68 those days seemed long distant and memories had grown short. Texas had lost four games in each of three consecutive seasons, falling twice each to Arkansas, SMU and TCU. After closing the '67 season with consecutive losses to TCU and rival Texas A&M, Royal turned down a bid to the Bluebonnet Bowl in Houston, the same bowl the Longhorns had played in to end their previous season. It seemed that Royal was downright embarrassed to go back a second time to a consolation bowl.

Changes would ensue. Royal reworked his staff, most significantly placing the Longhorns' inert offense (just 186 points in 10 games in '67) in the hands of 40-year-old linebackers coach Emory Bellard. It was a curious choice—Bellard had been in college football for all of one year after coaching 17 years of high school football at three different stops in Texas. On Dec. 17, 1966, Bellard's team from San Angelo Central High in West Texas had beaten Spring Branch High of Houston 21–14 for the Texas State Class 4A championship at Memorial Stadium in Austin. That victory had come on Bellard's 39th birthday, and soon thereafter Royal summoned him to the state university. "Every year since 1954 I had opportunities to go to at least one school in the Southwest Conference," says Bellard. "But I loved the high school atmosphere. Then Darrell called, and of course, that's the only place I would have gone."

Bellard was disappointed in what he found. "We had a really poor football team," he says. "We went 6–4 that season, nothing like what I would have expected from the University of Texas." He was on the road south of Abilene in central Texas recruiting a linebacker that spring when Royal called to inform him that Bellard would now be calling plays in the autumn. *Lord help me,* thought Bellard. But he knew the freshman squad—first-year players were ineligible for varsity in those days—was strong, led by fullback Steve (Woo) Worster and wide receiver Charles (Cotton) Speyrer. As the spring unfolded, Bellard began installing a basic split-T formation offense, which had first been used by Don Faurot at Missouri in the 1940s and included rudimentary option plays. He had a different idea in his head, but that he took home with him, letting it rattle around his brain, imagining what it could do, as the Texas spring turned to summer, the temperature rising and the pressure building.

Forty years later Emory Bellard, 80 years old, stands on the back patio of his ranch home in Georgetown, Texas, a half hour north of Austin. The house abuts a golf course, and just off the porch is the tee box for the 3rd hole, a long dogleg right. Bellard doesn't play much golf anymore, but slim and vibrant in a green sweater and khaki pants, he looks like he could tee it up just fine.

He holds the wishbone close to his soul. In a sense it was the perfect marriage of man and method, an offense for the overmatched created by a small-sized man working in a big man's game.

Like almost all football coaches, Bellard paid his dues toiling for years at the lowest levels of the game. Born in Luling, Texas, south of Austin, Bellard was raised in the small South Texas town of Port Aransas but didn't play football in high school until he was a junior, a single wing tailback at Aransas Pass High. (He was also on the track team and claims he once did 63 chin-ups in one minute while competing in a now extinct state championship event called the rural pentathlon.) He enlisted in the Army shortly after graduating in the spring of 1945, but the war ended soon after, and Bellard headed off to the University of Texas, a 5' 9", 165-pound scatback joining the biggest nationwide influx of college football players in the history of the game. He played on the freshman team in the fall of '45 and broke his leg. "Went from 10-flat in the hundred to 11-flat," he says. He never won a letter in Austin and finished up at Southwest Texas State Teachers College. He became a coach in the fall of '50 at Alice High, west of Corpus Christi, where he worked under former Detroit Lions offensive lineman Ox Emerson, who taught him the basics of scouting and strategy. He would spend 16 more seasons coaching at three more Texas high schools and win three prized state titles.

It was during Bellard's last year at Ingleside High in 1954 that he began to experiment with the roots of what would become the wishbone. "We had a good athlete playing quarterback that year and another good one coming up," says Bellard. "They could both do a lot of things. There were some things I thought we might be able to do with the quarterback and the fullback." Option football was not new; when Royal played at Oklahoma, the Sooners ran a straight down-the-line option with no fake to a fullback. Other teams had done likewise, sending the quarterback to the corner of the line with the "option" to keep the ball or pitch it out, based on the reaction of the contain player on the edge. But Bellard started thinking of ways to incorporate the fullback, for a third option. (In keeping with the overlapping nature of the history of football innovation, Barry Switzer would later suggest that Bellard may have picked up some of his ideas from Charles (Spud) Cason, a junior high school coach in Fort Worth in the '50s, who is said to have experimented with similar schemes.)

Between 1955 and his arrival at Texas in '67, Bellard was endlessly sketching possibilities for his new offense. He was clearly influenced by Bill Yeoman, the University of Houston head coach; it was Yeoman who truly introduced the triple option to college football, in the form of his split back "veer" offense in 1965. Yeoman was a Midwesterner who had played for coach Red Blaik at Army just after World War II and got his first head coaching job at Houston in '62. After starting out a promising 7–4 in his first season, Yeoman's Cougars slipped to 2–8 in '63 and were 2-4-1 in November of '64, preparing to play Penn State at home, when they happened onto the triple option by accident.

"We were getting ready for Penn State, Coach" recalls Yeoman—he calls his interviewer "Coach" throughout a long conversation. "And I wanted to run an old power sweep into a short slot. For some reason, I don't remember why, we had the two halfbacks lined up behind the guards on each side. Well, we ran a dive inside there, and the defensive tackle came way upfield and we cut it up inside him. The next morning we looked at the film and I said, 'Hold on a minute, let's look at that.' And we put it in against Penn State, and even though we got beat, Coach, we ran for a whole bunch of yards."

In the spring Yeoman installed the veer, so-named because the front-side halfback "veers" slightly to the outside while the quarterback puts the ball in the halfback's belly and either gives it to him (option 1) or keeps it, depending on the movement of the defensive tackle. After that initial read, the quarterback would either run upfield (option 2) or pitch it to the trailing halfback (option 3) from the back side of the formation. Early in the '65 season Yeoman got cold feet and didn't often run his new triple-option veer, and the Cougars started out 1–5. Before a Halloween weekend game against Tennessee-Chattanooga ("Good thing it was Tennessee-Chattanooga," he says), Yeoman told his team, "We're going to run this thing the way we ran it in the spring."

The Cougars went 3-0-1 in their last four games and went 47-15-2 over the next six seasons, half a step ahead of America in running the triple option. "We weren't going to be able to muscle anybody out," remembers Yeoman. "But with the veer, at least for a few years, nobody knew what we were doing, so they couldn't stop us." It helped that from 1965 to '67 Yeoman had a brilliant halfback named Warren McVea and in '67 and '68 a smart, slippery quarterback named Paul Gipson.

Bellard was watching Houston's success and kept tinkering with his own version. He conceived three building blocks, some of which mirrored Yeoman's offense, and some of which did not:

1) *Formation* Instead of two running backs behind the quarterback, there would be three. They would line up in a fashion similar to a straight-T full house (which was not new), except that the fullback—the middle of the

three running backs—would be moved forward. Conceptually, this would allow the first option (the fullback dive) to hit more quickly, speeding up the entire offense and forcing quick decisions from the defense. Visually, it would look like a letter Y.

2) *Reads* The triple option, right or left, was the basis from which all wishbone plays would develop. Its first movement, again, had the quarterback putting the ball in the belly of the fullback and reading the defensive tackle, *who was not being blocked*; instead, he was allowed to come free. If he attacked the fullback, the quarterback pulled the ball out of the fullback's belly and continued on down the line for the second and third options. If the tackle ignored the fullback, driving straight upfield to impede the quarterback's movement down the line, the quarterback gave the ball to the fullback. If the quarterback kept the ball, he would sprint down the line of scrimmage until he encountered an outside defender, usually a defensive end or outside linebacker, but occasionally a strong safety. If that defender attacked the quarterback, the QB would flip—pitch—the ball outside to a trailing halfback. "If you're doing it right, there are two defenders on the line of scrimmage who you don't even have to block," says Fisher DeBerry, who ran the option for 23 seasons at Air Force. "You're just reading them both with the quarterback."

3) *Blocking* Not only was Bellard proposing to read two blocks on the offensive front (Yeoman's veer read only the outside defender), but he was also using the front-side halfback (the one closest to the corner) as a lead blocker. While the quarterback worked down the line of scrimmage, the trailing halfback accelerated into open space to receive the pitch (ideally slashing upfield just as the quarterback flipped the ball to him). The lead halfback would barrel forward, blocking any defender in the gaps.

THERE WERE other wrinkles in the offense that Bellard had in mind, and other coaches would later add many more. "It all came down to one-two-three," he says. "One, somebody has to take the quarterback on the outside. Two, somebody has to take the pitch man. Three, somebody has to cover the deep third or you can beat 'em with the vertical passing game. And we did that." As summer arrived in '68, Bellard still wasn't ready to bring his offense to Royal. In the backyard of his Austin home he lined up his sons—Emory, Jr. was 18, and Bob was just eight—and one of their friends in his new formation. Bellard played quarterback himself. Just to see it with live bodies. And it looked like it worked. He went over to the Texas campus and rounded up some football players who had exhausted their eligibility, and he again played quarterback while they ran the other positions. Again, it looked viable. "One thing I knew," says Bellard. "If I could run it, I knew durn sure I could teach good athletes to run it."

Still, he kept his baby under wraps. Royal was under intense heat from spoiled Texas alums; for Bellard to suggest a virgin offense, virtually untested, was a mighty risk. Bellard found a former UT quarterback named Andy White, who had been with the Longhorns in '66, and asked him to run the formation with Bellard's band of postgrads. Again, it seemed to click, and at last Bellard felt ready to take it to the head coach. He went to Royal's office in Gregory Gym, Bellard smoking his ever-present pipe, and drew the new scheme up on a chalkboard. Then he walked Royal down to the field in Memorial Stadium, where White and his ersatz teammates were waiting to demonstrate. Royal watched impassively at first and then began to coach. After little more than an hour of repetition, he turned to Bellard and said, "Let's go with it."

To this day Bellard is humbled by the thought of that. "People hardly remember how tough those times were," he says. "Darrell had gone 6–4, 7–4, 6–4, and here I am suggesting something *way* out of the mold. But he looked at it, and he understood it, and he put his stamp on it. That took a lot of guts."

They would need the right quarterback to run it. At the start of two-a-day practices in the summer of 1968, Bill Bradley was the Texas Longhorns quarterback. Bradley had been dubbed Super Bill for his high school exploits; he was a Texas schoolboy legend in a state that worships at the altar of Friday-night football and exalts its young heroes more fervently than most. His reputation took root in the fall of '64. As a senior quarterback at Palestine High ("God's country!" a wisecracking Bradley would hoot more than four decades later. "The Holy Land!"), Bradley led his team to the Texas Class 3A state title. He was a righthanded quarterback who sometimes threw with his left. He punted too, and Texas teammates would recall that, just for fun, he would occasionally launch a high hanger during practice and then sprint down the field and catch it, cackling all the way. At Texas he had presided over the last two of Royal's four-loss seasons, but it never occurred to anyone that the mediocrity was the fault of Super Bill.

As the starter for the '68 season, Bradley would operate the new offense, which did not yet have a name. The halfbacks would be senior Chris Gilbert and junior Ted Koy (whose father, Ernie Sr., had been a Longhorns star in the early 1930s and whose older brother, Ernie Jr., was in the NFL with the New York Giants). Steve Worster, the heralded sophomore, was installed as the all-important fullback. The pieces were in place. And they almost instantly crumbled.

Texas was tied by Houston 20–20 in the season opener at Memorial Stadium. But Bellard's offense did get its name that night when Royal met with a group of sportswriters at the Villa Capri Hotel in Austin. According to historian Bill Little, one of the reporters asked Royal what he should call this new offense, albeit such an unsuccessful one in the opener. Said the writer, "It looks like a Y."

From near the door Mickey Herskowitz of the *Houston Post* said, "It looks like a pulley-bone." That sounded about right to Royal, who said, "O.K. The wishbone."

It appeared the name might die a quick and quiet death. A week later in Lubbock, Texas Tech beat the Longhorns 31–22, a loss that would knock Texas from the national rankings. Bradley was struggling with Bellard's offense. "One of the greatest athletes I've ever seen," recalls Bellard. "But he was Super Bill, and he had created so many things in his mind that he just had to do, and he was trying to do it all. And nobody can do it all."

In the spring of 2008 Bradley was employed as the defensive backfield coach for the San Diego Chargers, as full of piss and vinegar as he had been as a teenager in Austin, and he remembered the start of the '68 season as if it had just happened. "Here's what you're lookin' at," says Bradley. "You've got a team that went 6-4, 7-4 and 6-4. Now we're 0-1-1 in 1968, and we're all flyin' on two twin-engine planes out of Lubbock in the middle of the night back to Austin. We've got an embryo offense and a quarterback who can't operate it properly. Got that? So we land at, I don't know, two or three in the morning, and then there's a knock on my door at 5:30 a.m. Sunday. I'm dead asleep. Voice on the other side of the door says, 'Bill, Coach Royal wants to see you in his office.' Well, you know what Coach Royal used to say: 'When you pass the ball, three things can happen, and two of them are bad'? Well, when you get called into his office at 5:30 on Sunday morning and you're the quarterback and you're 0-1-1, there's about five things that can happen, *and all of 'em are bad.*"

Bradley dragged himself over to the same Gregory Gym office where

Bellard had sold Royal on the new offense two months earlier. Royal, a dominant and intimidating figure in the game and in the state, fixed his eyes on Super Bill and said, "Bill, we're fixin' to make some changes, and I'm startin' with you."

Says Bradley, "I'm 20 years old. And I am devastated." Royal shuffled four or five other positions that day, but none, of course, was more important than quarterback. Super Bill would be replaced by his backup, James Street, a 5' 11", 170-pound junior out of Longview, Texas. Everybody called him Rat, short for River Rat, because on a team canoeing trip he had tipped over and helplessly fought the cold water, terrified and panicking because he didn't swim well. He wasn't half the athlete that Bradley was. "But he was a competin' jackass," says Bellard. "He was wound up like a nine-day clock." Street had finished the Texas Tech loss and injected some life into the Texas offense in garbage time. There had been a little spark, and that was enough of a catalyst for the change.

Four decades later James Street is a wealthy man, running The James Street Group out of an office building in Austin. His company specializes in structured settlements, arranging long-term disbursements to claimants in personal injury and wrongful death cases. He is the father of five boys; the oldest, Huston, is a major league pitcher, now the Colorado Rockies closer and one of the game's best relievers. James still walks and talks with the jaunty confidence of a little man with something to prove. In 1968, he was close friends with Bradley when he replaced him, and they remain close friends to this day. Surely their friendship was cemented during the first practice after the change.

"Monday after the Texas Tech game, we come out onto the field for practice, and I'm nervous as hell," says Street. "Bradley comes out and lines up with the split ends, because he's not a quarterback anymore. Everybody is kind of tight because we're 0-1-1 and we've got a new quarterback. So Bradley lines up to run a pattern and he unties his pants, so as soon as he starts running, his pants fall down around his ankles. And that just broke the ice for everybody.

"Then we get to the next game, and we're playing Oklahoma State at home," says Street. "Before the game Bradley stands up. He's the captain. He tells everybody to be quiet and he says, 'All right, the Rat's gonna lead us to victory today. We all gotta support the Rat.' He threw his full support behind me that day, and it was big, because he was still Super Bill. What he did that week, and every week after that, allowed me to do everything I did." One more schematic change helped: Bellard and Royal moved Worster back one step, still in front of the halfbacks but not quite so close to the line of scrimmage. It gave both Street and Worster a split second longer to read the dive option, while keeping pressure on the defense.

All Street did was win every game he started, 20 in a row, from a 31–3 rout of Oklahoma State in that first week all the way through a 21–17 win over Notre Dame in the Cotton Bowl on New Year's Day in 1970. During that stretch Texas averaged nearly 39 points a game and opponents floundered trying to decipher the option attack. Street's decision-making was flawless. Worster attacked the first option with abandon, often turning the quick-hitting fullback dive into a long gain. Koy and Gilbert were perpetually loose on the corner, and just as Bellard had predicted, confusion and missed assignments often left wide receiver Cotton Speyrer open deep. In a 47–26 rout of Baylor in '68, Gilbert (212 yards), Worster (137) and Street (108) all cracked the 100-yard mark. On New Year's Day 1969 in the Cotton Bowl, the Longhorns trampled Tennessee 36–13 and finished the year ranked No. 3 in the nation. And the next season would be even better.

After sputtering in a 17–0 season-opening win over California in Berkeley, Texas tore through eight consecutive opponents by an average margin of nearly 37 points a game. Sophomore halfback Jim Bertelsen had seamlessly filled Gilbert's spot, and Street, Koy and Worster seemed to get slicker with every game. On a raw afternoon in December in Fayetteville, Ark., the No. 1–ranked Longhorns beat No. 2 Arkansas in the second so-called "Game of the Century" in modern college football history. (The first had been three years earlier, when No. 1 Notre Dame and No. 2 Michigan State had played to a 10–10 tie.) The Texas-Arkansas matchup turned on a single play that is central to the history of the sport and to the lore of the wishbone.

Trailing 14–8, Texas faced fourth-and-three on its own 43-yard line. Royal called Street to the sideline and shouted into the ear hole of his white helmet: "*53 Veer Pass.*" Street paused and looked at Royal. The coach repeated, more loudly, "*53 Veer Pass,*" and sent Street back onto the field. It was a fairly standard wishbone play that included a fullback ride to the tight end (strong) side. Except on this play Street pulled the ball from Worster's belly, dropped back five yards and threw deep up the seam to tight end Randy Peschel, the only receiver in the pattern. The ball was thrown with perfect touch, and Peschel made a beautiful catch on a ball that came directly over the top of his helmet in tight coverage. It was a 44-yard gain. Two plays later Bertelsen scored the tying touchdown and Happy Feller kicked the winning extra point. Even before Texas wrapped up its first national title since 1963, Street was a legend.

"You know what I'm known for, more than anything else in my life?" says Street. "Fourth down and three, I could get it done. And I've lived my whole life that way."

The ensuing spring was a once-in-a-lifetime whirlwind for Street. He met John Wayne. He hung out with Elvis Presley. He *turned down* a chance to visit former president Lyndon Johnson at his ranch because, says Street, "Shoot, that sounded boring." Publications of the day kept referring to Street's sideburns, as if his facial hair underscored his cool. "How lucky I had to be that I was in the right place at the right time," Street says. "They changed the offense, and it was new and it fit my style. And I take no credit. Hell, the first time Emory showed it to me and Bradley in training camp, we said to each other, 'What in the hell are they doing?' But it just took off, and for the rest of my life I'm quote-unquote James Street and people treat me differently." (For his part, Bill Bradley eventually moved from wide receiver to defensive back, started the last few games of his senior year at Texas and played nine years in the NFL, eight of them for the Philadelphia Eagles. Super Bill, indeed.)

It was at a 1990 reunion of the '69 Longhorns that Street connected with billionaire Houston attorney Joseph Jamail, an ardent supporter of their alma mater. As Street tells it, Jamail said, "Street, I'm fixin' to buy some life insurance; I'll buy it from you." Soon thereafter, Jamail's tax attorney introduced Street to the world of structured settlements. Says Street, "I got lucky."

On the football field the Longhorns' wishbone didn't slow in Street's absence. Eddie Phillips stepped in at quarterback, and Texas went 10–0 in the 1970 regular season before losing a rematch with Notre Dame in the Cotton Bowl on New Year's Day 1971. But by then the wishbone was already sweeping through the sport like a Texas windstorm, being copied frantically throughout the game.

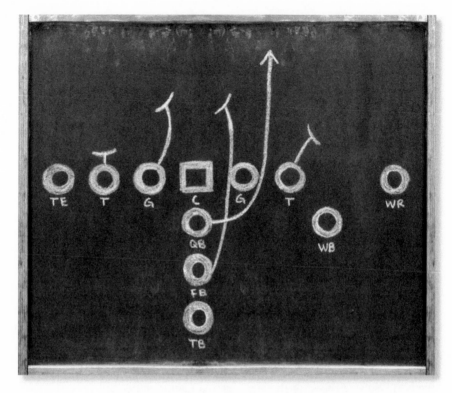

I-BONE MIDLINE OPTION

The Nebraska Cornhuskers of the mid- and late '90s used the midline option with huge success behind quarterbacks Tommie Frazier, Scott Frost and Eric Crouch. They ran it out of a wishbone variation called the I-bone, in which the fullback and tailback are positioned in a straight line ("I") directly behind the quarterback. As in the wishbone, the quarterback "rides" the fullback into the middle and, reading the reaction of the defensive tackle, decides whether to give the ball to the fullback or pull it back. If he keeps it, instead of running along the line of scrimmage and making the keep-or-pitch read with the tailback, the quarterback follows the fullback (2) into the inside hole behind blocks by the fullback and the play-side guard. The speedy Nebraska quarterbacks often reached the second level of the defense before the linebackers had even read the initial fake.

CHAPTER 5

OPTION FEVER

How the wishbone's connected to the flexbone, and the flexbone's connected to the I-bone. . . .

I T IS a given in football that when something works, it will be copied. The football world watched as Texas dominated the college game with its innovative attack. The wishbone worked. And it was copied. Emory Bellard recalls that by the spring of 1970, a steady stream of coaching staffs passed through Austin to watch the Horns practice and then sit for a tutoring session on this fabulous new offense. "Around our offices during spring training, you couldn't swing a stick without hitting half a dozen coaches," says Bellard. "It was just unreal."

He found himself doing clinics on almost every off day, all over the Southwest. He wrote manuals to help coaching staffs teach the wishbone. If some of those beseeching Bellard for his wisdom were seeking to emulate Texas's domination—and, of course, some were—many were simply attracted to the utilitarian qualities of the wishbone. It wasn't a power-based attack that required offensive linemen to open holes with power drive blocks. Rather, it used finesse blocking schemes in which linemen simply walled off their defensive counterparts or slanted inside and blocked half their bodies. The fact that two defenders were left unblocked and read by the quarterback made it more attractive. Defenses were forced to play conservatively, carefully, making sure that all options were adequately defended. It was perilous to blitz, because wishbone plays often broke the first level of containment. "All of a sudden," says Bellard, "every play can be a touchdown."

Darrell Royal would never forget these facets of the wishbone. In the summer of 1998, in the members' grill at the Barton Creek Country Club, where Royal played golf in retirement, he was asked by a visitor to recall the spring of '68, when the Texas wishbone altered the landscape of college football. It was furnace-hot outside, and though the grill was air-conditioned to meat-locker temperature, Royal was still flushed from his round in the sunshine.

He immediately began reaching over the black marble tabletop for condiment containers, arranging them with his gnarled, arthritic 74-year-old hands. A salt shaker was the quarterback, a jar of mustard the fullback, bottles of Tabasco sauce and ketchup a set of halfbacks. Royal rode his mustard with the salt and then slid the glass vessel toward the edge of the table while dragging his Tabasco halfback nearby, pushing it faster. Royal imagined defenders trying to find the ball, trying to keep their responsibilities straight, trying to play at full speed. "This will take care of those fancy pass rushers straight away," he says, joyfully smacking the table with his open right hand.

Back in 1968, when the mustard was Steve Worster and the ketchup was Chris Gilbert, a few onlookers were taking note of what Royal was up to. One was Jim Brakefield, coach at Wofford College in Spartanburg, S.C. When Brakefield had been an assistant at Wofford in the late '50s, the team had included an undersized wingback named Fisher DeBerry. When Brakefield became head coach, he made DeBerry, who'd been coaching high school ball in South Carolina, an assistant. They installed the split-back T formation, and Wofford endured four-win seasons in '67 and '68.

"People weren't real ecstatic about Jim's record those first two seasons," says DeBerry. "Well, Jim saw Texas play Tennessee in the Cotton Bowl after the '68 season, and he liked what Texas was doing. We were already using some real wide splits [between players] on the offensive line and running some splitback Houston veer, and Jim thought maybe he could mesh that with the Texas wishbone. Coach Royal sent up some film, and we studied and decided to put it in."

The result was much as it had been in Austin. Wofford lost the first two games of the 1969 season and then won 20 straight. When Brakefield moved to Appalachian State, he took DeBerry with him. They stayed nine seasons before Ken Hatfield hired DeBerry to bring the wishbone to the

Air Force Academy in 1980. Four seasons later DeBerry took over as head coach, and for 23 years DeBerry's Air Force teams used the wishbone to overcome a weekly deficit in size and speed. The Falcons won 169 games and went to 12 postseason bowls, along with mixing in the occasional epic upset, like the Beau Morgan–engineered victory over Notre Dame in 1996.

"Let's be frank," says DeBerry. "We had a system, and that system was the wishbone. And that gave us a chance to win. We couldn't recruit the same athletes as Colorado and Nebraska and Notre Dame. The wishbone is an offense that's based on routine and repetition; and routine and repetition are built into an Air Force Academy cadet's every day. I think the offense and academy go hand-in-glove." (The same was later true for Navy and Army, each of which prospered with the wishbone and its hybrids.)

DeBerry did not stand pat. He was among the first coaches to widen—or "break"—the wishbone by taking the halfbacks and lining them up as wing-backs, outside and just behind the offensive tackle (or tight end). It was called the flexbone, and it forced defenses to cover more options laterally—clearly among the precursors to the spread offenses (Chapters 12–15) that proliferated in the first decade of the new millennium. When Urban Meyer was coaching at Utah, he sought out DeBerry for advice on the option of-fense and later used a spread option to win two national titles at Florida and turn quarterback Tim Tebow into a Heisman Trophy winner.

Wishbone growth was not limited to the small and outmanned. Among the first coaches to approach Royal and Bellard was Paul (Bear) Bryant of Alabama. Bryant had been ensconced in Tuscaloosa since 1958, and in the eight years from '60 to '67, the Bear's teams lost only eight games and won two national championships. But in '68, '69 and '70 Alabama lost a total of 13 games, with back-to-back five-loss seasons. It appeared there was no magic left in Bryant's houndstooth hat, and surely none in the pro-style pass-ing game that was operated by his quarterback Scott Hunter. Bryant called Royal and asked for help. Royal and Bellard went to Tuscaloosa and holed up with Bryant and his staff in a hotel room, teaching the wishbone. The tutor-ing session lasted for four days. In the ensuing '71 season, Alabama went 11–1. From '71 to '79 the Tide rolled up a 97–11 record and won two national titles.

But there was another wishbone conversion that had far more impact on college football. The Oklahoma Sooners were in transition through the mid-1960s. Bud Wilkinson had retired his whistle after the '63 season.

Gomer Jones went 9-11-1 in two seasons, was replaced by Jim Mackenzie, whose team went 6–4 in '66 but was rocked when Mackenzie died suddenly of a heart attack after a spring practice in April '67. Mackenzie was replaced by assistant Chuck Fairbanks—but the far greater influence would come from a little-known offensive assistant named Barry Switzer.

Fairbanks's Sooners went 10–1 in 1967 but lost to one of Royal's four-loss Texas teams; for the next three years Oklahoma fell to the Longhorn wishbone, including a 41–9 pasting in '70. OU had been using the two-back Houston veer, but Switzer had grown antsy watching Texas run its wishbone.

"We were struggling with the veer," says Switzer. "So now it's 1970, and Texas is running up and down the field on everybody with the wishbone. So I'm talking with Larry Lacewell, who's running our defense, and I'm saying, 'Lacewell, this wishbone is what we should be doing. We've got a better quarterback than James Street [Jack Mildren]. We've got Gregg Pruitt and Joe Wylie. We've got better players than them." The racial element played heavily in Switzer's thinking. The 1969 Texas Longhorns were the last all-white national championship team; Switzer at the same time was recruiting black players, which he viewed as a distinct advantage. "Darrell wasn't even recruiting black athletes," says Switzer. "We were getting the best black athletes out of Texas." In fact, they were getting many of the best white athletes out of Texas too. Mildren was from Abilene and was white. Pruitt, who would become a two-time All-America as one of the most dynamic wishbone halfbacks ever, was from Houston and was black.

After losing to Oregon State in the third game of the 1970 season, Oklahoma had a week off. Switzer and Lacewell persuaded Fairbanks to work in some wishbone plays for the upcoming Texas game. That was the 41–9 loss. "Texas kicked our asses pretty good," says Switzer, who became the head coach in 1973. "But you could see we were getting better at it. And the next year we kicked their asses."

Indeed, in 1971 Oklahoma ran the Longhorns into the ground, 48–27. In one year they had become the most potent wishbone team in history. The '71 Oklahoma Sooners would average 472.4 rushing yards per game, a record still comfortably standing in 2010. "We were having a track meet every weekend, hanging half a hundred on everybody," says Switzer, invoking two of his favorite wishbone phrases—track meet and half a hundred. Switzer's teams seemed to play at a speed that was visibly faster than their opponents', as a succession of wishbone quarterbacks and halfbacks laid waste to the Big Eight and the nation. In his first 30 games as head coach, Switzer went unbeaten; the Sooners wishbone would lose just 33 games over 18 years and win three national championships, including in '74 and '75.

In a bizarre twist Oklahoma was hit with NCAA sanctions for recruiting violations prior to '73 that were invoked during the '74 and '75 season; the Sooners were banned from appearing on television in both seasons and from playing in a bowl following the '74 season. All of this notoriety lent an even more mythic air to the ripping Sooners wishbone, as if it were a slice of cowboy folklore, and Switzer was the perfect black hat. In '74 he told SI, "They can keep us off TV and ban us from the bowls, but nobody said that we couldn't win and have some fun."

Looking back, Switzer says, "I had a great run, but I'll tell you something: We had great players. For quarterbacks I had Jack Mildren, Steve Davis, Thomas Lott, J.C. Watts, Jamelle Holieway. For running backs I had Kenny King, Joe Washington, Billy Sims, Horace Ivory, Elvis Peacock. Great, great players. And with the wishbone, they couldn't stop us."

What is most remarkable is that Texas *gave* the wishbone to the archrival Sooners. After being routed by Texas in that 1970 game, Fairbanks called Royal and asked for help. The Sooners had picked up the big strokes of the wishbone from film but needed work with the subtleties. Royal was an Oklahoma alumnus, with some lingering loyalty to the Crimson and Cream. He called Bellard.

"Emory," he said, "Chuck Fairbanks is gonna lose his job up there if they don't do something about their offense, so I want to help him out. Barry Switzer is gonna be calling, and I want you to tell him whatever they need to know to put in the wishbone."

Bellard was stunned. As much as he had been willing to help other teams, the thought of handing over his prized weapon to the rival Sooners was too much to swallow. "Darrell, you gotta be joking," said Bellard.

"Nope," said Royal. "I'm just as dead serious as I can be."

Royal was the boss. Bellard backed down. Switzer called a week later and kept on calling for several months. "Anytime he had a question about what to do in a certain situation or against some defense, he would just call me right up," says Bellard. "We gave the whole thing to 'em."

Nearly four decades later Switzer insists the Sooners would have figured it out anyway. "Aw, sure, they helped us a little bit," he says. "But Emory had done a bunch of lectures, and we had all the Texas film, so it's not like there were a lot of secrets. By the time the 1971 season came around, our offense had it rolling, and we just about changed college football for the next 20 years or so."

After turning the wishbone over to his alma mater, Darrell Royal never beat the Sooners again as a head coach, losing every year from 1971 to '75 before salvaging a 6–6 tie in '76, his last year as coach of the Longhorns. More than 20 years later, in the summer of 2007, Bellard and Royal got together for an afternoon, two old coaches trading stories. In the middle of it all, Royal turned to his old assistant and said, "Emory, if I had it to do all over again, I probably wouldn't have been so benevolent."

Among the many coaches casting his eyes to the Southwest was Lou Holtz, who was hired as a 32-year-old in 1969 as head coach at William & Mary. He had been an assistant with Woody Hayes's powerhouse program at Ohio State and rolled into Williamsburg, Va., intent on running a little of everything on offense. His first team went 3–7, and in spring meetings he began studying an option offense that coach Jimmy (Red) Parker had once used at Arkansas A&M and The Citadel. It fascinated Holtz and, even better, it looked to him like a lifeline.

"Going into our second year at William and Mary, I sat down with my staff and said, 'O.K., let's list our assets,' " says Holtz. "We had a fine center. We didn't have a running back who'd gained a yard in a varsity game. We had one receiver who had caught three passes. On the offensive line we had problems everywhere but center. I said, 'How are we going to move the ball?' "

Replied his assistant, Larry Beightol, "If I were you, I'd just worry about making sure it doesn't go backward."

Holtz installed the wishbone and won the Southern Conference title in 1970 and went to the Tangerine Bowl. Two years later he began a four-year run as head coach at North Carolina State and took the Wolfpack to four consecutive bowls. Holtz coached 26 more years at four schools and always kept the option at the core of his offense, always forcing opponents to prepare to defend it, even if some Saturdays he chose not to run even a single option play.

When Holtz took his dream job at Notre Dame in 1986, he committed wholly to the option game. The problem was that, initially, he didn't have an option quarterback, having inherited senior Steve Beuerlein from previous coach Gerry Faust's failed regime. Beuerlein would play 14 years and start 102 games in the NFL, but at a statuesque 6' 3", 220 pounds, he was glacially slow. Holtz tried to run the option just the same, instructing Beuerlein never to keep the ball. In a summer practice he kept the ball on an option play and ran 20 yards upfield and was stunned to see Holtz chasing him from behind. "Steve Beuerlein, don't you *ever* run the ball again!" screamed Holtz. "You see that fast guy behind you? He's the runner. Pitch the ball to him and get out of the way."

A year later Beuerlein had been replaced by Tony Rice, a quarterback Barry Switzer would have loved: quick, strong, decisive and, just to further torment defenses, with a strong arm to exploit the deep defensive third of the field. Rice led Notre Dame to the national championship in 1988 and to the No. 2 national ranking a year later when the Irish knocked off previously unbeaten Colorado 21–6 in the Orange Bowl.

That win was significant because one year later Colorado would share the national championship running an I formation hybrid of the wishbone installed by offensive coordinator Gerry DiNardo under head coach Bill McCartney. That championship came nine years after McCartney was hired and five years after switching to the wishbone's cousin, the I-bone. "And I certainly think it was done out of desperation," says DiNardo.

Colorado had gone 7-25-1 in McCartney's first three seasons. "Bill wanted to throw the ball, so we threw the ball," says DiNardo. "I remember the headline in the Boulder *Daily Camera* said something like BUFFS WILL BE THE BYU OF THE BIG EIGHT. Even as we started to recruit better players, we still couldn't win. To me, from an analytical perspective, we were throwing too much on first-and-10. That's such an important down. It's the only neutral down in football. It's the only down where the defense has to defend everything. But we were throwing so much on first-and-10 that even against equal talent like Kansas and Kansas State—we were bad, they were bad—we were constantly in second-and-10. And second-and-10 favors the defense.

"So we started looking around at what other people were doing offensively," says DiNardo. "And we are absolutely desperate. At that point, we're talking 1984, you've got Lou Holtz running a form of the wishbone at Minnesota. You've got Oklahoma with Switzer and Larry Lacewell. You've got Jim Wacker at TCU, Ken Hatfield at Arkansas and, of course, you've got Fisher DeBerry at Air Force. So after all those years of second-and-10, we've got to find a way to get four yards on first down. Well, we felt like if we read the triple option correctly, it was pretty much unstoppable for four yards on first down. So we put it in for 1985 and sold our kids on the theory that if we could play first-and-10, second-and-six, third-and-two and stay on schedule 50 percent of the time, we would win every game. And it darn near worked out that way."

Not at first. DiNardo met with DeBerry, Hatfield and Lacewell in the winter of 1985 and installed the option at spring practice. He took the practice tape to Lacewell to view during a national coaches' convention. When DiNardo walked out of the room with his tape, Lacewell said to his fellow coaches, "I feel bad. They'll be lucky to win a game." The transition was comically painful. DiNardo recalls a preseason gathering in Denver with a booster club. One of the gentlemen in the audience stood up and, having heard of the conversion to the wishbone, said to McCartney, "Please tell me the first play of the season isn't going to be a dive up the middle, because I don't think I can stand that."

McCartney let the question hang and then answered: "You might want to come for the second play."

With athletes recruited to play a passing game, the Buffaloes improved from 1–10 in '84 to 7–5 in '85 to 8–4 in '88, settting the stage for a two-year run at the national title. "The switch to the wishbone allowed us all to keep our jobs long enough to start recruiting players," says DiNardo. They did exactly that, picking up the quicksilver quarterback Darian Hagan, a classic, tough and slippery wishbone QB, and running backs Eric Bieniemy and J.J. Flannigan. In their prime the Buffaloes ran their option from an I-bone, with two backs directly behind the quarterback and the second (lead blocking) halfback offset to the side, which DiNardo felt give him a better angle to throw a load block on the corner.

Colorado won 11 straight before losing to Notre Dame in the Orange Bowl following the '89 season and beat the Irish a year later, 10–9, to earn a piece of the title with Georgia Tech. "Not only did we stop a very bad slide, but we won a national championship," says DiNardo. "Which is pretty good."

Nebraska's option offense won *three* national titles, in 1994, '95 and '97 (shared with Michigan). That number could easily have been five had it not been for one failed two-point conversion in the '84 Orange Bowl and an upset loss in the '96 Big 12 championship game. For all of the success that Texas and Oklahoma achieved in the '70s and '80s, Nebraska's I formation–based option attack was arguably the most innovative and surely one of the most effective in the game's history. Unlike many of his peers, Nebraska coach Tom Osborne did not turn to the option out of desperation—in his case it was out of frustration.

In a 25-year head coaching career that began in 1973 when he was selected to replace his mentor, Bob Devaney, Osborne won nearly 84% of his games and never won fewer than nine in a season. "But we had trouble with Oklahoma," he says. "And I really came to admire what they did with option football." In Osborne's first eight years at Nebraska his teams lost a total of 20 games; however, they beat Oklahoma only once.

In 1981 Osborne installed an I-based option. "I didn't want to leave the I and go to the wishbone entirely," says Osborne. "We still liked the idea of having a great runner back there who could run the ball at any point on the field. Oklahoma had Billy Sims ['75, '77–79] in a wishbone, and he was a great player, but he was a little limited in how much he could carry the ball because of where he lined up."

The Nebraska I option (or I-bone) was an immediate success, largely because of three-year starting quarterback Turner Gill, who had been the object of a furious recruiting war while a quarterback at Arlington Heights High in Fort Worth. "The biggest mistake I ever made in coaching was taking for granted that Turner Gill was coming to Oklahoma," says Switzer. "February 1980, I'm fighting my ass off for a linebacker. I get a call from Turner Gill. He puts a stake in my heart and tells me he's going to Nebraska. So not only do I lose him, but I lose him to Nebraska, and I gotta play their ass!"

With Gill operating the Nebraska attack, the Cornhuskers went 12–1 in both 1982 and '83 and narrowly lost the '83 national title when Osborne famously played for a winning two-point conversion and lost to Miami 31–30 in the Orange Bowl. Not long after, the balance of power in the Big Eight would shift back to Oklahoma and, briefly, to McCartney and Colorado, always with the wishbone or some form of the triple option as the basis of the offense. But through the middle of the '90s, Osborne sped the evolution of Emory Bellard's old game, stringing together a series of innovations and nearly landing four consecutive national titles. Among Osborne's variations:
• Pulling tackles and guards from the back side of the play to trap aggressive defenders—such as gap-blitzing linebackers, who had become a popular defensive answer to the triple option—and creating new seams in the defense. (Even the NFL was watching; Washington Redskins coach Joe Gibbs

[Chapter 7] would later credit Osborne with birthing the blocking schemes that led to the development of the Counter Trey running play that the Skins rode to Super Bowl victories at the end of the 1987 and '91 NFL seasons.)

• Creating plays in which the quarterback follows a lead blocker, instead of optioning off of unblocked defenders. Tommie Frazier (1992–95), Scott Frost ('96 and '97) and 2001 Heisman Trophy winner Eric Crouch (1998–2001) all flourished in the system.

• Running option plays with the quarterback in a shotgun formation. Osborne, who like so many of his peers is loath to claim invention of anything, says, "That one, running the option out of the shotgun, I think we were at least *one* of the first teams to try that. We got a lot of ideas from the service academies and from Oklahoma. With them, we had them on the ropes in a number of games over the years, and their quarterbacks would make a great play to get them back in contention. We wanted to develop some things where our quarterbacks could make plays like that."

Switzer says, "Here's what Tom did: He has the quarterback read the tackle, like always. Now, the linebacker is watching that read, but he doesn't know the tailback is hauling ass right behind the fullback and he's going to block the linebacker. Right when that happens, the quarterback ducks into that seam, and the first guy with a shot at him is the three-deep safety. Tom got teams in fourth-and-three, and he'd go for it, and by then I'm out of college coaching and I'm watching on TV, and I would just start laughing my ass off because they don't know what's about to hit 'em. Next thing you know, the Nebraska quarterback is running 50 yards untouched."

By the turn of the century, though, the wishbone (and all forms of the triple option) had all but vanished from the college game. Recruiting was clearly a factor, as the option became stigmatized as failing to prepare star players for the pro game. "The wishbone in particular became a service-academy offense because the major programs running it could no longer successfully recruit the great quarterback, the great running back, the great left tackle," says DiNardo. "When we were running it at Colorado, I can't tell you how many programs beat us up in recruiting by telling kids, 'You won't be able to play in the NFL because you won't be learning the passing game.' And eventually most of the option teams just caved in, and it gradually went away."

In related fashion, and just as significantly, there was a rush to install spread offenses and numerous other throwing systems. Eventually they, too, would incorporate option principles. But as for the pure wishbone, its practitioners dwindled to a precious few. One of them was Paul Johnson, a North Carolinian who was at his third assistant coaching stop at age 27 when he was named offensive coordinator at NCAA Division I-AA Georgia Southern in the spring of 1985. He had played on a wishbone team in high school and had watched on Saturday afternoons as Oklahoma tore up the midlands and Alabama the South with the wishbone. "Here was the biggest thing for me," says Johnson. "When I was on defense, I thought the option was really hard to defend well, if it was run right. So I wanted to run it." In his two years at Georgia Southern, his offense averaged 36 points a game and won 26 of 30.

Ten years later Johnson was back at Georgia Southern with his first head coaching position, and he wishboned—flexboned, really—the Southern Conference and all of Division I-AA into submission. In five years the Eagles went 62–10, won two national titles and five conference championships. True to early wishbone strategy, defending it left Georgia Southern's opponents susceptible to the passing game. "Some of those teams, we scored 50 points a game for stretches, and our guys were playing half the game," says Johnson. "We could have scored 70 every game if we wanted to."

It galled Johnson then, and it galls him now, that the wishbone fell into such disfavor and was so roundly criticized, like fashion worn a year too long. To his mind, it never stopped working. Coaches just stopped using it because something else was available. "All of a sudden there was this stigma attached to it, that you're not supposed to use it anymore," says Johnson. "Well, why not? I think it's because some of those really strong Miami teams beat some Oklahoma option teams by throwing the ball. And that was about it. Then they would say it's an offense for overmatched teams, when you don't have equal talent. At Georgia Southern we had equal or better talent than the team we were playing, and we went 62–10."

Ironically, Johnson would prove the overmatched theory in his next job. In 2002 Johnson became head coach at Navy. The Midshipmen went 2–10 in Johnson's first year and then 43–19 in the next five. That got him hired at Georgia Tech late in 2007, where he promised to bring the wishbone back to major-college football. In his first season at Georgia Tech, in 2008, the Yellow Jackets finished 9–4 and Johnson was named ACC Coach of the Year; in 2009, he finished 11–3—all the while running the triple option. He kept his promise. The 'bone still had some pop in it.

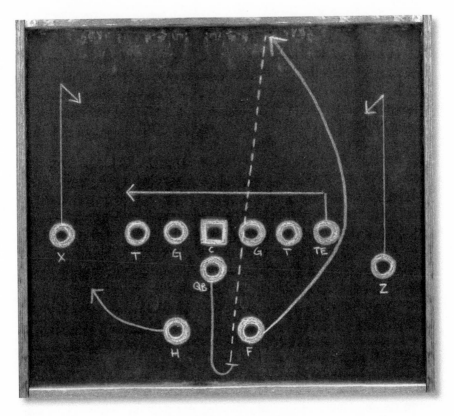

525 F POST SWING

One of the staples of Don Coryell's revolutionary vertical passing game was the post swing. In Coryell's digit system, pass plays are numbered across the formation. On this play both outside receivers (X and Z) run "5" routes (15-yard comebacks) while the tight end (TE) runs a "20" route (a shallow cross). Thus, reading the routes horizontally, 5-20-5 or 525. The comeback routes occupy the two cornerbacks and the cross route attracts the linebackers. Meanwhile, the "F" receiver—sometimes a running back, sometimes a second tight end—runs a post-pattern option route to the middle of the field ("F post"), reading the deep safety and cutting accordingly.

CHAPTER 6

AIR CORYELL

In the '60s, a squeaky-voiced coach decided there was only one way to beat a better team: Throw like hell

Pasadena, Calif.
February 1, 1993

ORV TURNER woke up on a Monday morning in possession of a Super Bowl title. As offensive coordinator of the Dallas Cowboys he had called plays the previous night in the Rose Bowl, guiding the Cowboys to a 52–17 rout of the Buffalo Bills. Dallas quarterback Troy Aikman had thrown four touchdown passes to three receivers and had been named the game's most valuable player.

The game would occupy an important place on the NFL time line: A storied franchise, and one of the league's most recognizable brand names, the Cowboys had returned to greatness following a decade of mediocrity and just three years after jarring change—most notably the ouster of beloved founding head coach Tom Landry by new oilman owner Jerry Jones. The victory would launch a minidynasty, as Dallas won three Super Bowls in four years.

The game was equally significant in another way. It had showcased Aikman and a Dallas passing game that would become an NFL staple throughout the '90s. On a warm California evening Aikman had peppered the Buffalo defense with scoring passes: a 23-yard touchdown to tight end Jay Novacek running straight up the middle of the Buffalo defense; a 19-yard slant score to Michael Irvin slashing diagonally across the field; another 18-yard touchdown to Irvin, planted at the right sideline; and, finally, a 45-yard bomb to Alvin Harper, wide-open far beyond the deepest Buffalo defender.

In front of his TV at his home in San Francisco, former Chargers quarterback Dan Fouts had watched Aikman's precision like a man staring in a mirror. On the morning after the game he called Turner, offered congratulations and then said, "O.K., let me see if I got this right. . . ." Fouts then recited the play calls on each of Aikman's four touchdowns, as if he had been standing in the Cowboys' huddle.

"Dan's on the phone, and he just runs down the calls," recalls Turner. "He's like, 'The first touchdown was 370, right? Then the second one was 839? The third one looked to me like 787 special. And then the last one was 989.' I can't remember the exact calls, but Dan remembered them back then. Perfectly. He called every single play, exactly." On the phone Turner had laughed out loud and Fouts laughed back, two men linked across time by another man's lasting genius.

Fouts had been a 27-year-old quarterback for the Chargers in September of 1978 when team owner Eugene V. Klein forced head coach Tommy Prothro's resignation and replaced him with a 53-year-old coach named Don Coryell. He had built winners at San Diego State and with the St. Louis Cardinals by installing an inventive, pass-first offensive system that attacked defenses as few others had before it. Eight years later Turner, who had come to the Los Angeles Rams from USC in 1985 as an offensive assistant coach, found himself working under Ernie Zampese, who had worked under Coryell with the Chargers. Fouts and Turner shared a passion for what came to be known simply as the Coryell offense, and they shared a fluency in its language.

Fouts rode the Coryell offense into the Hall of Fame, directing the explosive Chargers attack that redefined offense through the 1980s. Turner took Coryell 101 to Dallas and taught it to Aikman and Irvin and the rest. There were many other Coryell disciples, and there would be many more in the years that followed, all because a former Army paratrooper turned football coach got sick of losing two games a year to deeper teams while coaching at San Diego State in the 1960s. So he built an offense that combined technical simplicity with daring downfield strikes written into almost every play. Pass routes were numbered in a basic 1 through 9 ladder. Quarterbacks were instructed to read from deep to short and to get rid of the ball quickly. Formations with four wide receivers became common, and eventually, players in motion became routine. On defense, an entire sport backpedaled.

Mike Martz watched Coryell's San Diego State teams while he was playing tight end at San Diego Mesa (Junior) College in the late 1960s. ("I pictured myself playing for Don, but I wasn't good enough," says Martz.) Three decades later, in 1999, Martz became offensive coordinator of the St. Louis Rams and directed an explosive offense to the Super Bowl title. Because they played home games indoors on artificial grass, the Rams came to be called The Greatest Show on Turf, but in truth it was just the Coryell offense, evolved. During the height of the Rams' success, Martz met up with Coryell, and the two were photographed together. Martz later sent the photo to Coryell with the following inscription:

> *Coach Coryell, we are all grateful to you for your impact on the game. You changed it forever. . . . the 'Godfather' of today's passing game.*

"And he is exactly that," says Martz. "He was way ahead of everyone in terms of innovation. There was this unspoken set of rules that you played by on offense. And everyone was running generally the same kind of plays. The formations were the same. The concepts were the same. Coryell changed all that. People immediately said, 'You can't do that.' Well, you can do that, and he did it. His whole approach to the game was different. He was going to beat you with the ball at any time. He had this aggressive mind-set. He was always attacking the defense, never going into this conservative mode where you try to win through attrition. And that's where football was at that time in history. Now, 40 years later, you're seeing the second and third generations of coaches running Coryell's system."

The recent history of the NFL is rich with success descended from the Coryell offense. Zampese won with it in Los Angeles. Joe Gibbs, who played for Coryell at San Diego State and also coached under him, took the playbook to Washington, expanded it and won three Super Bowls. Turner took it to Dallas, then Washington, then San Diego. Martz turned the league upside down in St. Louis. Jason Garrett (Aikman's erstwhile backup) called Coryell's plays into Tony Romo's helmet as the Cowboys' offensive coordinator. Players have been made famous by running signature patterns in the offense: Irvin on the Bang 8 slant; Jay Novacek, then Marshall Faulk and most recently Antonio Gates on the F post.

By the start of the 2008 NFL season, there was scarcely a team in the league that didn't incorporate some piece of the Coryell passing game into its offense, whether by the numbering of pass routes or spacing concepts or individual plays. By 2010 several teams—most notably Baltimore, Dallas, San Diego and San Francisco—relied almost exclusively on the Coryell offense.

"If you brought Don Coryell to Dallas and handed him our playbook," said Garrett in the fall of 2007, "without ever having watched one of our practices or games, he would still recognize an awful lot of stuff in that book."

Puget Sound, Wash.
March 2008

THE WORD coming through the football pipeline was that Don Coryell, 83 years old, had become a recluse, living a quiet life far from the mainstream, resistant to questioners and in poor health. Some of this, it turns out, is true: Coryell resides far from the noise of Sunday afternoons and has done few interviews in recent years. He has slowed with age. But he is not a recluse. It's just that inquisitors must go to him, and even in a world made small, that is not easy.

It is a 66-mile drive north on Interstate 5 from Seattle to Burlington, and then 16 miles west on Route 20 from Burlington to Anacortes, a staging point for many of the ferries that service the San Juan Islands floating at the nexis of Washington State, Canada's Vancouver Island and the Olympic Peninsula. From a pier in Anacortes, one boat stops first at Lopez Island and then continues on 20 minutes later to Friday Harbor, a village of 2,200 year-round residents, the only incorporated town on San Juan Island, the second largest in the chain. A late-model SUV slows to a stop along Front Street, parallel to the shoreline, with Coryell at the wheel.

The old coach wears a heavy fleece pullover, baggy sweat-style pants and walking shoes. A baseball cap covers thin gray hair, his blue eyes are full of vigor. He is slender in the manner of a former athlete, but he also explains that a recent knee replacement has left him hobbling, and he has a set of hiking poles in the backseat to prove it. The ride is 25 minutes over rolling, pastoral hills and sweeping roadway curves from downtown Friday Harbor to Coryell's home across the island, a three-story natural wood house overlooking a peaceful, horseshoe-shaped inlet called Neil Bay. Coryell and his wife, Aliisa (who died in December 2008), bought the home while he was still coaching in the NFL; he now lives there year-round.

The drive across the island is plenty long enough for Coryell to unfurl the story of his life: raised in Seattle, played football at Lincoln High School, enlisted in the Army in 1943 and spent 3½ years as a paratrooper. He returned to Seattle and the University of Washington in the fall of 1946 and played defensive back for the Huskies. "I wasn't good enough to play offense," he says. "Even on defense, I think I started one game, and that was in my senior year." He also began sliding, almost accidentally, toward his calling.

"I started out as a forestry major," says Coryell. "I wanted to be a forest ranger. But there was a lot of science, and there was no way I could get through all that science. So I withdrew before I flunked out and switched over to physical education." He graduated in the spring of 1950, and after getting a master's degree from Washington in physical education, embarked on what was another of those classic coaching odysseys: two years at high schools in Hawaii, two years as head coach at the University of British Columbia, a year at Wenatchee Valley College in Washington State, a year coaching a military team at Fort Ord in Northern California; three years as head coach at Whittier College in suburban L.A. and a year on John McKay's staff at USC before taking over at San Diego State in 1961.

At every stop Coryell tinkered. "You look at your players, and you figure out what the hell they can do," he says. Coryell had been a single wing quarterback in high school. In 1955 Wenatchee's lone outstanding running back was injured during the preseason. "We took one of our fullbacks and put him at tailback. The other fullback played fullback, right in front of the halfback. We called it our hash marks offense because we'd use it on the hash marks and put the other halfback to the wide side. For us, it was backs-left and backs-right."

Football historians call it something else: The power I. It would come to dominate college football in the 1970s (including at USC, where Coryell had worked with McKay). As with so many football creations, its precise origins are unclear. It might have been Frank Leahy at Notre Dame in the early 1950s or Tom Nugent at Virginia Military Institute in the middle of the decade who first ran the formation. But Coryell was certainly one of its pioneers, and Wenatchee went from winless to unbeaten in one season.

At Whittier he endlessly ran the power I, yet he remained fascinated with the possibility of expanding his offense and read a book by TCU ath- letic director and coach Dutch Meyer titled *Spread Formation Football*. In his third year at Whittier, Coryell moved a tailback to quarterback, spread out his wide receivers and began throwing passes.

Whittier went 23-5-1 in Coryell's three years. After his one season at USC he was hired to salvage football at San Diego State, winner of just seven games in the previous four seasons. Coryell made the Aztecs better immediately, winning 38 games in his first five seasons. Yet they also lost two games a year, and it was those losses that galled Coryell. "Two games, every goddam year," he says. He was scouring California junior colleges for players who had escaped the grasp of USC and UCLA, but still San Diego State usually found itself with a talent deficit against major-college programs. But not a skill defi- cit. Coryell concluded that the best way to win was to make full use of quar- terbacks and wide receivers and beat more complete teams with the pass.

"I just decided, hell, you can't just go out and run the ball against better teams," he says. "You've got to mix it up. You've got to throw the damn ball if you're going to beat better teams. So we started throwing the ball."

Joe Gibbs played at San Diego State during Coryell's first three seasons and was an assistant coach for the next three. "When I first came there in 1961," Gibbs says, "Don was a killer running coach. I formation, power running. Just killer. But then it's amazing the transition that took place. Don switched to throwing it like mad, and he was very creative. He was not afraid to try anything."

Over the next six seasons San Diego State was 55-9-1, becoming a national phenomenon, forcing recognition by pounding nonelite opponents, but forc- ing fans and media to wonder just how good they might be. "USC or UCLA might be wise to steer clear of the Aztecs," wrote SPORTS ILLUSTRATED in October 1966. SDSU sometimes drew more fans than the Chargers, who were then a power in the American Football League. Among Coryell's as- sistant coaches were Gibbs, Zampese and John Madden.

The recognition all came on the wings of the passing game, though the conversion was gradual: In 1961, Coryell's first year, San Diego State quar- terbacks threw a total of 124 passes; three years later it was 250. In 1964, se- nior Rod Dowhower (later head coach at Stanford and with the Indianapolis Colts) led a passing attack that accounted for 2,083 yards (nearly double the '61 total). Junior flanker Gary Garrison (who would become an AFL All-Star with the Chargers) caught 78 passes in '64 and 70 more from Don Horn a year later, with a total of 26 touchdowns. Haven Moses, Ken Burrow and Isaac Curtis would follow Garrison's tracks into pro football. At quarterback, Dennis Shaw followed Horn, and Brian Sipe followed Shaw; all played in the NFL, as did at least two dozen other of Coryell's San Diego State players.

That was just the beginning. Coryell would guide the St. Louis Cardinals to two divisional titles in the brutal NFC East and the Chargers to two divisional championships in the AFC West. So how, exactly, did he do it?

ON THAT chilly winter afternoon in 2008 Coryell sits at the dining table in his waterfront home, ignoring a fruit and cheese plate as he becomes absorbed in explaining his offense. From a canvas shopping bag he pulls a thick, three-ring binder, a small index card affixed to the front: SAN DIEGO CHARGERS: 1979. "Right here," Coryell says, smacking the front of the binder with his right hand, the one adorned with a ring from the College Football Hall of Fame. "This is how we did it."

Football historians often point out that Coryell created his modern, effective game at the same time Sid Gillman was coaching the Chargers and using a daring air offense with quarterback John Hadl and receivers Lance Alworth and Garrison. It has been suggested, more than once, that Coryell devised his offense after watching Gillman's. Coryell says it's not so. "Sid Gillman threw it down the field, and I probably watched Sid's teams," says Coryell. Then he smacks the binder again. "But this is *our* stuff."

Coryell's offensive system is based on three elements: simplicity, spacing and timing.

It is unclear which early sideline mavens first used numbers, rather than names, to identify pass routes. What is unquestioned is that Coryell's numbering system has been the most enduring and efficient. The foundation: Routes for the outside receivers in a formation (typically designated the X and Z receivers) are assigned single digits, from 1 to 9; routes for an inside (or Y) receiver are assigned multiples of 10, from 10 to 90. A basic pass play might begin with the number 837, which means the outside X receiver runs an 8 route, the inside Y receiver runs a 30, and the outside Z receiver runs a 7.

Coryell flips through pages in the binder until he arrives at a page entitled "Routes for X and Y." Half the page is filled with a basic diagram showing half an offensive line and a single wide receiver. A series of lines emanates from the lone wideout, each one numbered. Below the diagram is a key, with a description of each route, in intricate detail. The numbering system would become not only intrinsic to the offensive language of the sport but also to the lexicon of the broadcast booth.

Here are some examples, for the X and Z receivers, which can be split ends or flankers: A 1 route is a basic out. A 2 is a hard slant. A 6 is a curl. An 8 (or a "Bang 8," with which Aikman and Irvin would get rich and famous in Dallas) is a skinny post. A 9 is a go route, or fly pattern.

The route descriptions are precise. For instance, from the list of routes for the Y receiver, which can be a slot player, tight end or running back, a 20 is explained like this: "Release inside and sprint across field aiming for 7 YD depth on the other side of formation." This is essentially what became know as a "drag" route, or in the West Coast offense (Chapter 8), a "drive" route.

Coryell created the numbering system for two reasons. The first is that it was easy to learn quickly. At San Diego State, Coryell relied so heavily on junior college players, who would only be available to him for two seasons, that quick study was a necessity. "You can get a guy and teach him the whole thing in two days," says Coryell.

Cam Cameron, who learned the system as Turner's quarterbacks coach with the Redskins, says, "At the NFL level, one of the highest compliments you can give the system is that you can bring new guys in on Tuesday and they can play on Sunday."

The second reason—a key explanation for the longevity of the Coryell system—is that the numbering system is *visual*, rather than cognitive. Whereas many prior, and subsequent, offensive systems would give each play a word name (Cowboy or Maverick or some such), the backbone of every Coryell play is a two- or three-digit number that doesn't just name the play but also describes what the play will look like. A play with the number 335 *shows* that the X receiver is running a deep out (3), the Z receiver is running a comeback (5) and the Y receiver is also running a deep out (30).

Even in the Coryell system, further word and letter additions are necessary to describe formations and routes for the running backs (labeled H and F), as in Scat (formation) 435 F Cross (an inside crossing route by a running back). But every play is built from the foundation of the digits.

"It was always a great thing for me," says quarterback Trent Green, who played in the Coryell system for Turner in Washington and later for Mike

Martz in St. Louis. "The first thing I do when a play comes into my headset is visualize it. In this system, with every play call, you're actually telling everybody what to do by what you say. Instead of saying, 'I Right Omaha,' or something like that, you're saying, 'R 428 H Stop,' and that tells everybody what to do, instead of relying on their memorization of something."

As Joe Gibbs puts it, "Using Don's offense, you felt like the quarterback had a picture in his mind of what was going to happen. If everybody in the huddle shut their eyes, they could all see the play, much more than just learning a name by rote."

Jason Garrett, who installed the system as coordinator of the Cowboys in 2007, says, "To me, there was so much simplicity in the way it's taught and the way it's learned. And that goes back to the three-digit system of digitizing the routes. Putting the whole passing game together is just a matter of putting the numbers together. It all flows so naturally."

The spacing element of the Coryell offense—in which every route is designed to maximize distance receivers, making them more difficult to cover—has its roots in the Dutch Meyer book that Coryell studied. "It's one of the huge keys to the entire offense—the spacing is just so important," says quarterback Kurt Warner, who operated the system for the Rams. "It's so emphasized to all the receivers: Get off the ball and get downfield, get great separation between your deep route and your six- to eight-yard route. The entire offense is very precise, and it comes down to spacing more than anything else, spreading out the defense." If the Coryell system is executed properly, as with any spread-style offense, defenders are forced to cover huge chunks of earth to blanket receivers.

The final component was timing; from the early days Coryell harped on the wedding of speed and precision. "We put a timing element on every one of the routes," says Zampese. "Say we were asking the X receiver to run a 1 route. We would tell the guy, 'Three steps, and when your third inside foot hits the ground, that's when you break! Just go ahead and change direction. No fakes, just timing. Third inside foot and break.' And the key was to run as fast as you can. Which we forced these guys to do. We told them not to round off their cuts, but we had them running the routes so fast that they had to round them off a little bit."

Just as important was the speed of the quarterback. Anyone who has played in the Coryell system can still hear an assistant coach—Zampese,

Turner, Cameron, Garrett—screaming in a quarterback's ear as he drops back from the center: *Get it out! Get it out! Get it out!*

"Urgency is critical," says Garrett. "If I heard Norv Turner and Ernie Zampese say it once to the wide receivers, I heard them say it 500,000 times: 'Run off the ball! Run off the ball! Get out of your stance and get going!' And it applies to the quarterback. 'Get out! Get away from the center! Get your back foot down and get rid of the ball!' Can you teach a guy this? I don't know, but I'll tell you this: It's going to be ground into the head of any guy running this system. Bang, bang, bang! *Get the ball out.* Over and over again."

The most obvious "Gillmanesque" quality in Coryell's system is its every-down homage to the deep ball, the way Sid liked to play. Nearly every play in Coryell's book includes some sort of downfield option, and quarterbacks are taught to read plays from deep to short—whereas many offenses read short to deep or some sort of other predesigned progression. "On Don's pass routes, normally there were three different parts to the route," says Gibbs. "And there's always a deep portion. And you'd have a medium portion and a short checkdown. Don's reads [for the quarterback] would always start with the deep shot, so you didn't have to guess and gamble by calling a specific deep shot. It was already there, built into all the routes."

Coryell drilled two other credos into his quarterbacks' heads: 1) "Never pass up an open receiver. If he's there, stop reading and throw it to him." 2) "Never, ever worry about an incompletion. You don't give a damn about incompletions. Just go back and get it the next time."

When Coryell arrived in St. Louis in 1973, his first move was to restore 29-year-old, eight-year veteran Jim Hart as the starting quarterback. Hart was the classic Coryell QB: durable and decisive, with a quick release. "Don came into St. Louis and looked at film on Jim Hart," says Jim Hanifan, who came to the Cardinals with Coryell from San Diego State. "Jimmy had been sitting on the bench. Don looked at the film and said, 'Screw that. This is my quarterback.'"

Coryell gave Hart one order: "Don't get hit." (Translation: Get rid of the ball.) The Cardinals took a year to master Coryell's system and then won 31 games in three years, including two divisional titles. Coryell expanded his offense, adding multiple formations and putting in several screen passes to best utilize his speedy little running back, Terry Metcalf. In 1974 and '76 Hart led the NFC in touchdown passes.

"Back in those years," says Hanifan, "a lot of teams would just sit back on defense and Don would feast on them. So they started to bring pressure, and Don would just say, 'We are not going to let this happen. We're going to attack.' "

Gibbs, also a Coryell assistant in St. Louis, says, "I'd be up in the press box calling plays, and Don would grab the headset and he'd say, 'Let's start getting after their butts!' Usually that means pound it down their throats, but with Don it meant 'Let's start throwing it.' Not running it on them, getting after them by throwing it."

Four games into the 1978 season, the Chargers hired Coryell as head coach. Coryell, who had returned to San Diego after the Cardinals let him go (St. Louis's owner got antsy after a 7–7 season in '77), was introduced to the Charger players on the morning of Monday, Sept. 25, 1978, one day after a 24–3 loss to Green Bay, the team's third consecutive defeat. More eerily, it was also the day on which 144 people were killed when a Pacific Southwest Airlines 727 jet collided over San Diego with a Cessna 172.

Dan Fouts picks up the story: "It was such a strange day. There is this huge disaster in the city. Then there's a team meeting. We're 1–3 at this point and going nowhere. Just got crushed by Green Bay, and we were awful. So they fire Prothro, and he talks to us, and then he walks out of the room. Now, our team was pathetic under Prothro, but he was this big, imposing Southern gentleman. And right after he walks out, in walks Don, and he's this smaller guy with a funny voice. (To this day, anyone who has known Coryell can imitate his urgent, nasal inflection.)

"Don stands up there," says Fouts, "and he says, 'People think I'm crazy to take this job. I'm still getting paid by the St. Louis Cardinals. And I'm sitting up on that hill, getting paid for doing nothin'. But I'm a little bit crazy. I'm crazy enough to turn this thing around.' And we're all just looking at each other, and I'm thinking, Holy shit, what a refreshing attitude. It was a breath of fresh air. And from that point on, we were just ready to take off."

Coryell recalls, "Gene Klein told me, 'I hired you to throw the football. Now throw it.' I said, 'That's a damn good idea.' "

It would be the true birth of what came to be known far and wide as Air Coryell. For one season Coryell moved conservatively, but the Chargers won seven of their last eight games to finish at 9–7. In the off-season, Coryell brought in Gibbs and his old buddy Zampese. Fouts was already positioned as the quarterback, and wide receiver Charlie Joiner had come by way of a trade from the Cincinnati Bengals in '76. Wideout John Jefferson had been the team's first pick in the '78 draft, and in the spring of '79 Coryell would take 6' 5", 251-pound tight end Kellen Winslow, a transcendent athlete from the University of Missouri.

What transpired was a splendid blend of players and system. Joiner was a brilliant, cerebral pass receiver, perfectly suited to an offense in which receivers had to make decisions based on how they were played by defensive backs. "I learned more from Joiner than he learned from me," says Zampese. Winslow was a wideout in a tight end's body. "If you put him in the conventional tight end position, linebackers would just pound him every time," says Gibbs. "So what we did is, we started moving him, putting him on the move and getting him spread out so they couldn't hammer him. And then they couldn't cover him, either." And Fouts had the unflagging courage to set, stand and throw, and then to take the pounding that inevitably followed.

To a system already revolutionary in its spreads and routes, Coryell now added motion and screens and more formations every day. Weekday game-planning sessions took on a giddy aura.

"Let's say it's a Wednesday," says Fouts. "It's nine o'clock in the morning, and they're putting up the plays that we're going to run against this week's team. Joe Gibbs would say, 'O.K., here's the way they read motion by the tight end, so we're going to run this play against it, and here's why it will work.' And he would do that with the whole game plan, and we walk out of the meeting and we've already won the game. Wednesday was a better day than Sunday.

"For me," he continues, "it came down to a feeling that I can't be wrong. If I got through my progression, if I do what I've been told by the coaching staff, we'll have a good play. And not only that, we've got a chance to make a big play on every snap. It was just a total confidence in every play that was called. You know how many times I audibled in 10 years? Maybe once or twice. Maybe. And I would get in the huddle on the first series on Sunday, and I'd just say, 'O.K., boys, 40 today.' Or, '50 today.' "

There was, always, a quirkiness to Coryell. He had that odd voice, for starters, and he had a piercing focus that often disarmed his colleagues—or made them laugh. Gibbs recalls once poking his head into Coryell's office, only to find the room in nearly total darkness, with Coryell sitting at his desk, scribbling terminology by the glow of a tiny desk light. On one morning Coryell climbed into his car for the drive to work after putting the family's garbage cans into the trunk, planning to leave them at the bottom of the driveway for the trash collectors. Before he put the car in gear, his mind had turned to football, and he arrived at work with the cans still in the trunk, where they fermented throughout the day in the sunshine. "It *was* funny," says Gibbs. "But his ability to focus was phenomenal."

Over the next four seasons the Chargers went 39–18 and twice played in the AFC Championship Game. They led the NFL in passing offense for six consecutive years beginning in 1978. Fouts passed for more than 4,000 yards each year from '79 to '81, including what were at the time the two highest totals in NFL history, long before such numbers became commonplace.

Signature plays emerged from the weekly brainstormings. Joiner caught 213 passes for 3,328 yards from '79 to '81, almost exclusively on crossing routes in the middle of the soft zone defenses that were typical in those years. "Charlie wasn't very fast, and neither was I," says Fouts. "But my drop-back and his routes seemed to just time out perfectly. There were times with Charlie, because I played with him for so long, that if you measured his heartbeat and my heartbeat, I'll bet you'd find they were just about the same."

A single play dominated the offense: F Post. There were dozens of variations, called endlessly, first by Gibbs and then by Zampese, who dialed up the F Post so often that throughout the NFL in later years it became known simply as an "Ernie route."

The most common call was 525 F Post Swing. Both outside receivers would run 15-yard outside comeback routes, carrying the corners to the outside. The Y receiver would run a 20, or a shallow cross, occupying the vision of the linebackers and safeties. The F receiver—sometimes a running back, sometimes a second tight end, depending on the formation—would then run an option post route, finding his own open path. A running back would run a short swing pattern. "It got to be an unbelievable play, the best play in the whole system," says Zampese. "And they still run it."

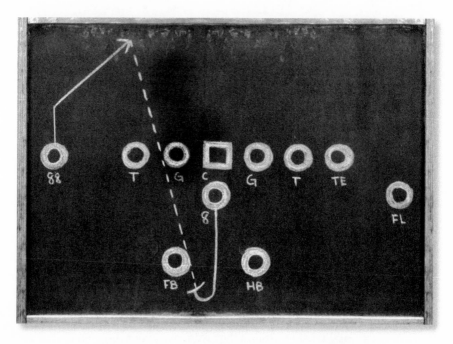

BANG 8 (THE SKINNY POST)

*The Dallas Cowboys of the '90s took one of the most simple and
basic of pass plays and, with endless practice and repetition, honed
it into a quick-hitting, surefire offensive weapon. Quarterback
Troy Aikman (8) took a five-step drop from center. Wide receiver
Michael Irvin (88) ran a skinny — or acutely angled — post
pattern (an "8" route in the original Coryell numbering system)
while reading the cornerback's movement and timing his cut based
on the coverage. As soon as Aikman's back foot hit the ground, he
released the throw to Irvin. It was an almost unstoppable play.*

CHAPTER 7

AIR HEIRS

The disciples of Don picked up where the great Coryell left off—and won more than their share of Super Bowls

I N NFL FRONT offices across the country, team execs watched Air Coryell take off. And, no surprise, it wasn't long before they began plucking off Coryell's assistants—obviously in hopes of replicating this new thing. First to leave for a top job in the NFL was Gibbs, hired to coach the Redskins in 1981. He installed the Coryell offense, then sought to take away any semblance of predictability by adding dozens of new formations and shifts from which to run the same plays; he also built in a power running game centered on counter plays. Gibbs's Redskins lost their first five games in 1981 but won the Super Bowl in '82, lost it in '83 and won twice more, in '87 and '91, a dynasty by any measure.

"No matter what you have in football," says Gibbs, "you need something you can do really well, and run it over and over again. We had the counter game." For much of the '80s, the Redskins operated the counter like a fine piece of machinery, using the inside zone counter and the outside zone counter, and then developing a third counter play which entered the language of football, fittingly enough, as the Counter Trey. Basically, it worked like this: The strong side of the offensive line delivered gap blocks while backside guard Russ Grimm would pull and trap the first defender outside the tight end; at the same time backside tackle Joe Jacoby would pull and lead first through the hole between the strong side guard and tackle, barreling upfield, 305 pounds in full, lumbering flight, leading John Riggins or George Rogers or Earnest Byner for big chunks of yardage.

The Counter Trey, among the most dominant single plays in the game's history, sprung from an unlikely source. "The whole counter started, to tell you the truth, when we saw some film on Nebraska in the early '80s," says Gibbs. "Tom Osborne was doing some really innovative things with his line up front, and we were watching it and thought, God, that's good stuff. So we stole it. We had no pride whatsoever, and really, nobody does in this game. We all steal things." (Told, years later, that Joe Gibbs had mimicked his blocking schemes, the forever taciturn Osborne said, "Well, I know Joe. I talked to him. But I never knew that. I'll be darned.")

Behind the Counter Trey Gibbs kept throwing Coryell's pass routes, adding the "bunching" of three wide receivers on one side of the formation. "We kept the numbering system, the pass tree, everything," says Gibbs. "The main thing we did that was different was that we ran the hang out of the ball to get [the defense] close to the line of scrimmage, and then we majored in the deep ball." Gibbs is as appreciative of Coryell's influence as anyone: "Mr. Cooke [longtime Redskins owner Jack Kent Cooke] once said, 'There are no geniuses in football.' But in a lot of ways— the terminology, the numbering of plays, the way you read routes and his passing tree, Don really was a genius."

While the Redskins were dominating the NFC East with their version of Air Coryell, the Rams were using their own version a continent away. With Zampese assisting head coach John Robinson, they melded the Coryell passing game with the USC-based running game (Chapter 10) that Robinson had learned from John McKay and used at Tailback U. With quarterback Jim Everett and lethal F Post runner Henry Ellard leading the way, the '89 Rams came up one win short of the Super Bowl.

They also launched another coach to prominence. After the 1990 season, Norv Turner, who had assisted Zampese with the Rams' offense, was contacted by Cowboys coach Jimmy Johnson. In two years since taking over America's Team, Johnson had improved from 1–15 to 7–9 but wanted more from his offense. He interviewed Turner and offered him the job as offensive coordinator—with the condition that Turner bring the Coryell scheme with him. It is hard to imagine a coach being more ready: Turner had been steeped in this offense.

In Dallas, Turner found an ideal set of players for the system. The third-year starting quarterback, Troy Aikman, who had thrown 36 interceptions and endured 58 sacks in two seasons, was a Coryell quarterback waiting to happen. "The entire passing game is predicated on having a quarterback who will turn the ball loose," says Turner. "Get on his fifth step, or his seventh step, and when that back foot hits the ground, the ball is out. And he has to have great anticipation, because you're throwing into holes. So in Dallas we inherit a guy, Troy, who is as good as anyone who has played in the system because he's such a good athlete. He would separate from the center quicker than anyone I've ever been around and still get set and get the ball out of his hand and make the throws. People teaching the offense in this league still show the first touchdown pass in our first Super Bowl [1992 season], when Troy throws the slant to Michael Irvin and the ball goes inches—I mean *inches*—above the linebacker's fingertips. That's a throw that Troy was willing to make, and you have to be willing to make it."

If the F Post defined the early years of the Coryell offense, it was a route called the Bang 8 that defined these Cowboys (the Bang 8 so named because it was a Coryell "8" route thrown very quickly—bang—and later generically called the "skinny post" throughout football because it was a post pattern but not run as deeply as a traditional post, thus run at a more severe—skinny—angle). Jay Novacek, to be sure, ran the F Post brilliantly from the flanked tight end position, but it was Aikman and Irvin who turned the skinny post into an almost undefendable weapon.

One player who watched the Aikman-Irvin show with interest was Trent Green, a quarterback with the Redskins at the time. From the Skins' sideline he watched Aikman and Irvin complete the Bang 8 with such proficiency that his frustration turned to admiration. "The Bang 8 is a five-step drop," he explains, "where you let the ball go based on the leverage of the corner. That dictates the angle of the route by the receiver and also whether the safety is in the middle of the field or in roll coverage [helping the corner]. Just to watch Troy and Michael run that play, you could tell that they had repped it so many times that they could almost make it a blind throw and complete it. From a Redskins standpoint, it was tough to watch because we couldn't stop it. But as a quarterback, with an appreciation of the offense, it was almost fun." Or, as Jason Garrett, Aikman's backup who saw the play countless times, puts it: "896 F Flat Bang 8 on the outside—if they don't roll the coverage over there, the ball is halfway there before the receiver turns his head. And tell me that's not your image of the Cowboys from that era: Michael Irvin catching a Bang 8."

By the time the Cowboys dynasty had captured its third Super Bowl, concluding the 1995 season, defensive coaches were working feverishly to counter this offensive surge, primarily with the invention of the zone blitz in Cincinnati by defensive coordinator Dick LeBeau, who then popularized it in Pittsburgh with Dom Capers (Chapter 18). In St. Louis, Mike Martz was committed to staying a step ahead of the defensive wizards. "With all the zone blitzes, what happened with offenses was they wanted to know where every defender was coming from," says Martz. "So offenses got real conservative again. Keeping another receiver in to block, that sort of thing. We decided to do just the opposite, and that was all about the Coryell system. We spread 'em out and said, 'Good luck finding the guy we're throwing it to.' We took the F Post and ran it with five different positions from every formation in the playbook. We ran it with Az Hakim, with Isaac Bruce—and Marshall Faulk was an unbelievable post runner. At one point I counted 137 different ways we could run the F Post."

Operating Martz's system was none other than Green, now a Ram. Green completed 28 of 32 passes in three exhibition starts, but his fun didn't last—he went down with torn ligaments in his left knee in the third preseason game. The offense was handed over to an unknown quarterback named Kurt Warner, a 28-year-old undrafted free agent, veteran of NFL Europe, Arena Football and, at one point, a grocery store where he stocked shelves. The system didn't miss a beat; the Rams went 13–3 and won the Super Bowl. Warner threw 41 touchdown passes, and a legend was born.

"I loved the system from Day One," says Warner. "I loved everything that it was about. I loved that it was deep first, then checkdowns. The design of the offense was to continually put pressure on the back end of the defense. It was all about getting chunks of yardage.

"The F Post was still a big part of the offense," Warner continues.

"The Bang 8 got to be a little tougher because in '99 and after that, coverages were starting to change. Instead of getting single high safeties, you would get a lot more four across, which made it harder to throw that skinny post. So we made a living off what we call a Big 4, a deep in pattern. Our inside guy would push hard on the safety and force him deep, and then we would throw inside with the Big 4, like 18 or 20 yards deep, and that's where my accuracy was really good, and I could separate myself from other quarterbacks."

IT IS October 2007, and Jason Garrett sits behind his desk in an office on the first floor of the Dallas Cowboys' sprawling suburban complex of Valley Ranch. The surface of the desk is half covered with play diagrams, and a whiteboard on the wall is peppered with game planning, like some sort of arcane graffiti. Asked to describe his offensive foundation, Garrett leans back and says, "It's what you would have to call the Coryell offense." More than 40 years have passed since Don Coryell grew tired of losing two games a year at San Diego State, but the offense he founded has endured like little else in football.

Garrett came to the Cowboys from Miami before the '07 season and immediately began teaching Tony Romo in the same way that Zampese and Turner taught Aikman. "Romo was pretty good from the start," says Garrett. "But we absolutely had to coach him to get away from the center. And we've had to coach receivers to get off the ball. Like Ernie always said: 'Speed, speed, speed.' None of that changes." There is still a 525 F Post in the Cowboys playbook. An Ernie route.

Half a continent away and five months later Coryell sat at that kitchen table in fading light after several hours spent piecing together memories, conjuring up ghosts from decades earlier. The coaches that Coryell so profoundly influenced are astounded that he has not been enshrined in the Pro Football Hall of Fame. "It's mind-boggling," says Martz. "I can't think of a coach who has had a bigger impact on what is done out there on the field than Don Coryell."

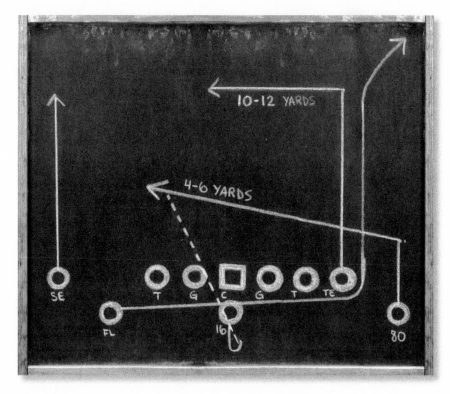

FLANKER DRIVE

What became the iconic play of the '80s was vintage Bill Walsh. It was built for his 49ers, and the goal was simple: Put the ball into the hands of wide receiver Jerry Rice in open space with Rice at full speed. The split end on the left runs his cornerback off the play, and the slot receiver (FL) from the left side comes across the formation and commands deep attention to the right. The tight end runs a deep cross, occupying the safety in the middle. Rice (80) runs three steps upfield, then "drives" across the field at full speed; he is too fast for the linebackers to track him. Quarterback Joe Montana (16), after a five-step drop, hits him, with an emphasis on leading him with the ball to allow Rice to continue running all-out. The play's design calls for Rice, as soon as he makes the catch, to turn upfield for additional yardage.

CHAPTER 8

THE WEST COAST OFFENSE

It really should be named the Cincinnati Offense, but make no mistake: This is the Bill Walsh's baby

Dallas, Texas
Autumn 1993

Offenses and defenses get their names in one of three ways: from what they look like (the Wishbone), how they work (the Zone Blitz) or where they come from (the Green Bay Sweep). Then there is the West Coast Offense, one of the iconic technical names in modern football, a name that can be heard endlessly on college and professional telecasts every weekend in the fall, a term that lands in the average fan's comfort zone like a tall, cold beer. Yet it fits none of the customary naming profiles: It describes neither the look of the offense nor its function. And while the name appears to derive from its place of origin, even that is off by more than 2,000 miles. The name is a mistake that took on a life of its own.

Here is how it happened: The Cowboys were in the middle of their minidynasty of the early and mid-'90s, a run that included three Super Bowl titles in four years, when SPORTS ILLUSTRATED's veteran NFL writer Paul Zimmerman—the esteemed Dr. Z—visited the Cowboys' headquarters in Irving, Texas. The Cowboys' offense was a sweet balance of run (Emmitt Smith and fullback Daryl Johnston) and pass (Troy Aikman to Michael Irvin and Jay Novacek, among others); Zimmerman, always fascinated by the technical underpinnings of successful teams, wondered what it was like behind the curtain.

Bernie Kosar, the gangly savant who had led the University of Miami to an unexpected national championship in 1983 and had started nearly 100 games at quarterback for the Cleveland Browns, was now in Dallas as Aikman's backup. Zimmerman sought out Kosar to learn about the offense.

Fifteen years later, at a pre–Super Bowl dinner in a steak house in Scottsdale, Ariz., two days before the Giants upset the Patriots, Zimmerman told the tale of what happened. It is a tasty slice of anecdotal football history: "I went to Kosar because I knew he would be able to explain to me what the offense was. He said, 'It's the West Coast offense. Norv Turner, Ernie Zampese, Don Coryell, Sid Gillman.' Bernie was right, and he knew his history."

Kosar was indeed correct. The offense he was describing—Air Coryell—was begun by Coryell at San Diego State and likely influenced by Gillman's San Diego Chargers teams of the 1960s. Coryell tutored Zampese, who tutored Turner, who ran the offense with the Cowboys. This attack is most accurately called the Coryell offense. Here again, Dr. Z's telling:

"I quoted Bernie talking about the West Coast offense, and it got picked up by somebody out West," he said. "I think it was a wire reporter. But that guy mistakenly attached the term "West Coast offense" to Bill Walsh's teams in San Francisco in the 1980s with Joe Montana. And the name stuck. It was wrong, but it stuck."

In the often murky history of football strategy, where one man's innovation spills into the next, there is no evidence that anyone but Kosar and Zimmerman coined the name "West Coast offense," as applied in Dallas. Its application to the '80s 49ers dynasty was inaccurate, except in the very loose sense that both Coryell and Walsh—like almost every modern coach—were influenced by Gillman. Coryell's and Walsh's systems were different, their terminology was different and their basic philosophy was different. The fact that both flourished on the West Coast, Coryell's in San Diego and Walsh's in San Francisco, only compounded the confusion.

What came to be known everywhere as the West Coast offense—for clarity's sake here, let's call it the Walsh offense—was the first passing strategy in football to effectively attack the field from sideline to sideline rather than from the line of scrimmage forward. The Coryell offense (the original West Coast offense) was a downfield attack. The Walsh offense used running backs as receivers in more extensive ways than any attack before it and, perhaps most significant, validated the *short* pass as an effective offensive weapon when most previous systems had lived and died by the long ball.

The irony is that Bernie Kosar and Paul Zimmerman accidentally named the West Coast offense 23 years after Bill Walsh invented it—but Walsh did not invent it in San Francisco or even in California or anywhere on the West Coast at all. The West Coast offense, as it's now known to all, was born in Cincinnati.

Cincinnati, Ohio
July 1970

THE CINCINNATI Bengals began play in the summer of 1968, an expansion team whose principal owner, general manager and inaugural head coach was the esteemed Paul Brown, who as coach of the Cleveland Browns had won four championships in the All-American Football Conference and three more in the NFL from '46 through '55. The Bengals won two of their first three games in that inaugural season but finished with a 3–11 record in the brutally competitive, premerger Western Division of the American Football League. In the spring of '69 they used the fifth pick of the draft to select 6' 4", 220-pound quarterback Greg Cook from the University of Cincinnati.

Cook was a sensational athletic specimen. "Greg Cook could have been the greatest quarterback in the history of the NFL," says Sam Wyche, who in 1969 would back up the rookie and went on to coach in the NFL for 18 years. "You could see it from the first day of training camp. He had everything—size, speed, rifle arm, accuracy. He had the head to run a system and he had the physical talent to improvise if it was necessary. He was an incredible player."

The job of schooling Cook fell to 38-year-old offensive assistant coach Bill Walsh, who had come to Cincinnati with Brown after a year as an assistant with the Oakland Raiders. Walsh had coached nine years before arriving in the NFL, one as a graduate student at San Jose State, two as the head coach at Washington Union High in Fremont, Calif., and three each as an assistant at California and Stanford. Upon joining the Raiders, Walsh's football apprenticeship accelerated. He was put in charge of running backs and from that perspective learned the system of head coach Al Davis, who was just one of many who had been influenced by Sid Gillman.

Davis will be remembered as a big-play, throw-the-bomb offensive coach, but in *Building a Champion*, a book Walsh wrote with Glenn Dickey in 1990, Walsh gives Davis credit for much more creativity than simply playing for the deep ball. "The pass offense [in Oakland] included an almost unlimited variety of pass patterns as well as a system of calling them, and utilized the backs and tight ends much more extensively than other offenses. . . . To develop an understanding of it took time, but once learned, it was invaluable."

Paul Brown, meanwhile, was arguably the most innovative thinker in the game's history. He is recognized as the first coach to use game film as a teaching tool, and he refined classroom-style preparation into the team-meeting model still used today. So early in his career Walsh was exposed to a rich confluence of football thinkers. He came to Cincinnati as the quarterbacks and receivers coach, ready to run an offense of his own. And Brown gave him the latitude to tinker. And in their second season together, 1969, he was given an athlete who could do it all.

As Walsh writes in his book:

> [Greg Cook] was the finest natural talent of any quarterback I have seen. He was a brilliant athlete—big, active, with a quick arm and great delivery—and he had the spontaneity of Joe Montana. . . . Those who saw Cook would have to say that physically he was the best ever to step on the field. He wasn't just a big Adonis who could throw the ball 100 yards. This was a quick, graceful athlete with a lightning-fast delivery and great instincts.

COOK BECAME the Bengals' starter as a rookie, and even though the team's final record that year was just 4-9-1, there was a promise of much greater success ahead. The Bengals started the '69 season with three straight wins, including a 24–19 home victory over the Kansas City Chiefs, who would go on to win the Super Bowl that year. In that game Cook was thrown to the artificial turf in Riverfront Stadium on a blitz by Chiefs All-Pro linebacker

Bobby Bell. Cook would miss parts of four games, but the full ramifica-
tions of his injury wouldn't be known until the off-season.

Cook finished the year with an NFL-rookie-record 9.41 yards per attempt and with an average of 17.5 yards per completion, a mark that has
been bettered just once in the four decades since. But he was also never
the same after Bell's hit, on a rollout that Walsh would later blame himself for calling. He played through the season with what was diagnosed
afterward as a torn rotator cuff in his throwing shoulder, an injury that
was regularly repaired in later years but which, in 1969, essentially ended
Cook's career. By the training camp of '70 Walsh found himself with an
offensive system designed for Greg Cook, but without Cook to run it.

Instead, the Bengals were looking for a quarterback. They had Wyche,
a two-year backup who had thrown just 89 passes and would ultimately
spend most of his career as a journeyman. They had Dave Lewis, a rookie
punter who had played quarterback in college. Brown and Walsh wanted
other options, so in the middle of training camp they acquired Virgil Carter
from the Buffalo Bills. Carter had previously spent three years in the NFL,
all with the Chicago Bears. He had started five games in 1968 (winning
four) but in '69 was benched in favor of Bobby Douglass, a rugged, 6' 4",
225-pound quarterback who was primarily a runner. "When I was traded
to the Bengals," says Carter, "I didn't even know how to spell Cincinnati or
where it was. I had to look on a map to tell my family where I was going."

Carter could not have been more different from Greg Cook. He was
listed at 6' 1", 192 pounds but probably was at least an inch shorter than
that. "Virgil couldn't throw the ball 20 yards," says Bruce Coslet, a future
NFL head coach who was a second-year tight end on that Bengals team.
Yet Carter did have skills. In 1965 and '66, Carter had been the first in
what would be a long line of effective passers at Brigham Young. As a senior he passed for 2,182 yards, an unspectacular total now but among the
nation's leaders then. All of those BYU yards, however, were accumulated
in a belly-series rollout passing game with pass-run options on the corner.
No drop-back passes, few multiple-receiver patterns.

"Greg Cook was a guy who could throw the ball down the field," says
Carter. "When it turned out that he wasn't coming back as quickly as they
had hoped, they were looking for somebody to fill the void until he did
eventually come back. I did not have a strong arm, but I was mobile. And

I had always been able to make decisions on the run as a play developed." The combination of a healthy Virgil Carter and an injured and uncertain Greg Cook presented Walsh and Brown with a dilemma. Walsh's solution was to design an offense for Carter. It is the attack that, many years later, would be labeled the West Coast offense.

"I'm not sure what they had for Greg Cook," says Carter. "As things moved along through training camp and into that [1970] season, Bill Walsh started putting in more things that played to my strengths—designed scrambles, designed waggles, quick out cuts, reading defense as you dropped back. There was very little of the seven-step drop, pat the ball and then fire it downfield."

Walsh would write:

> Virgil was a nifty athlete, but he was not considered to have a strong arm. We had to devise a system to fit his abilities. The timing of our passing game now became very important. Virgil would take three steps, throw, five steps, throw—short, quick throws within 10 yards of the line of scrimmage. . . . Or we would have him sprint out, to take advantage of his mobility, and again throw the ball short.

THE EMERGENCY system was wildly successful. The third-year Bengals, after a 1–6 start, won their last seven games to finish at 8–6 and qualify for the playoffs. (They were beaten by the Baltimore Colts 17–0 on the day after Christmas; the Colts would go on to win the Super Bowl.) Carter finished a respectable 14th in the NFL in passing, seventh in the AFC.

As Walsh wrote:

> With Carter at quarterback, we won our division with a 'nickel-and-dime' offense. It was very effective because we controlled the ball. . . . Our specific objective was to make 25 first downs a game and control the ball with short passing and selective running. . . . Other people in the NFL couldn't believe Virgil could be that effective and that we could win that way.

The offense, created out of desperation, fed perfectly into Walsh's strengths as a cerebral football coach. "Bill's thinking was completely different from the usual football mind-set of smash, crush, destroy," says Mike Holmgren, who in 1986 would join Walsh in San Francisco and later take the West Coast offense to success, and Super Bowls, in Green Bay and Seattle. "It was a chess game. And that really was the fun part of coaching. With Bill, it was always, 'Let's figure out how we can beat this.' "

From a technical standpoint the creation of the West Coast offense was a watershed moment in the history of the forward pass, and one that would influence offensive systems four decades later. "Look at the NFL right now," said Holmgren in the late summer of 2009. "It's almost easier to count the teams that are not using some form of this system. If a team doesn't have a shutdown defense, like Pittsburgh or Baltimore, and if a team isn't committed to running the football, like Miami or, again, Pittsburgh, they're probably using some form of this passing game. Because there's no other way to win."

From the beginning Walsh's offense was different, in several specific ways. 1) It was the first pass offense in which *timing* was the critical element. While Coryell's offense at San Diego State at the same time also relied on precise quarterback-receiver timing, Walsh's scheme put more emphasis on shorter, more horizontal routes. Receivers in the Walsh offense were expected to arrive at specific locations across the field in precise segments of time, syncing up perfectly with the quarterback's drop-back, set and delivery. In previous offenses a receiver tended to run a pattern down the field and the quarterback would observe him and throw if the receiver broke open—and sometimes even if he didn't. In 1969 NFL quarterbacks completed 52.6% of their passes; in 2008 that figure was 61.0%, a game-altering leap in efficiency. Before Walsh, the forward pass came with significant risk; since Walsh, it has been a much more reliable chain-moving tool. Says Wyche, "The timing and coordination of routes had to be perfect, and that was very different from anything I had learned previously. The theory of every play was a designed coordination between the quarterback and the receivers."

2) Walsh's passing system was the first that relied on a sequence of potential receivers, giving the quarterback a first, second, third and fourth option, which he would tick off one by one on his drop-back. "It was a progression passing game," says Coslet. "If the first guy was open, you'd throw it to him. If the second guy was open, you'd throw it to him. If the third guy was open, you'd throw it to him. And if they

were all covered, you always had the back coming out of the backfield. One-two-three dump."

3) It was the first offensive system to assign and incorporate what came to be commonly known as "hot" receivers. Walsh called them "blitz" receivers. In his book Walsh wrote, "We were always looking for ways to beat the blitz. . . . [Opponents] assumed that when facing a total blitz, teams would naturally keep both backs in to protect the passer." Instead, Walsh's teams would routinely send a running back into the void vacated by a blitzing linebacker.

4) It was the first pass offense to conceive the attack horizontally rather than just vertically. The difference is more subtle than the language may imply. Certainly offenses had historically included pass routes in which receivers ran across the field, and of course Walsh's offense included patterns in which receivers ran straight down the field. But Walsh's offense used countless routes in which receivers—sometimes multiple receivers—would run all the way across a formation, virtually sideline to sideline, forcing a defense to stretch itself across the field until openings inevitably developed. "Bill always talked not only about vertical stretch but also about horizontal stretch," says Holmgren. "The horizontal stretch exposed where the voids were in the defense."

5) Walsh's offense turned conventional thinking about sustaining a drive on its head. "At that point in time, the league was knee deep in power running and taking long shots down the field," says former Ravens coach Brian Billick, who briefly worked as a p.r. man with Walsh's 49ers and later used the offense in both Minnesota and Baltimore. "Bill really introduced the concept of using high-efficiency intermediate passing routes as basically an extended running game."

Walsh wrote, "Many coaches didn't understand that style of 5-to-6-yard completions. . . . It was very effective because we controlled the ball."

The Walsh offense was a technical marvel, to be sure. But as time passed, it was not only the schematic qualities of the West Coast offense that emerged but also the very coaching style that Walsh would carry forward through the years of the 49ers' dynasty. The enduring success of the West Coast offense has much to do with the way Walsh taught it in the classroom and on the field, with every aspect preached and drilled in minute detail.

"Bill really believed in the value of running after the catch, and I think he was one of the first coaches to stress that," says Wyche. "Even back in Cincinnati he would always preach to receivers, 'Your first move has to be toward the goal line. Never mind trying to make that first guy miss. Screw that. Get two yards upfield. Then try to make somebody miss.' In order to make this happen, he was obsessive about where the ball was completed. He always wanted passes completed above the waist so the receiver didn't have to go to the ground."

Says Coslet, "If the ball wasn't thrown 1½ feet in front of the receiver, Bill would go ballistic. He was a real stickler for accuracy. And he never wanted his quarterback in the shotgun, because that meant looking down to catch the snap, and then he wouldn't be looking at the defense and his receivers."

In Walsh's world there was no room for good plays with sloppy execution. "I remember vividly one practice in San Francisco," says Holmgren. "Joe [Montana] threw a ball that Jerry [Rice] had to reach back for. Just slightly. But Jerry was so great, he just reached back, caught the ball and turned upfield. I said something like, 'Nice job.' Well, out of the distance I hear this voice. *Miiiiiiike.* Bill would drag it out in this whiny tone. *Don't you want that ball thrown six inches in front of the numbers?* And that's the way Bill would do it, too. He would yell at the coach, and the players would subtly get the idea and work harder so their position coach didn't get yelled at by Bill. It was a very interesting philosophy."

In Walsh's eight years in Cincinnati, his offense flourished. In the third round of the 1971 draft the Bengals selected Ken Anderson out of tiny Augustana College in western Illinois. Anderson sat one year behind Virgil Carter but quickly developed into an even better pilot for the Walsh offense. He was decisive, efficient and reliable, if unspectacular. ("Anderson has received the kind of acclaim usually reserved for a shoe salesman," wrote SI in 1975.) He also had a stronger arm than Carter and was just as accurate.

The Bengals became playoff contenders. In 1975 they went 11–3 but lost to Oakland 31–28 in the first round of the playoffs. It would be Walsh's last season in Cincinnati; he left embittered when Paul Brown, upon his retirement, named Bill Johnson his successor instead of Walsh. Walsh was gone, on to a one-year stop in San Diego and two years at Stanford. In '79 he was hired as coach of the 49ers, where he orchestrated a near-perfect union of players and system.

In his first draft with San Francisco in '79, Walsh selected Notre Dame quarterback Joe Montana in the third round, famously low for a player who would become what many feel is the best ever to play the position in the NFL. "Physically, he was not off the charts," says Holmgren. "He had a good arm but not a rocket arm. He was thin with skinny legs, and while he moved pretty well, he wasn't fast. But he was so accurate. He was like a ballerina back there, and he was always in such perfect rhythm with Bill's style of offense."

In that same '79 draft Walsh found Dwight Clark, a slow, 6' 4", 212-pound receiver from Clemson, in the 10th round. He too was a perfect fit for the Walsh system, a diligent route-runner with good hands who could find horizontal holes in a defense, turn upfield and gain positive yardage, again and again. "Dwight Clark couldn't run," says Coslet, "but he was a great receiver."

Clark also possessed a quality that Walsh craved in his wideouts: toughness. "Bill wanted his receivers to turn upfield and make yards, often in the middle of the field," says Billick. "They were going to get hit. Bill wanted big guys who could take a physical pounding."

The system got better as the players got better, and there would be more. The 49ers drafted running back Roger Craig out of Nebraska in the second round of the 1983 draft, and Craig became the model for a West Coast offense flare-route receiver. He would catch 566 passes in his career, including 92 in '85. "Roger Craig was a guy who could stay on the field," says Wyche. "Other teams in a passing down, they would have to bring in another wide receiver. Roger Craig was already as good at catching the ball as most wide receivers." Adds Holmgren, "You always have to adapt the system to your personnel. When I was at Seattle, we had Shaun Alexander, and he was a great running back. But he was an average receiver and a horrible blocker. So in certain situations we had to get him off the field. Bill could just leave Roger Craig on the field."

In 1985 came Jerry Rice from Mississippi Valley State. "He broke the mold," says Holmgren. "A big guy [6' 2", 200] who could run and who was tough." John Taylor, a poor man's Jerry Rice, was drafted a year later. It was the ideal collection of players to run Walsh's system, no accident. Walsh knew exactly what he needed.

Signature plays developed. Whereas the Coryell passing game featured plays described principally by numbers, plays in the Walsh offense were named with words. Example: What was termed 585 H Angle in the Coryell scheme was 22 Texas in the Walsh scheme. The play any football fan has seen most in four decades of the Walsh offense is X Shallow Cross. In its most basic form, from a set with a tight end and two wide receivers, the tight end runs a 10-yard cross, stretching the linebackers horizontally, while the "X" receiver runs across the formation from the opposite side, capitalizing on the chaos created by the tight end. The X either finds a hole in the defense and sits down for the ball or continues across. Dwight Clark ran it. John Taylor ran it. Larry Fitzgerald runs it for the Arizona Cardinals now. Rarely is an NFL game played—or a college game for that matter—without somebody running X Shallow Cross.

The West Coast offense began spreading when Wyche took it with him to Cincinnati—back to its place of origin—as head coach in 1984 and eventually molded pieces of the system into a no huddle offense that he took to the Super Bowl in the '88 season. Walsh left the 49ers after beating Wyche's Bengals in that game, Super Bowl XXIII, and was replaced by assistant George Seifert. The 49ers repeated as world champions in '89; Holmgren stayed for two more seasons, leaving to become head coach of the Green Bay Packers. His replacement as offensive coordinator in San Francisco was 39-year-old Mike Shanahan, a driven football thinker who had endured two tumultuous seasons ('88–89) as head coach of the L.A. Raiders and in '90 and '91 had been quarterbacks coach under Dan Reeves with the Denver Broncos, tutoring John Elway.

In San Francisco, Shanahan was taking on a veteran team, where his offensive chops would be challenged every day. And he knew it. "I was walking onto a team that had Joe Montana, Steve Young, Jerry Rice," says Shanahan. "You walk into that situation, you better know more about the offense than they do. And they knew a lot."

Here is where Bill Walsh's brilliance visited itself upon Shanahan. Throughout his tenure at San Francisco, Walsh had videotaped all meetings—whether with the full team and coaching staff or simply with the offense or just the quarterbacks. "Bill had a library of every meeting," says Shanahan. "I watched every one of those tapes. I was watching a coach who had won three Super Bowls in nine years, and I was watching every meeting he conducted. It was exciting for me. It's like I was there."

After helping the 49ers win Super Bowl XXIX in 1995, Shanahan became head coach of the Broncos, where he installed huge chunks of the Walsh offense for Elway and added new wrinkles to fit Elway's considerable talents. "There were no seven-step drops in the West Coast system, but John had a very strong arm and wanted some seven-step drops, so we put them in," says Shanahan. "John was great out of the shotgun, so we put the shotgun in."

An equally significant germination was taking place in Green Bay, where Holmgren had taken over the Packers; shortly after his hiring, the club traded for an unknown second-year quarterback name Brett Favre. Favre had a powerful arm that would become mythic. "I go from the ballerina [Montana] to this wild stallion," says Holmgren. "It was like Bill going from Greg Cook to Virgil Carter in Cincinnati, except in the other direction."

Holmgren stayed true to basics of Walsh's offense but opened up the formation. Where Walsh usually had two wide receivers, Holmgren began using three. His coaching staff included Jon Gruden, who would become a head coach in 1998 at age 34, and Andy Reid, who would take over the Eagles a year later at age 40. Both took the Walsh offense with them and added their own touches—Gruden using many more sets and men in motion, Reid adding a zone-blocked power running game. Both went to Super Bowls.

As Walsh acolytes permeated the league and more teams incorporated the controlled, short passing game, defenses predictably sought answers. The best response came in the form of the Cover Two descendant built by Monte Kiffin and Tony Dungy with the Tampa Bay Buccaneers in the '90s and called Tampa Two (Chapter 16). The central philosophy of the Tampa Two was to allow the short passing gains but tackle well, forcing teams to sustain long, slow scoring drives.

"In this offense," says Holmgren, "huge chunks of yardage will happen. But more often you were scoring on an eight- or 10-play scoring drive. Carving up the defense a few yards at a time. The times when we really struggled were against the teams that played that Cover Two scheme really well. They would get in that two-deep look, tackle well and really make you earn the yards, make you execute all the way up the field.

"And all of us calling the plays would eventually get impatient," says Holmgren. "You're making first downs and moving up the field, but it's like watching paint dry. You get emotional and you think, 'Enough of this b.s. Let's try something down the field. And, of course, that's playing right into the defense's hands.'"

ON JAN. 10, 1982, Virgil Carter watched on television as the San Francisco 49ers played the Dallas Cowboys for the NFC championship and a place in Super Bowl XVI. Carter, 36 years old and five seasons out of football, had secured his place as the first quarterback ever to play in the West Coast offense, although that distinction would seldom be recognized outside the game's inner circles. However, on this late evening he would understand better than most as he watched one of the most memorable plays in the history of the NFL.

The play was called Brown Left Slot—Sprint Right Option. It is known now to all good football fans as simply The Catch, Montana's six-yard, game-winning completion to Clark in the end zone with 51 seconds to play. The play lives eternally, run again and again by way of NFL Films: There is Montana rolling right, drifting and drifting farther until he is nearly at the sideline, twice cocking his arm and resetting before throwing high and deep to the back of the end zone. Clark has run a cross to the inside and adjusts to Montana's roll and jumps high to catch the ball behind Dallas cornerback Everson Walls.

Montana's first read was slot receiver Freddie Solomon, who was covered. He threw instead to the back line as he floated dangerously close to the sideline, and it is still on occasion speculated that he was throwing the ball away and got lucky when Clark leaped to the rescue.

Virgil Carter knew better. "That first year in Cincinnati, 1970, Bill Walsh put in a play called Scramble Right," says Carter. "We would work on it in practice every day. I would move right, and the outside guy would clear, just like Freddie Solomon did, and the deep receiver would run across the back of the pattern, just like Dwight Clark did. By '82, they might not have been calling it Scramble Right anymore, but Joe Montana knew that Clark was back there. I knew it, too, as soon as he threw the ball."

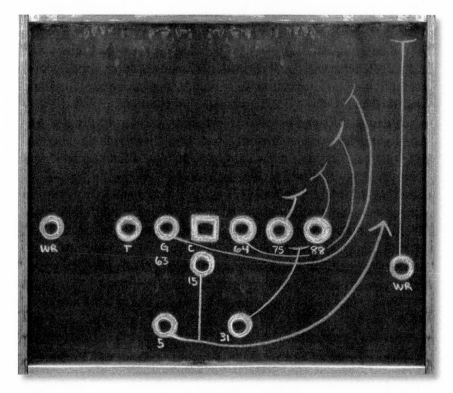

49 SWEEP RIGHT

*Vince Lombardi loved the single wing's power concepts, and his famous
Packers sweep would come to define his great teams of the '60s. It was a
simple play but continually effective—thanks to Lombardi's insistence on
practice, practice, practice. At the snap, both left guard Fuzzy Thurston
(63) and right guard Jerry Kramer (64) pull and roll to the outside.
Quarterback Bart Starr (15) executes a straight handoff to halfback
Paul Hornung (5). Fullback Jim Taylor (31) seals off backside pursuers
along with right tackle Forrest Gregg (75). Tight end Ron Kramer (88)
throws the most difficult and most critical block, on the outside linebacker.
Thurston and Kramer block downfield as Hornung follows.*

CHAPTER 9

LOMBARDI'S POWER SWEEP

Here was one man's proof that a key to football will always be knocking the crap out of somebody else at the line of scrimmage

Miami, Fla.
Oct. 25, 2009

THE NEW Orleans Saints arrived in South Florida on this afternoon unbeaten in five games to begin the 2009 season. They had scarcely been tested and possessed the league's most lethal passing game. Head coach–play-caller Sean Payton's hybrid offense (a mix of systems, including the West Coast and Coryell) had been made surgical in the hands of veteran quarterback Drew Brees. The Saints had scored six passing touchdowns in the season opener against Detroit and hadn't let up. Next would be the Miami Dolphins, who had bounced back from an 0–3 start to win two consecutive games.

What happened in the first two quarters of this game veered significantly from the anticipated script. The Dolphins' 3–4 defense, with natural edge pass rushers Jason Taylor and Joey Porter lined up as the outside linebackers, sold out on the run to focus instead on effectively pressuring Brees. Late in the first half the Saints trailed 24–3 before scoring late to narrow the gap to 24–10. In those first 30 minutes the Saints ran 30 offensive plays, the Dolphins 32; the Saints threw 22 passes and ran eight times; the Dolphins threw 10 passes and ran 22 times.

In the second half, though, the roles were reversed. The Dolphins virtually abandoned the ground game—inexplicably so—with inexperienced quarterback Chad Henne throwing 26 passes; Miami ran the ball just seven times. The Saints, meanwhile, also changed their strategy entirely and employed a more balanced split of 19 runs and 16 passes, enabling them to seize control of the line of scrimmage, slow the Dolphins' pass rush and stage a furious rally to win the game, 46–34. The Saints pounded Miami for 115 yards on the ground in the second half, transforming themselves at halftime from stunt plane into bulldozer.

After the game the Saints' offensive linemen sat in their dressing cubicles in the belly of Land Shark Stadium stripping tape from knees and ankles. As with most of their peers on the O-line, they look to be an unathletic lot, with their thick legs and jiggling bellies (for power, and for protection). Yet they remain, as always, the foundation on which every offensive play is built. Jon Stinchcomb, the hulking right tackle, stiffened and fell backward onto a chair in the middle of an interview. "Little cramp there," he said, pointing to his left foot, which was twitching like a hooked trout on a dry dock.

The game had turned into their kind of contest. In the second half the offensive line had been freed from the passive restraint of pass-blocking, backpedaling to try to control an onrushing defender; instead the line was allowed to attack the defense to create holes for the running game. Ask any offensive lineman at any level if he would rather run-block or pass-block and you'll get the same answer. "Being able to run the ball sets up everything in this league," said Saints left tackle Jermon Bushrod, enjoying the victory. "When you push out and run the ball, teams just can't load up and rush the passer the way they were doing in the first half. And every offensive lineman would rather hit somebody than sit back and get hit. That's human nature."

Said Stinchcomb, "Anytime you're able to have some offensive balance and keep a defense respecting both aspects of your game, you're going to have more success. We see that time and time again. Today, we had to get the game back to a manageable point differential, then we could mix the run in with the pass."

This is hardly a new concept; it is fundamental football. Yet for the Saints of '09, dedication to the run was a recent addition to their repertoire. The Payton-Brees passing game, in which the Saints elevated a group of relatively unheralded wide receivers to a potent unit, had made the Saints competitive. The running game, with backs Mike Bell, Reggie Bush and Pierre Thomas and a stout offensive line executing a zone-blocking scheme, made them whole.

These Saints represented a something of a reversal of the obvious and essential order of football. Historically, the run came first, followed by the pass. The sport is built on the idea of physical domination, with the running game at its core. Yet as modern football moved into the mid-1950s, the pass and run were in a subtle tug-of-war for ownership of the game. Passing was still simplistic, but seductive. The running game had grown stale.

Coaches anticipated the birth of something new and innovative to carry the running game into the latter half of the 20th century. What they got, instead, was a very old school coach, Vince Lombardi, building the power sweep from the same principles that had once made the single wing effective. First he used his power sweep in New York as an assistant with the Giants and then, more famously, in Green Bay after arriving there in 1959.

In short, the new phase in the evolution of the ground game wasn't new, it was old. It wasn't complex, it was simple. It was football at its most basic: survival of the strongest and the toughest.

THEY SAT inside a picnic shelter on a summer afternoon signing autographs. Max McGee, then 69, affixed his signature to a stack of artist's prints depicting his epic—and unlikely—two-touchdown performance in the first Super Bowl. "I *sort of* remember that day," says McGee, who notoriously stayed out all night on the eve of the game, delivering a well-practiced line with convincing fogginess. Paul Hornung, 66, sits next to McGee, signing a classic picture from 1960, in which he is running onto the field, bright sunshine illuminating his blond curls, eye black edging his cheekbones, a green-and-yellow Green Bay Packers helmet dangling from his right hand.

Hornung, the erstwhile Golden Boy, is not so Golden anymore, and certainly not a boy. His head is still full of hair, but it is silvery now. McGee is bald, much as he was as a player, and he reminds the crowd with vaudevillian style, dipping his mug toward Hornung, "He's the one with the gray hair. I don't have any gray hair," says McGee. It is a small crowd in a small town, and an adoring one. Chuck Roeske, 62, a maintenance machinist at the local Veterans Administration hospital, regards them with awe. "These guys were the greatest," he says. "Real football players."

The Green Bay Packers of Vince Lombardi left a lasting imprint on football in America, images handed down through four decades of fans. Most often it is the image of the man in the glasses with the gaps in his teeth, fedora atop his head, pacing the sideline. And no part of Packers lore has a more vibrant afterlife than Lombardi's prized creation, the power sweep, the chalkboard emblem of the first dynasty of the modern NFL.

It was this single play that would represent the cool efficiency that made Lombardi's Packers great, and it was these charismatic Packers that gave the NFL a foundation on which to build its future, offering a '50s simplicity and sociability as comfortable as a suburban backyard cookout. For opposing defenders, though, the power sweep wasn't comfortable at all—that apparent simplicity was instead almost maddening. Yet the sweep had its own sweet complexity, perfected only through endless repetition. "It wasn't a simple play," says Ron Kramer, the 6' 3", 234-pound tight end from Michigan who played on Lombardi's first six teams. "But when you run it 25 or 30 or 50 times a day, it starts to become very simple, and that's exactly what we did."

The sweep was most often run by Hornung, the dashing, dynamic 1956 Heisman Trophy winner from Notre Dame. For so many football fans it is an indelible picture: Hornung, the ball in the crook of his arm, dancing to the outside; guards Fuzzy Thurston and Jerry Kramer, each barely bigger than a modern wide receiver, barreling out in front; fullback Jim Taylor and right tackle Forrest Gregg in their trench labor being swallowed along the path. It is arguably the most lasting image in NFL history.

Pewaukee, Wis.
July 1959

LOMBARDI'S PACKERS gathered for the first time in the summer of 1959, the vestiges of a franchise that had won just a single game in the

1958 season and hadn't had a winning season since going 6-5-1 under Curly Lambeau in 1947. Lombardi was the head coach, but he had run the New York Giants' offense under Jim Lee Howell and he would run the Packers' offense as well. He introduced the sweep to his team on the very first day of practice. "He told us, 'This will be the key to the whole running game,' " recalls Hornung. "He told us it was something we had to do perfectly."

It was no surprise to the Packers' veterans. They had seen the Giants run the sweep with Frank Gifford carrying the ball. "Lombardi showed us films of the Giants every day," says Hornung. "We watched Frank Gifford run that play over and over again. He brought his whole offense with him from New York to Green Bay, but the sweep was the thing he really made us work on. And we knew it was coming."

In truth, the sweep went back much further than the Giants, back to the roots of modern power football, the single wing. Lombardi played college football at Fordham from 1933 through '36. He was a 5' 8", 185-pound guard on the Rams' offensive line that was nicknamed the Seven Blocks of Granite. During that same era, Jock Sutherland over-saw a dynasty of sorts at Pittsburgh from 1924 through '38. Running the single wing, Sutherland took Pitt to four Rose Bowls and won pieces of several national titles.

The single wing revolutionized football with intricate backfield fak-ing and ballhandling but also featured punishing offensive line play that included athletic pulling and trapping, as well as fierce double teams at the point of attack. Single wing backs were also called upon to read blocks and cut back accordingly. Lombardi was enamored of all these elements, even as a college opponent. "I was impressed playing against the Single-Wing sweep the way those Pittsburgh teams of Jock Sutherland ran it," Lombardi wrote, together with W.C. Heinz, in his book *Run to Daylight!* "And I was impressed again in those early days of attending coaching clinics when the Single-Wing was discussed. To-day our sweep has a lot of those Sutherland qualities, the same guard-pulling techniques, the same ball-carrier cutback feature, and there's nothing spectacular about it. It's just a yard-gainer."

If Lombardi's interest in the sweep began at Fordham, it was solidi-fied at West Point, where Lombardi worked from 1949 through 1953

When Pride Still Mattered: A Life of Vince Lombardi, David Maraniss writes, "Since his days at West Point, [Lombardi] had based his coaching philosophy on Red Blaik's belief that perfection came with simplicity. The theory was to discard the immaterial and refine those few things that one did best." He put the sweep in with the Giants in 1955, Gifford's fourth year with the team.

In Lombardi's own writings he makes it clear that the power sweep—49 Sweep in the Packers' playbook—would be his core play and that its proper execution would achieve not only yardage but larger goals. "It is our number one play, our lead play, that 49 Sweep," he wrote in *Run to Daylight!*

> It is our bread-and-butter, top-priority play, the one we have to make go and the one our opponents know they must stop. All teams have them. Detroit has that fullback slant for Nick Pietrosante, the Bears have that pitchout for Willie Galimore, the Browns use that fullback wedge with Jimmy Brown. Continued success with it, of course, makes a number one play because from that success stems your confidence. And behind all that is the basic truth that it expresses you as a coach and the players as a team and that they know full well when they execute it and it's completely right.

"THAT FIRST training camp in '59," recalls Ron Kramer, the tight end, "we had a seven-man blocking sled on the practice fields. Every day we would go out at the start of practice, and we'd get on the seven-man sled. Bart Starr or one of the other quarterbacks would stand off to the side, calling out a cadence: *Set. Four-22. Hut! Hut!* And we would crack into that sled. Lombardi would be standing on the sled, and he'd yell, 'O.K., one more time!' And we would do it again until finally Lombardi was smiling and he'd say, 'That's the way I want it done!'!"

Inside the repetition was a precise division of labor. "In football, no one can take all the credit for making a play successful; that's the beauty of the game," says Kramer. "It has to be everybody together." Over time the Packers' sweep has come to be most closely identified with the two pulling guards, Thurston and Jerry Kramer. "But everybody had a key block," says Ron Kramer. "Everybody had to do a job."

body had a key block," says Ron Kramer. "Everybody had to do a job." (Devotees of vintage reels from NFL Films may recall a classic piece on Lombardi in which he is standing at a chalkboard, apparently outdoors on a practice field, diagramming the power sweep: *What we're trying to get is a seal here and a seal here and run this play in . . . the . . . alley.* In this instance the importance of the precision of each assignment is clear, and the scene has routine stamped all over it.)

In his book he writes, "I've diagrammed it so many times and coached it so much and watched it evolve so often since I first put it in with the Giants eight years ago that I think I see it in my sleep."

The sweep was run from a splitback formation, with a flanker (it was usually Boyd Dowler) to the strong side, outside the tight end. (Ron Kramer, whose legacy would become entwined with this play, was returning from a year of military service and first had to beat out Gary Knafelc to get the starter's job.) The line was balanced, a tackle and a guard on each side of the center. Starr was under center, and the backs were split behind him. In the early years those backs were most often Hornung and Jim Taylor, with Hornung on the left and Taylor on the right, each lined up on the outside leg of the guard in front of him. The sweep was most often run to the right, largely because Hornung ran it better—and Taylor, a tough-as-nails inside hammer, excelled at everything else, particularly running between the tackles.

"And there was another reason for running right," says Hornung. "If you ran it to the left, you'd have Max McGee out there blocking for me on some linebacker and, crissakes, nobody wanted that."

While the mythology of the sweep exalts the pulling guards, in truth the three most challenging blocks were delivered by tight end Ron Kramer, fullback Taylor and center Jim Ringo. Most important of those was Kramer, who at the snap was responsible for blocking the player across from him, usually the outside linebacker. "Never allow penetration to the inside or over you hard," wrote Lombardi in describing the tight end's role. "If he penetrates inside, he knocks off both our pulling guards." In other words, the play would be blown up. To the inside of Ron Kramer, right tackle Gregg and Taylor were responsible for working as a pair—in a style that, looking back, is suspiciously similar to the "zone blocking schemes" that were yet to prevent the defensive end from disrupting beyond the line of scrimmage. If any of these three players failed, the sweep could not work, and Jerry Kramer and Thurston, the pulling guards, would not ramble into space ahead of Hornung.

Jim Hanifan was coaching high school football in California in 1959, watching the Green Bay sweep from afar; he would later become one of the most successful offensive line coaches in league history. "I tried to coach that damn sweep in college ball," says Hanifan. "It was really, really hard to do. You were asking for two key blocks from the tight end and from the lead back and tackle. And both of those blocks had to be successful, and that was not easy to get done. Green Bay in those early years with Lombardi had a great, great tight end in Ron Kramer, and he would just kick your ass. And then Gregg and Taylor usually did a good job, and then you get the guards out there and make some money for yourself."

On a Friday fall afternoon in 2009 Ron Kramer was driving from Chicago to Green Bay with his old pal Hornung and became just a little bit emotional when recalling Lombardi's appreciation for his work on the edge of the sweep. Said Kramer, "The nicest compliment that Vince Lombardi ever gave me—and it gives me chills to think about it—was that having Kramer at tight end was like having 12 men on the field because he didn't have to worry about double-teaming anybody. That meant so much to me when he said that."

Ringo's block at center was also difficult. He had to execute what is called a "reach block" (extending laterally to block a defender who is in a seemingly advantageous position), in this case on the play-side defensive tackle to prevent him from achieving any penetration. Once all of these blocks were delivered—and it all happened in less than two seconds—guards Kramer (from the right) and Thurston (from the left) were free to barrel down the line of scrimmage, turn upfield and pick off defenders in the open field. And they were brilliant at doing it, as was Hornung at reading their blocks.

The exchange from Starr to Hornung was a straight handoff. Starr would reverse pivot—turning to his left—while Hornung began running. Starr would stick the ball into Hornung's belly with his left hand. "I'd run two steps to the right and then as soon as I got the ball, I'd deepen

run two steps to the right and then as soon as I got the ball, I'd deepen by a yard and a half," says Hornung. "That would give me and the guards both a chance to make a cut off Ron's block. We all had to watch what Ron was doing with the linebacker. If he took the linebacker inside, me and Jerry and Fuzzy would run outside. If he took him outside, we'd run up inside. I think everything moved quicker to the inside. But the whole key was watching Ron and that linebacker."

The play was made even more effective by the possibility that Hornung might throw the ball, an "option pass" in the language of the day. He had been a quarterback at Notre Dame, and though he was primarily a runner and threw only 55 passes in his entire nine-season NFL career, the threat of the option pass helped keep cornerbacks honest and enabled flanker Dowler to deliver a better block on the deepest defender.

The sweep was the backbone of Lombardi's attack, operated by the perfect combination of athletes. Ron Kramer was a horse, bigger and stronger than most outside linebackers at the time. Gregg was a powerful man-on-man blocker. Thurston and Jerry Kramer were not giants (247 and 245 pounds, respectively), but they were terrific athletes, capable of engaging defensive backs in the open field. "It wasn't a game-breaking play," says Ron Kramer. "It was a solid five, six, seven-yard play every time. It was made to keep the ball and wear out the defense."

Says Hornung: "Lombardi loved to show us the sweep on film after the game. Boy, he got his jollies when we did it right. More that anything else, I think."

Bill Yeoman, who in the 1960s invented the triple option Houston veer, recalls attending a Lombardi clinic in the late 1950s. "Vince would get so excited talking about the sweep," says Yeoman, "I thought he was going to have an orgasm right there at the chalkboard."

Lombardi's beloved sweep set up two other plays: Right 47 (off-tackle, with a lead blocker) and Right 43 (a quick-hitter straight up the middle with the lead back), each requiring less finesse than the sweep. Taylor was a battering ram on both, and he ran for more than 1,000 yards in each of five consecutive seasons from 1960 through '64. Together the sweep and the inside power plays formed a devastating

On this foundation Lombardi quickly righted the Packers. After a five-game losing streak in the middle of the 1959 season, Lombardi's first in Green Bay, the Packers closed with four straight wins to finish at 7–5. They went 8–4 and lost to the Eagles 17–13 in the '60 NFL Championship Game but returned the next year to win 11 games in the regular season and crush the Giants 37–0 for the team's first championship since '44. And the power sweep was the signature play of the new champions. In his book Lombardi referred to it as the "pay-off-the-mortgage" play.

But as early as that first championship season, Lombardi saw other teams begin to adapt, as he wrote in *Run to Daylight!*

> In 1961 it started falling off a little as play recognition by the defense began to develop. But in that 1961 championship game against the Giants, Hornung made one 19-yard gain with it. Then the Giants adjusted and when they drove Jim Katcavage, their left end, upfield hard, we used the counter [with Taylor]. We ran inside instead of outside, using cross-blocking, because a play's value is not only in that play itself, but in the counter it sets up.

The Green Bay power sweep would ultimately fall victim not only to film and familiarity but also to the quickening of the modern game. "It was a slow-developing play, where Hornung would run outside to the numbers, where, we used to say, the grass is still green," says Howard Mudd, an offensive lineman with the San Francisco 49ers of the 1960s and later a respected NFL line coach. "It was a play that went sideways and up."

Defenses became faster. Inside-out pursuit became a more common factor in defending outside players. If a halfback like Hornung waited for blockers, he would be caught by backside and inside chasers. As speed became paramount and precision less valuable, a new sweep—a quicker, more dynamic sweep—would take root, half a continent away.

But the Green Bay power sweep left a deep imprint on the soul of the sport and on the men who ran it. Hornung, riding shotgun on the drive with Kramer back up to Green Bay, told tall tales on his old bud-

drive with Kramer back up to Green Bay, told tall tales on his old buddy and then made sure that a passenger understood that he might be stretching the truth. But not about everything. As the flat, Midwestern landscape raced past the car windows, Hornung declared, "They never did stop our sweep."

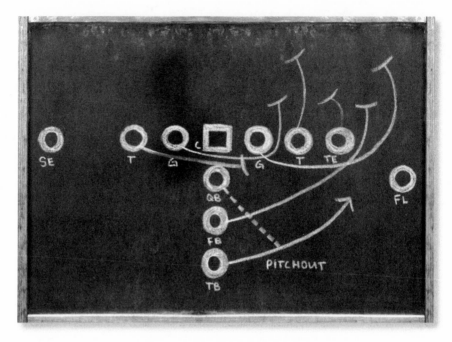

USC SWEEP RIGHT

At Southern Cal in the '70s and '80s, the Trojans incorporated many of the principles of the Lombardi sweep but used their speed to hit the defense more quickly. Both guards pulled, but unlike in the Lombardi sweep, only the play-side guard attempted to get out in front of the ballcarrier and move downfield. (Sometimes the Trojans pulled the backside tackle as well.) The USC sweep was run from an I formation in which the quarterback would pitch the ball to the tailback (unlike the Packers handoff), enabling the runner to get outside more quickly.

CHAPTER 10

STUDENT BODY RIGHT

The play made guys like Ricky Bell and Marcus Allen legends at Southern Cal. Oddly enough, even Bobby Bowden was involved

Los Angeles, Calif.
June 1995

ATHLETIC FACILITIES have come a long way. Once upon a time they were gyms with offices tucked into dark corners, or field houses with offices stuck somewhere behind the bleachers, and you had to work hard just to find the coach. Gradually they have become, of course, something much more, giant palaces erected in homage to the money of some alumnus. They have elaborate workout rooms and shiny office suites overlooking the field.

USC's Heritage Hall is something altogether different. It is not a palace, because it is not new or vast or opulent. But it is a shrine, and that is apparent from the seven Heisman Trophies on display, under glass, in the first-floor lobby. In Heritage Hall—even the name is instructive—it is impossible to forget who has trod the floor beneath your feet.

On this day, USC coach John Robinson, who will turn 60 at the end of the following month, is sitting in a meeting room on the second floor of the building. Robinson is beginning the third year of his second tour as coach of the Trojans. (The first was from 1976 through '82; this second run would last from '93 through '97.) He is sitting in darkness, his profile illuminated by an overhead projector that spins out past Trojan glory, much of it orchestrated by Robinson.

The viewing isn't Robinson's idea. "I don't spend a lot of time reminiscing," he says. But once the show begins, he assumes a coach's pose: loafers on the table, remote control resting in the palm of his right hand with his thumb at the ready.

On the screen there is an image of the late Ricky Bell, who played for USC from 1973 through '76 and was the starting tailback on Robinson's first team as head coach. The narrator on the film intones, *"One of the highlights of Robinson's first year in '76 was the play of senior tailback Ricky Bell."* He gained 1,433 yards that year and scored 14 touchdowns as the Trojans went 11–1.

"Great player, collision runner like Earl Campbell," says Robinson. His voice cracks slightly. Bell died of sudden heart failure in 1984; he was only 29 years old. "This guy was a great kid," says Robinson. "A big-time human being."

Now the screen is lit with action of the 1980 Rose Bowl, in which No. 3 USC beat No. 1 Ohio State 17–16. Narrator: *"USC trailed undefeated Ohio State in the final minutes and then began one of the most devastating victory drives in the history of the Rose Bowl. . . ."*

"I told Paul Hackett, our offensive coordinator, 'Give the ball to Charlie White and run behind Anthony Muñoz,' " says Robinson. "Muñoz was a senior, played the first three plays of the first game of the season and got hurt. He came to me in December and said, 'Should I play in the Rose Bowl or redshirt?' I told him he really should play, and if he plays well, he'll get drafted anyway. Hell, he was the third guy picked in the whole draft. Charlie White broke his nose in that game, blood all over his face. Toughest player I've ever been around. His fullback was Marcus Allen. One hundred eighty-five pounds."

The show goes on for nearly an hour. Highlight films like this have a way of making the ordinary seem extraordinary. But the USC production that Robinson is watching is a true cavalcade of greatness. Sam Cunningham, Charlie Young, Lynn Swann, Anthony Davis, Pat Haden, Bell, Marvin Powell, Clay Matthews, Paul McDonald, Muñoz, White, Allen, Ronnie Lott, Dennis Smith—it's like a football fantasy camp. Robinson coached all of them, either as an assistant (1972–74) or head coach, before moving to the NFL for nine years as coach of the Rams.

The flow of talent running through USC during the Robinson years was unprecedented in the college game. "Big man on big man" is what renowned former USC assistant Marv Goux would call the Trojans' practices. "We has so much talent and we played so hard during the week," recalls former tight end Charlie Young, "our practices were harder than the games." Through all those years there was a relentless, punishing offensive system built on foundation plays that became known throughout the college game as student body right and student body left. They were power sweeps run with mammoth linemen leading fast, tough tailbacks out of the I formation; they were descendants of the Green Bay power sweep but operated by a generation of better athletes, most of whom would also wind up in the NFL.

The modern running game began with Lombardi, who was the first to take the ancient principles of the single wing and modernize them. But coach after coach after coach will tell you that the next link in the chain of innovation was the USC power game, which would later become the Los Angeles Rams' power game. And it started well before John Robinson got to Southern California.

Douglas, Ga.
Summer 1956

BOBBY BOWDEN was 26 years old when he signed on as coach of football, basketball and baseball at South Georgia College. Hedging against the possibility that he might not be busy enough, Bowden was also the athletic director. But his future lay in football, and he knew it. And he also knew he needed an offense. The closest major university was 126 miles southwest in Tallahassee, where Tom Nugent was about to begin his fourth year as coach at Florida State. Bowden and his assistant coach, Vince Gibson (who would later be the head coach at Kansas State, Louisville and Tulane), piled into a car and went to see Nugent—because Nugent, a known football innovator, had something they wanted to see.

When Nugent had taken over as coach at Virginia Military Institute in 1949, the predominant offensive attack in college football (and, indeed, in professional football as well) was the T formation. Nugent was looking for something different to run. He designed a formation in which all three backs lined up directly behind the quarterback, in a single line, perpendicular to the line of scrimmage. Just as the T formation was named for its appearance, so was this: the I.

Nugent did not run the I in his inaugural season; that would begin in 1950. In his history of VMI athletics, *The Corps Roots the Loudest*, Thomas W. Davis writes:

> Nugent's second season was one of the most unusual in VMI's gridiron history. It started with a high note of success, a 25–19 night game win over William and Mary in Roanoke, the first loss by [William and Mary] to a Virginia team in 10 years; a contributing factor was Nugent's unveiling of the I formation, its first use in college football.
>
> Later, Davis writes, "Tom Nugent's third season resulted in a 7–3 record and a Southern Conference championship that VMI shared that year with the University of Maryland. Using their coach's I formation with great success, VMI's offense averaged 28 points in each of the seven wins." Nugent stayed one more season before taking his offense to Florida State.

BOWDEN, BEFORE his arrival at South Georgia, had been an assistant at Howard College (now Samford) in Birmingham, his hometown. "We ran the dead, straight T formation at Howard," says Bowden. "We didn't split anybody out. But I wanted to see what Tom Nugent was running at Florida State. Well, he was running the pure I formation, with all four backs, including the quarterback, in a straight line. Tom gave us the playbook. I still remember it today. The off-tackle play was called the Blast. The outside play was called the Roll. And they had a play action pass off both of them."

The I formation was a power offense with slightly more deception than the T. With the I, offenses could run a power play off tackle by sending the lead back one way for a fake and still have a back as lead blocker at the point of attack. "Back in those days," says Bowden in his familiar drawl, "there wasn't a whole lot of imagination."

Bowden ran the I formation for three years at South Georgia, and when he went back to Howard/Samford as the head coach in 1959, he switched to the wing T. But by the time he landed in West Virginia in '66, he was running a pro-set I formation, with two backs behind the quarterback. It would remain the foundation of the Bowden offense for more than three decades and was called the multiple I. And to this day Bowden says, "You never can tell who invented anything, but it wouldn't surprise me if Tom Nugent invented that thing."

AT THE same time Bowden was visiting Nugent, a continent away Don Coryell, athletic director and football coach at Fort Ord, a U.S. Army base near the Monterey Peninsula, was tweaking the two-man I formation for the 1956 season that he had used with success at Wenatchee Valley College the year before.

After his one season at Fort Ord, Coryell ran the I formation for three years at Whittier College, then went to USC as an assistant coach under John McKay in 1960. USC history generally credits McKay with installing the power offense that would eventually become student body right, and clearly he deserves much of the credit. Says Robinson, "There's no doubt McKay was the guy who developed the USC offense in that era. But he talked to a lot of people about it. I always heard there was a high school coach somewhere in L.A. who was running the I formation offense. And Don Coryell was somebody that McKay talked to a lot."

Once committed, McKay went all in on the power I. Willie Brown became the first in a long line of brilliant, durable USC tailbacks. In McKay's third year Brown rushed for 574 yards on just 88 carries, and USC went 10–0 in the regular season, beat Wisconsin in the Rose Bowl and won its first national championship since 1939. The Trojans would win four more in the next 16 years.

Robinson explains the USC power philosophy in all its breathtaking simplicity. "Number 1," he says, "you were going to have a tailback that you really featured. McKay wanted to develop one player who really dominated the scene. You were going to give him the ball 30 times a game. Hell, I gave it to Ricky 53 times in one game. People wanted to kill me." (Actually Bell carried *only* 51 times, for 347 yards in a 23–14 win over Washington State in 1976.)

"Then," Robinson continues, "McKay worked really hard on getting the best offensive linemen, and really physical offensive linemen. The goal was to physically dominate the defense, control the line of scrimmage and feature the tailback. Beyond that, we wanted a smart quarterback who could manage the game and throw individual routes when defenses singled the wide receivers. That was Pat Haden, Paul McDonald."

The USC power offense was clearly informed by Lombardi's power sweep. The Trojan and Packer offenses were similar in that both aspired to get two solid blocks (in most cases the tight end and play-side tackle) on the front side of an outside play and attack the edge of the defense. But McKay and USC refined the play in two important ways. First, where Lombardi's sweep began with a handoff from the quarterback to a halfback running across the back of the formation from behind the backside guard-tackle gap, student body right began with a quick toss from the quarterback to the tailback, who lined up directly behind the quarterback.

"It hit faster than the Green Bay sweep," says Robinson. "By the quarterback flipping the ball to the tailback, who was already running to the outside, we got the tailback outside much faster than Lombardi did. But it was similar to the Green Bay sweep in concept, in that it broke sideways, turned upfield and tried to ram the ball down your throat."

Second, while the USC sweep, like the Green Bay sweep, pulled both guards (and sometimes the backside tackle), the blocking scheme was altered. Says Robinson, "The backside pullers didn't attempt to get in front of the tailback. Only the onside guard got in front." In truth, the USC sweep was too fast-hitting for both guards to get out ahead of the tailback. The backside guard instead picked off backside chasers.

And while the toss sweep was to become the most famous of USC's power running plays, it was but one of four base calls. The others were isolation (or, in coachspeak, *iso*), power strong and power weak. On the isolation call, the tailback ran straight over the middle of the offensive line, with a double-team block on the nose and the fullback leading. Power strong was an off-tackle play to the tight end side, and power weak had a fullback leading the play away from the tight end side. "It was an offense that you could draw up real simply," says Muñoz. "But it required real tough, effective man-to-man blocking by the tackle and the tight end on the play side."

In 1965 Mike Garrett won the Heisman Trophy running behind sophomore offensive tackle Ron Yary, who two years later would win the Outland Trophy and eventually become an All-Pro with the Vikings. Five years later, in '70, McKay took the Trojans to Alabama to play Bear Bryant's Crimson Tide at Legion Field in Alabama. Rare is the game that becomes an implement of social change, but not long after USC sophomore Sam Cunningham trampled Alabama for 135 yards, Bryant began to plead with his university to integrate the program.

Eight years later, under Robinson, the Trojans went to Birmingham again, this time with an offensive line that included Muñoz and Keith Van Horne as the tackles, Brad Budde at one of the guard positions and Hoby Brenner at tight end. Charles White was the tailback, and blocking for him was an undersized freshman stud, who Robinson just had to get on the field somewhere—Marcus Allen. It was one of the most talent-stuffed college football teams in the game's long history. The Trojans beat the Tide 24–14, and nothing better illustrated USC's power game than Van Horne's dominance of Alabama defensive tackle Marty Lyons. "All we heard all week was what a tough matchup it was going to be for Keith against Marty Lyons," says Muñoz. "Well, I can say to this day is that Keith did an outstanding job."

Robinson left USC after the 1982 season to take over the Rams. "We brought a lot of the same stuff to the Rams that we had been running at USC," he says. As at USC, Robinson developed offensive linemen and a featured tailback, in this case a 6' 3", 220-pound blend of speed and power named Eric Dickerson, who entered the NFL the same year Robinson did and rushed for nearly 7,000 yards in his first four seasons. He ran behind the likes of right tackle Jackie Slater, who would land in the Hall of Fame, and six-time Pro Bowl center Doug Smith, who made the L.A. power series hum. But by the end of the '80s, the Rams were learning a different system altogether. It was called zone blocking.

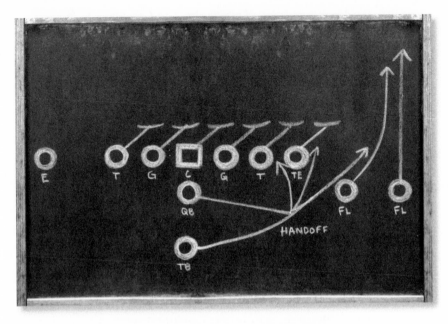

OUTSIDE ZONE RIGHT

In zone blocking schemes, offensive linemen attempt to use the speed and pursuit of the defense against itself. Each offensive lineman, instead of firing forward and blocking the defender directly in front of him, slides in one direction, together with the others—"like on a railroad track," as Anthony Muñoz describes it. In an outside zone scheme, as the defenders chase the play, the offensive linemen use that momentum to carry them farther outside, spreading them, which opens running lanes. The quarterback takes the snap and runs wide to make a direct handoff to the tailback. Once the TB receives the ball, he reads the gaps in the defense and cuts upfield when he sees an opening.

CHAPTER 11

ZONE BLOCKING

It's all the rage in the modern running game, but don't try to tell an old hard-core offensive line coach it's a revolution

Terre Haute, Ind.
August 2009

AT NOON on a midsummer day the Indianapolis Colts shuffled off their training camp practice field at the Rose-Hulman Institute of Technology. They had gone through a light session under a rising morning sun; a much more stressful afternoon workout would follow, under more painful conditions. No energy was wasted as players walked slowly off the artificial turf onto the asphalt path that led to air conditioning, medical treatment and food. It was eerily quiet, except for the occasional Colts fan beseeching an autograph. And, of course, the ear-splitting engine noise when 67-year-old offensive line coach Howard Mudd roared off the field in a four-wheel all-terrain vehicle.

Golf carts are everywhere at a pro football practice, with all manner of support personnel scooting about; small flatbed tractors are common too, for transporting tackling dummies, Gatorade buckets and, on bad days, injured players. But Mudd has raised the vehicular bar, tearing around the Colts' camp in an open-top roadster that looks as if it belongs in some sort of extreme sports competition. "When we finish talking," says Mudd, "I'll get this thing up to speed for you. We can even go back on the trails, if you're interested. There are some great trails around here."

If Mudd were not a real '60s-vintage professional football player dragging his wounded body into old age with little complaint, he could play one on television. He has the barrel chest and broad shoulders of a faded offensive lineman, a middle gone soft over the years, a right knee swollen and scarred grotesquely by no fewer than three total knee replacements. His face is leathery and reddened by four decades of training-camp summers; a gray-and-white beard finishes the package with a professorial touch that is fully appropriate given his standing in the O-line community.

Mudd, who grew up in Midland, Mich., played on the offensive line at Hillsdale College from 1960 through '63, then spent nine seasons in the old school NFL trenches: six with the San Francisco 49ers, three with the Chicago Bears. He played in three Pro Bowls but went out in '71 with a knee injury that still hounds him today.

He coached offensive linemen at the University of California in his first two years out of the NFL and took his first coaching job in pro football at the age of 32, with the 1974 San Diego Chargers. He has been in the league ever since and has spent more time watching large men's backsides than most people spend watching television. He knows blocking.

In the language of football, certain terms become part of the vernacular overnight, or seem to. "Zone blocking scheme," and its relatives "inside zone play" and "outside zone play," have suddenly become ubiquitous, often exalted as something brand-new. Yet there has been considerable commentary in the coaching community—some of it downright dismissive—as to whether there is anything at all new about zone blocking. Hell hath no fury like an old coach being told that a thing is new when he's been watching it for decades. Zone blocking is one of those things.

Jim Hanifan, who coached NFL offensive lines in the 1970s, '80s and '90s (and was head coach of the St. Louis Cardinals from '80 through '85), says, "I get a kick out of people saying zone blocking is something new. Yeah, it's new all right. It's only been around for 50 years or more. It's part of the game. Some people are acting like it's part of a revolution. Bullshit!"

Hanifan played at the University of California in the early-to-mid-1950s and shortly afterward coached high school football in California for seven seasons. "And I coached zone blocking there," he says. "We've been using it forever." Hanifan's insistence—shared by almost every old school

O-line guru in the sport—grows from the hazy definition of the term. It sounds simple enough: zone blocking. Different from man-to-man blocking. But, of course, it's more complicated than that.

"Zone blocking has always been there," Mudd says. "Maybe people called it something else, but it's always been part of the game." Here Mudd becomes the teacher. He is sitting in his turbo golf cart in the glare of summer, but he might as well be in a classroom, writing on a whiteboard with a grease pencil. He grabs his "pupil's" notebook and pen and begins sketching diagrams to explain what it is and to postulate on its heritage. In football evolution, few areas are grayer than zone blocking. But let Mudd explain the basics:

"Man blocking is just what is sounds like," he says. "You've got one man blocking another man. When the play gets called in the huddle, the offensive player has an assignment, to block a particular player on the other team. That's man-to-man blocking, and you really don't see a lot of that anymore. Zone blocking, well, in the simplest terms, the offensive players are blocking an area. Instead of trying to block a particular player and move him to a particular place, they're blocking whatever is in front of them."

Anthony Muñoz, an integral part of the man-to-man blocking scheme that fueled USC's famous sweeps, would later play left tackle on the '80s Cincinnati Bengals teams that brought zone blocking into the NFL mainstream. "Think of it this way," says Muñoz. "If you're man blocking, you've got this guy across from you, number 71. You're job is to block him. That's your man. Zone blocking, you're on a track, like a railroad track, with your buddy, or all your buddies on the offensive line. If a defensive lineman or a linebacker crosses onto the track, your job is to take him and move him."

As the offensive linemen, working in unison, take advantage of the defenders' own momentum, the running back, following, reads those blocks before finding his seam and hitting it. The best thing about zone blocking schemes," Muñoz continues, "is that it doesn't matter what the defense is doing. You can use your strength and your power to your advantage. You can say, 'Let's not see where the defense wants to move to; let's dictate where they go by where we move along that track and then use their movement against them to create seams.' "

The concepts of zone blocking have, indeed, been a part of football since the turn of the 20th century. (And, arguably, before that; after all, the flying wedge was technically a zone blocking play, albeit with inter-locked limbs. A group of players, arm-in-arm, ran up the field plowing over anything in their way, without regard to any personal blocking as-signment.) Pop Warner's single wing was rooted in double teams and trap blocking rather than pure body-on-body blocking. Tubby Raymond's Delaware wing T was also built on a foundation of traps and team blocks or "buddy blocks."

Among the first mainstream college coaches to effectively use the mod-ern concepts of zone blocking was Bill Yeoman at Houston. It was Yeoman who began running the veer in 1965, using what were essentially zone blocking techniques, even if they weren't called that at the time, for more than a decade. And through the '70s and '80s, at both the college and the NFL level, as defenses became so much more sophisticated—linemen slanting and stunting in ever more unpredictable ways—it became nearly impossible for an offensive lineman to simply block the man across the line because often that man wasn't rushing directly at him. Offenses needed some way to counteract these more elaborate defenses.

HOWARD MUDD arrived in Cleveland in 1983 to work as the Browns' offensive line coach under Sam Rutigliano. The Browns went 9–7 in that first year and won just one of their first nine games in '84; Rutigliano was fired and replaced by defensive coordinator Marty Schottenheimer, an old-school former AFL linebacker who would build a successful coaching career on the philosophy that the best way to win was to use the running game to pound the football. For the '85 season he charged Mudd with rebuilding the Browns' offense into a power running machine.

Mudd will not take credit for inventing the NFL version of zone block-ing. He says the Seattle Seahawks, where he coached from 1978 through '82 under Jack Patera, had been using a few zone blocking plays. That surely helped shape Mudd's thinking as he worked up his run game for the '85 season. There was another influence too. When Mudd played for the 49ers, one of the team's running backs was John David Crow (Heis-man Trophy winner at Texas A&M in '57), near the end of his impressive 11-year NFL career. Mudd and Crow would later coach together with the

San Diego Chargers in the mid '70s, and Mudd picked Crow's brain about how running backs find holes.

Says Mudd, "One day I said to John David, 'What do you look at when you're hitting the hole?' I asked him because we were always telling running backs, 'Look at the butt of the blocker you're following.' So I wondered if that's what they actually did. John said, 'I'll tell you what: I'm not lookin' at [the blocker]. I'm looking at that sumbitch that's gonna hurt me.' Well, that really helped me because then I realized that running backs aren't watching offensive linemen, they're watching defenders. That's a big difference."

For Mudd this signaled a change: Instead of assigning specific blockers to open specific holes, why not try to have the entire offensive line work as a flowing team, creating movement in the defense and letting the holes open up wherever they opened and letting the running back see them. "I was thinking, Let's cover up their color with our color," says Mudd, "and then encourage the ballcarrier to run toward the defense and then go where they aren't going. Hit 'em where they ain't, you could say."

Everybody in football in the 1980s had played—or coached—the wing T at some point in his career, Mudd included. He started there. "The wing T is built on principles of the double-team block up front," says Mudd. "So with Cleveland in 1985, what we installed was a system where we tried to double-team at the point of attack, and as soon as the double team is engaged, we would come off and get the 'backer on the second level." This would become the bedrock of the modern zone scheme: flow, double-team and release to the second level.

There was also a bonus. "Zone blocking is easier to teach," Mudd says. "There are fewer things that can go wrong because you're creating this mush, where guys are working with the guy next to him and there's just less space for things to go wrong. Now, with this, of course, you're going to lose some of the techniques that I grew up with—the angle blocking and pulling. But it's just easier. Over the years I've been in so many meetings where we said, 'Ah, hell, let's just zone-block it.' And that's what we did."

Another concept became apparent. Whereas running backs in the old man-to-man blocking system would generally accelerate at the snap and receive the ball—by toss or handoff—while running at full speed, zone blocking schemes called for more patience. "It became important for the ballcarrier to have speed *through* the hole, not speed *to* the hole," says Mudd.

The 1985 Browns started four offensive linemen who had not been regulars in the previous season. They also started second-year man Earnest Byner at tailback and rookie Kevin Mack at fullback, and each rushed for more than 1,000 yards, the only double-thousand backfield in the NFL. A year later the rushing numbers dipped, but with Bernie Kosar at quarterback, the Browns reached the AFC Championship Game (losing to John Elway and the Broncos on "The Drive") and eventually strung together three straight double-digit-win seasons.

THE LEAGUE was watching. In Cincinnati 42-year-old Jim McNally was half a decade into his first NFL coaching job, handling the offensive line for head coach Sam Wyche. McNally, who would become one of the most respected O-line coaches in the game, already had anchors at left tackle (Muñoz) and right guard (Max Montoya). In '86 he started implementing Mudd's zone system with the Bengals. "Howard Mudd really ran one play, an off-tackle play, exceptionally well with a zone scheme," says McNally. "We copied that play and ran it a little wider, starting with [running back] James Brooks."

In fairness to McNally, it's not as if he'd been sleeping on the sideline for five years. He had seen the defenses increasingly attacking gaps in the offense, making it more difficult to block for a traditional man-to-man running game. "When defensive lines started to pinch and slant," says McNally, "you'd get a situation where a [defensive end, or tackle in a 3–4 alignment] would line up over your tackle and he would slant to the inside. Well, your guard is firing out to get the linebacker, and the slanting defender would pick him off." That would kill the play, often letting a linebacker shoot the gap untouched.

McNally's answer was to have his linemen take a step backward with one foot—counterintuitive to everything linemen had been previously taught—and then launch into a series of lateral double teams. In the summer of 1986 McNally introduced two movements to his offensive line: the "drop step" and the "bucket step."

Muñoz was part of those early practice field sessions and recalls, "People were asking, 'How can you run-block when you're taking a step backward?' I remember a couple years later, the Rams were putting in a zone blocking system, and [Hall of Fame tackle] Jackie Slater called me and said, 'Anthony, they want me to start by going backward! I want to fire out and hit somebody.' I told him that's the beauty of the drop step and bucket step. Once you learn to do them properly, you're stepping backward to get your hips in position to move, but your shoulders are moving forward. When everybody takes that same step and gets moving on that track, you look like a bunch of dancing bears. But it's effective."

It took two seasons for the Bengals to become efficient with the scheme. James Brooks rushed for 1,087 yards in '86, and the Bengals went 10–6. A year later they slipped to 4–11 in a strike-interrupted season, but in '88 the Bengals were an offensive machine. Brooks, a 5' 10", 180-pound scatback from Auburn, rushed for another 931 yards, but it was rookie Ickey Woods, a 6' 2", 231-pound battering ram, who exploded behind McNally's dancing bears.

Patriots coach Bill Belichick says, "To be a great running back in the NFL, you've got to be a truly instinctive runner." Woods, for one season, was truly that: He had superb instincts for following the nascent zone blocking, seeing and feeling the seams and bursting *through* the hole (as Mudd would have it). Woods rolled up 1,066 yards, 5.6 yards every time he touched the ball. The Bengals led the NFL with 2,710 yards on the ground, nearly 200 more than any other team.

Woods became famous for his Ickey Shuffle touchdown dance, which he performed 15 times in the regular season and three times more in the postseason. Using McNally's zone blocking scheme in combination with Boomer Esiason running Sam Wyche's no-huddle offense, Woods and the Bengals won the AFC title and lost to San Francisco in the Super Bowl 20–16. (Ickey Woods would tear his left ACL in 1989; he never returned to the form that made him a one-season superstar.)

IN THE 1990s zone blocking became ever more prevalent. Theories abound on why this happened. Bruce Coslet, who was offensive coordinator on the Wyche-McNally Bengals teams of the late '80s, suggests the reason was that linemen kept growing larger, becoming less capable of executing the man-on-man blocks that characterized so many earlier running schemes.

"They couldn't trap, they couldn't pull and they couldn't run," says Coslet. "Before the early '80s everybody was running sweeps and using angle blocking and trapping. But as linemen got bigger and bigger, you just couldn't do that stuff. Our linemen with the Bengals, we called them the Road Graders. They would just knock the shit out of the guy in front of them with a double team, and then whoever got off that block would get to the second level and knock the shit out of the linebacker. That's all zone blocking was for us."

Mudd doesn't disagree. "In a sense, we've lost a lot of the techniques I grew up with," he says. "The taking angles, the trapping. And there's no question that when you get people 340, 350 pounds, they're not going to be able to run around the corner and leverage people. They just can't."

But there is a middle ground where many offenses have taken up residence. While it's true that many NFL offensive linemen of the 1990s became almost grotesquely outsized and opened holes more or less by leaning on defenders, Muñoz argues that the most effective zone blocking is accomplished by big, but not massive, men who can move. "We had guys in Cincinnati," he says, "who weighed 300 to 310 pounds, and you had to be nimble and agile to run the system. You had to move, and you had to get to the second level."

The direct descendant of Bill Yeoman, Howard Mudd and Jim McNally is Alex Gibbs. A former running back and defensive back at Davidson, Gibbs started coaching offensive linemen at the age of 34 when he took a job at Ohio State under Woody Hayes in 1975. His greatest impact would come more than two decades and eight jobs later, when he coached the Denver Broncos' offensive line from 1995 to 2003, under head coach Mike Shanahan.

Gibbs installed a zone blocking scheme that relied not only on adroit movement and double teams at the point of impact but also—controversially—on cut blocks at the second level. In a four-year period starting in 1995 and culminating in back-to-back Super Bowl victories to end the '97 and '98 seasons, Terrell Davis ran for 6,413 yards. Eight different offensive linemen started at least 14 games for the Broncos;

all of them weighed less than 300 pounds. They were quick and athletic, and if their cut blocking rankled opponents who deemed it dangerous and career-threatening, it was also well within the rules. No less an authority than Muñoz says, "Cutting has always been a part of offensive line play. Those guys at Denver in those years did a terrific job of getting to the second level."

Gibbs, who became the Houston Texans' offensive line coach, remains at the vortex of NFL offensive line play. As for the question of whether there is or isn't anything new about zone blocking, Gibbs, like his peers, surely has opinions; but he's not the one who will resolve that debate—he doesn't grant interviews.

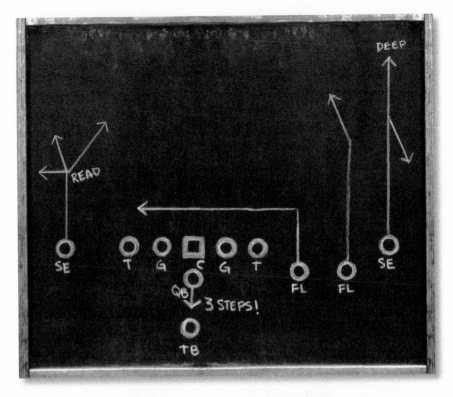

THE RUN-AND-SHOOT

The concept was borrowed by Mouse Davis from Tiger Ellison: Spread the field with your offensive formation (thus stretching the defense) and rely on the quarterback and his receivers to be in perfect sync. Mouse unleashed his version in the late '60s. In this play, the three receivers to the right side run assigned routes: a deep "go" on the outside (if he can't beat the defender, he breaks it off with a 15- to 18-yard curl to the sideline), a seam route in the middle and a shallow cross on the inside. The lone receiver on the left side simply reads the defense and runs away from the coverage. The quarterback makes the same read; it is up to him to decide which of the three receivers presents the best target. Three-step drop, quick decision, delivery.

CHAPTER 12

THE SPREAD OFFENSE

How Mouse met Tiger, horrified the football establishment
and—40 years later—made Vince Young famous

T HE COLLEGE quarter-
back sat in the dark with
a remote clicker in his
right hand and two cell-
phones on the table—one for close friends only and the other for lesser
acquaintances. This was early in the summer of 2005, and Vince Young
was poised somewhere between urban legend and mythic hero. Five
months earlier he had led the University of Texas to a Rose Bowl victory
over Michigan, setting the stage for a run at the national championship
in the fall of '05.

Young represented vastly different things to different constituencies.
To die-hard fans of the Longhorns, he was a savior, a modern-day James
Street, a quarterback who would return the Horns to their rightful place
at the top of the college football world. To inner-city football players, he
was the image of survival, an athlete who refused to be dragged into any
of the many evils infecting his Houston neighborhood—and who also refused to be moved from quarterback to any other position on the field.
To pure football fans, he was the next link in the evolutionary chain of
offensive innovation.

Young watched himself on a video screen in the basement of the
Texas football facility. Outside the room the hallways were lined with

plaques celebrating Texas's proud football history; at the far end of the building was a sprawling weight-training center, where players came and went seemingly all day long. Up on the screen came images from a Texas victory over Kansas the previous fall, Texas trailing 23–20 with just more than a minute to play and facing fourth-and-18 on its own 45-yard line. From out of the shotgun Young ran right to the corner of the formation, darted farther outside and made a lone defender miss a tackle before running out-of-bounds with a 22-yard gain that would lead to a game-winning touchdown pass five plays later. "Me and one guy trying to make the tackle," Young says. "I like that matchup. I just gave him a little two-step."

Another game, this one on a home Saturday night against Oklahoma State. The Longhorns had fallen behind 35–7, embarrassing themselves in front of a well-oiled home crowd. Young brought them all the way back to a 56–35 win and stamped the victory with a slaloming 42-yard touchdown run with 6:57 to play. Again from the shotgun, Young slid the ball briefly into the belly of the lone running back, Cedric Benson, then pulled it out and ran to the outside. "The outside guy takes me, I give it to Ced," says Young, explaining the mechanics of the play. "If he slants real hard to get after Ced, then I keep it and go to the corner. He slanted real hard." It is a sequence that would become endemic to Saturdays in the fall (and even some Sundays).

The video session lasts for more than an hour as Young takes a visitor through the high points of his redshirt sophomore season. It all has the feel of something different from ordinary football, as if the University of Texas and Young had discovered a new way to play an old game: A shotgun snap, a quarterback running wild or throwing from elongated formations.

It was the result of a process long under way when Texas signed Young out of Houston's Madison High in February 2002. What would come to be known as the "spread offense" had percolated in various forms at various locations for more than half a century before Vince Young turned it into a highlight film at Texas. Dutch Meyer coached at TCU from 1934 through '52, and among his quarterbacks were the legendary Sammy Baugh ('34–36) and Heisman Trophy winner Davey O'Brien ('37–38).

Meyer embraced the idea of using the full breadth of the football field in ways that now seem obvious but were radical notions at the time that he began with them. In his landmark manual *Spread Formation Football*, published just after his final season at TCU in 1952, Meyer wrote:

> We found that by moving out both ends and two or three backs, it became imperative for the defense to scatter too. As a result the entire defensive line was spaced so much wider that *natural* holes were created and much of the power blocking necessary on closer formations was no longer needed.
>
> Regarding the passing game from spread formations, Meyer concluded, ". . . it can be quickly seen that potential receivers, placed out from the main body of the formation and away from a congested defense, can move rapidly into the opponent's secondary and will have much freedom of movement as they deploy into set patterns."

MEYER'S WRITING, in its simplicity, neatly described the essence of spread football: Make the defense cover the entire field.

Texas offensive coordinator Greg Davis is a football junkie who found his comfort zone. In 37 years of coaching at two high schools and six colleges, Davis has never worked on the defensive side of the field. In his world defenders are one-dimensional cutouts that have only fronts, but no backs. They are just letters squeaked onto a whiteboard with a Sharpie. "I was a high school and college quarterback," Davis says. "I've always been fascinated by offense and the ways you can find to move the football." For the majority of his career, what that involved was the forward pass.

He coached Gary Kubiak at Texas A&M and they remained close as Kubiak climbed the college and NFL coaching ladder. Under head coach Mack Brown at Texas, he helped make dangerous passers of Major Applewhite and Chris Simms. But in the early years of the new century Davis saw change unfolding. He saw Rich Rodriguez employing a wide spread offense as offensive coordinator at Tulane and Clemson and then as head coach at West Virginia. He saw Urban Meyer take Utah into the BCS with a combination run-pass game. And in 2002 he signed Vince Young, a 6' 5", 195-pound quarterback with a gift for open-field running.

"His mother said to me, 'You're not going to have my son just dropping back and passing the ball, are you?' " says Davis. "I said, 'No ma'am, we're not just going to do that.' "

On Jan. 4, 2006, Young led Texas to a 41–38 victory over USC in the Bowl Championship Series national title game. He passed for 267 yards, ran for 200 more and, with 19 seconds to play, bolted nine yards for the winning touchdown, denying the Trojans a third consecutive national crown. Young was dazzling, and he looked like something new, a startling change in the game. Yet it was a change imagined long before that night in Pasadena. Vince Young was simply the perfect result.

Portland, Ore.
Autumn 2008

SUMMER IS gone early in the Pacific Northwest; a cold wind ripples across the urban campus of Portland State University, tucked into the southwest corner of the city. The Vikings play football games here in a minor league baseball stadium but practice on a field hidden among academic buildings and dormitories at the center of the campus, invisible from a block away. On a September morning the team shuffles off the field at 9:15 a.m. after an early-Thursday practice; last to leave the field are coach Jerry Glanville and his offensive coordinator, Darrel (Mouse) Davis.

Wrapped in a black windbreaker, Davis throws his arm around a visitor. "You want to get some breakfast?" he asks him. This is what Mouse does after nearly every single morning practice: He walks off the Portland State campus, then two blocks to the corner of 6th and College and through the doors of the Cheerful Tortoise, a musty, dark-wood saloon that serves a rib-sticking breakfast. Mouse takes a seat near the front of the room, orders two basted eggs, hash browns and, after much more consideration than one might expect from a man who calls football plays every 40 seconds under duress, chooses sourdough toast over wheat.

At the age of 76 Davis revels in the sudden and vast popularity of all spread offenses because three decades ago, when he was rolling up ungodly numbers with quarterbacks like June Jones and Neil Lomax at Portland State, he was accused of crimes against football by the keepers of a staid game.

"At my age," he says, hoisting a fork and stabbing at the eggs on his plate, "it's nice to know that I'm not a complete fucking idiot after all."

Mouse—and it's best to dispense with "Darrel" right here and now because nobody calls him that—is also an honorable man. For decades journalists and coaches alike have attempted to credit him with the creation of the run-and-shoot offense. (Sometimes this was a compliment, but often it was not.) Just as quickly as the title was bestowed, Mouse would make a correction. And he does it again now. "This stuff," he says, "it all started with Tiger Ellison." And the story of how Mouse Davis came to find Tiger Ellison is a classic case of football socialism: Everything belongs to everyone, especially the diagrams on a board or the plays on a film.

Mouse was one of five siblings who grew up together in the town of Independence, Ore. They all had nicknames: Birdie, Blackie, Teancie, Tickie and Mouse. (In 1979, SPORTS ILLUSTRATED's Kenny Moore wrote that "Their mother's call to dinner sounded like an appeal for an exterminator.") Mouse was the youngest, and he earned his nickname by failing to grow. He was 5' 6" and 135 pounds as a high school senior, too small to play quarterback. But he did. Certainly he was too small to play quarterback in college, but he did that too (at what is now Western Oregon University). He became a coach immediately upon graduation in 1955, and by '62 he was the head coach at Milwaukie High in the suburbs south of Portland.

Mouse ran a basic I formation, with a tight end, slotback and wide receiver, and he was forever trying to use players like himself, of which there was no shortage. "Little pissants," he says. "At Milwaukie in 1962 I had a lot of good players, but they weren't big, physical players. That's the case at a lot of high schools. More of your good athletes are little pissants. Good athletes, but small.

"As a coach, everything you do comes from some previous experience," Davis continues. "At different parts of my playing career I had been a quarterback and a receiver. And I was a little pissant. So my attitude was, you take the little guys and put them out in space and they're pretty good. You put 'em in a slug-it-out kind of game, they're pretty average. So we were putting them out in space."

On a spring Saturday in 1965 Davis was doing a series of "car clinics" with a group of his coaching buddies. "You do a clinic, jump in the car and go do another clinic," he says. "That's why we called them car clinics." En route from one stop to the next, one of Davis's colleagues handed him a book entitled *Run and Shoot Football: Offense of the Future*, written by one Glenn (Tiger) Ellison. Davis read the book and it resonated instantly.

The forward was offered by Woody Hayes, who wrote:

I lured Tiger Ellison away from Middletown, Ohio, where he was firmly fixed in a coaching position he often said he would never leave. He was totally dedicated to the town and to its high school, most especially to its football program. I got him in 10 short minutes with one long word: dedication.

"Ellison," I said, "you're the forward-passingest coach in the country, and they say I'm the most non-passing coach that ever lived. Yet I want you at Ohio State because of the one thing you possess: dedication—to your family and to your school and to your community and to the great game of American football."

In [this] book Ellison goes further toward opening up the game than any other coach I have known. His daring departure from traditional football will amaze you. But I have seen his teams play. I have studied their movies. His fantastic offense had fantastic success. It is a crowd pleaser. You could almost bet every year that his quarterback would make the all-state team. Yet those quarterbacks seemingly possessed only average physical ability. I suspect that their success can be wrapped up in one word: dedication—to their coach and to their cause.

I am sure that every coach regardless of the level on which he works will profit from a study of the revolutionary ideas expressed in this book.

W.W. Hayes, Head Football Coach,
Ohio State University

GLENN ELLISON had met Woody Hayes when they were football teammates at Denison University. In 1933 Ellison returned to his home of Middletown to join the staff of his high school coach, Elmo Lingrel, as a line coach and the school's faculty as an English teacher. (Apparently his work in the classroom was often as compelling as his work on the practice field. His youngest daughter, Carolyn, later wrote of him, "Glenn decided to make poetry . . . come alive. He would recite several poems to [his students] and ask them to listen for the drumbeat in it and to tap the drumbeat out on their desks. That drumbeat was a pulse beat that gave it excitement, a heartbeat that made poetry come alive!")

After 12 years as an assistant coach, Ellison succeeded Lingrel; he would coach the Middletown varsity for 18 years and adopt a familiar persona for a mid-20th-century high school coach: all hellfire on the practice field (hence his nickname, Tiger, bestowed in his very first year as an assistant) and all inspiration off it, filling halftime locker rooms with Rockne-esque oration, leaving young men willing to run through walls on his behalf.

And his teams won, consistently. But in 1958, his 14th season as a head coach, everything turned sour. Middletown went 0-4-1 in its first five games. Not since the school began playing football in 1911 had it experienced a losing season, but with five games remaining, that result seemed a distinct possibility. Ellison had long coached smashmouth football. In his book he would write, "Our motto was: 'Hit 'em so hard and so often with so much that they simply cannot stand up in front of us!' This was serious football. We lifted weights all winter, ran our hearts out all spring and dug ditches all summer to prepare for the fall grind."

Now, suddenly, this utilitarian approach to the game had failed Tiger. So, in a desperate attempt to save the season, he turned in a completely different direction. He concocted a thoroughly nontraditional offense that he called the Lonesome Polecat, in which the center lined up alone on the ball and the rest of the offensive line was split out far to his left, two receivers far to his right and the quarterback alone in a shotgun formation. The quarterback was encouraged to scramble and to find open receivers. Middletown won its first game 34–0 and finished the season with five consecutive victories. "The Lonesome Polecat taught us that an average passer with average receivers can move the football," wrote Ellison. "Average boys can become better-than-average passers and receivers if their coach will permit them to throw and catch."

Following the '58 season Ellison refined the Lonesome Polecat into something better, something more sound. In his book he says the Polecat "revealed that football can be fun and that fun football can win ball games," but also that it was "a departure into insanity, an escape from reality." Still, Ellison was committed to this new brand of football. He took many of the Polecat's basic principles and applied them to his new offense.

His previous offense had had one passing play—called the run-and-shoot—so that's what he named his new one. It had 20 runs and 20 passes. Middletown lined up in a double-slot formation with two split ends uniformly 17 yards from the ball, but no closer than six yards from the sideline. Blocking schemes were identical for runs and passes, so as not to tip off the defense, and Ellison made a sincere effort to make "every pass look like a run and every run look like a pass."

It is impossible to overstate the degree to which this was different from the norm. Middletown used the run-and-shoot for 4½ seasons and with it won 38 of 45 games. Ellison's team won one game 98–34; over the life of the offense, the team punted an average of just 1.2 times a game.

When the time came seven years later to write the story of his new offense Tiger Ellison did not cheat his readers by thinking small. His 2½-page introduction begins like this:

This is the story of a revolution. A revolt started in the mind of a football coach and ended in a new order of things on the football field. The revolution awakened a sleepy community into wide-eyed enthusiasm and caused a veteran coach, squirming with frustration on the threshold of his first losing season, to wake up and enjoy life to its fullest. In the wake of that revolution came an explosion of touchdowns popping at the rate of one touchdown every ten plays or five touchdowns per ball game for four years. . . .

[And later, this:] "Yet, have you been lately to the football stadium where you found twenty-two musclemen with their heads on each other's shoulders pushing and pulling and howling and growling while somewhere beneath them hidden from view was the oval-shaped 'bone of contention?' The only time you saw the football was when one side kicked it over to the other side. What you were witnessing was a sample of possession football the way it has been presented to the public the past dozen years, ever since the rules makers unwittingly foisted upon the colleges the horse and buggy football which became the vogue in the early '50's. Three-yards-and-a-cloud-of-dust football returned to the American gridiron because the college coach found it no longer expedient to divide his squad into offensive and defensive units with each unit spending its entire practice time perfecting the fundamentals of that particular phase of the world's most intricate teamwork sport. The coach had to split his practice time, half for offense and half for defense, even though there has never been since the game began quite enough practice time to get an offense polished to perfection. . . . High school coaches, although not restricted by the new rules, nevertheless followed suit because coaches are copy-cats, and high school coaches, including me, tend to copy the colleges.

[And finally, this:] However, the future of this great game suddenly looms bright because football can now start growing up again, for the college rules makers have recanted—two-platoon football in our colleges is back on the American scene. College football will soon become the greatest sports spectacle of all time, provided college coaches will open their eyes and stir their imaginations and put the oval-shaped ball on display before those who come to see exciting entertainment.

I was a high school coach for thirty years. For the first twenty-five and a half years I was a possession coach, a slave-driver, a blood-and-thunder guy, a coach whose constant motto on the field and in the classroom and at home was: 'Root, hog, or die—dig, little pig, or starve to death!'

I have changed. The revolution came. This book is the story of that revolution.

THIS WAS the book that was handed to Mouse Davis during his car clinic in the spring of 1965. Already predisposed to run a spread formation that would free up his pissants to run amok, Mouse took Ellison's theories—and even more than that, his formations—and escalated his own attack. He spent the last 12 years of his high school career using the evolving run-and-shoot. His last team, at Hillsboro High, won the 1973 Oregon State Championship. A year later he was the offensive coordinator at Portland State, and a year after that, in 1975, he was the head coach.

In Davis's first season in charge, quarterback June Jones threw for a then–Division II record of 3,518 yards (a record that stood for a decade) and over two seasons averaged 266.2 yards a game in total offense. Jones's successor, Neil Lomax, became the alltime NCAA Division I-AA total offense leader (Portland State had jumped up one division) until being surpassed in 1994 by Steve McNair. Football purists recoiled. Davis adopted a casually defensive posture. "We were told that this wacko offense would only work in high school," Davis told SI in '79. "So it was fun to succeed with it in college."

Now Davis likens the run-and-shoot to the triple option in one key way: "With option reads and with run-and-shoot pass routes, the offense gets the chalk last," he says. That's coachspeak. The expression derives from the practice of coaches scheming offenses and defenses together on a chalkboard, passing the chalk back and forth in response to each other's moves. He who moves last has the advantage. All of the elemental run-and-shoot plays involved option—or readable—pass routes, where the receiver is reacting to the defense and the quarterback is reading the receiver. Says Davis, "I get to keep the chalk even after I snap the ball."

The core philosophy of the run-and-shoot never changed. "The whole thing is, when you boil it down," says Davis, "if I play a pissant, you've probably got to cover me with a pissant. And the more of the field that you use, the cleaner your reads."

In the Cheerful Tortoise, with breakfast finished and the plates cleared away, Mouse takes the visitor's notebook and diagrams a play. He scribbles four wide receivers, each of whom breaks off the line of scrimmage. As he draws in the notebook, Davis explains that each receiver then determines his next cut, based on the reaction of the defense. The quarterback is simultaneously reading the defense and throwing to a spot where the receiver should be. For more than three decades, when it was well-executed, the run-and-shoot was a gridiron symphony when it worked well.

Yet there was loud and predictable criticism of the scheme at every turn. Mouse was further from the football mainstream than Tiger Ellison had been from Woody Hayes. "People said our offense was unsound," says Davis. "They called it flag football. That's because football has very conservative roots, and coaches have traditionally been a very conservative lot. You ought to be able to knock somebody's head into the dirt or you're not a real football coach. That was the thinking."

Mouse left Portland State after the 1980 season. In the ensuing years he had two opportunities to implement the run-and-shoot in the NFL: with the Detroit Lions from '88 through '90 as offensive coordinator under Wayne Fontes and from '94 through '96 with the Atlanta Falcons as quarterbacks coach under his old Portland passer June Jones. Neither venture was ultimately successful. The Lions under Fontes and Davis went 15–22 in 2½ seasons, and the Falcons with Jones and Davis went 19–29 in three. Still, five Falcons receivers went over 1,000 yards in those three seasons. "Both places," says Davis, "we moved the shit out of the ball."

But it was in Houston that the run-and-shoot really moved, with three different teams: the Houston Gamblers of the United States Football League, the Houston Cougars of the NCAA and the Houston Oilers of the NFL. For nearly a decade, beginning in 1984, Houston was run-and-shoot central.

Former NFL linebacker Jack Pardee coached in all three places. With the Gamblers both Davis and a tall, cocky Texan named John Jenkins—nearly nine inches taller than Mouse—were offensive assistants. The quarterback was Jim Kelly, who would later take the Buffalo Bills to four Super Bowls while running a slick no-huddle (Chapter 21) as one of the last NFL quarterbacks to call his own plays. "I tell everybody I learned the passing game from Mouse Davis in Houston," says Kelly.

He had been a college star at Miami but says, "I had never learned proper footwork. I had never learned to throw on the run. When I got to Houston, I was almost starting from scratch. But Mouse, he was almost like a college professor with me. He had a way of explaining the run-and-shoot that let you really understand the reads and the options. I was a believer from Day One."

Kelly left the ill-fated USFL after the 1985 season. Pardee also left that year and took Jenkins with him in '87 to the University of Houston, where Jenkins installed the run-and-shoot. In the '89 season Andre Ware passed for a then–NCAA record 4,699 yards—an unheard-of number—and won the Heisman Trophy, prompting an outcry that a gimmick system had hijacked college football. It would get worse. (Or better.)

When Pardee went to the NFL in 1990, Jenkins took over the Cougars and rode the run-and-shoot to a 10–1 season in which they scored more than 50 points five times and on the night of Nov. 17 in the Astrodome beat up on Eastern Washington 84–21, with Houston quarterback David Klingler throwing 11 touchdown passes. Three weeks later in a game in Tokyo, Klingler shredded Arizona State for 716 passing yards. Both records are still standing to this day. Comfortably. In a SPORTS ILLUSTRATED story that was written in the summer of 1991 Cougars assistant Tony Fitzpatrick said, "Jenks is so far ahead of everybody else, it's a joke. Mouse comes in here now, looks at our films and even he doesn't understand them. Spreading the field? Mouse had [the Gamblers'] slot guys split arm's length from the tackles. Jenks would have them start their routes over by the Gatorade carts if they could."

The epilogue is less glorious. Jenkins's second and third Houston teams went a combined 8–14, and by '93 he was gone.

But Pardee proved that the run-and-shoot could be employed effectively in the National Football League. From 1990 through '93, with Warren Moon at quarterback, the Oilers averaged more than 10 wins a season and went to the playoffs in four consecutive years. Other devotees always returned to it. When June Jones became the head coach at the University of Hawaii in 1999, he installed the run-and-shoot and went on to win 75 games in nine years, while quarterbacks Timmy Chang and Colt Brennan rang up dazzling numbers.

From 2004 through '06, Davis was one of Jones's assistants before returning to Portland.

Football archeologists understood that even when the run-and-shoot did not lead to big victory numbers, it always advanced the cause of innovative offense. As an even more compelling measure of its worth, the run-and-shoot became immensely popular with high schools populated by Mouse Davis's physically overmatched pissants. Tiger Ellison would have been proud. A revolution, indeed.

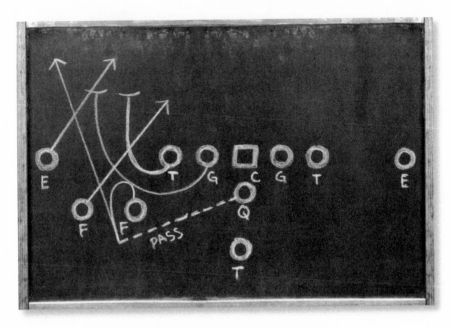

BUBBLE SCREEN LEFT

When Joe Tiller first ran this play at Purdue in 1997, even he was stunned by its effectiveness. Defenses were just getting accustomed to playing against four-wide passing offenses, and the bubble screen was a totally unexpected new wrinkle. The action is all on the three-wideout side. At the snap the two outside receivers run inside-leaning routes, in effect taking away at least two inside defenders and creating left-side space. The inside receiver uses a slip move into the backfield, moving forward then looping back, a bubble-shaped pattern that gave the play its name. The quarterback hits the bubble receiver with a quick pass and the receiver turns upfield where the playside guard and tackle both block for him.

CHAPTER 13

THE ONE-BACK SPREAD

An L.A. high school coach took a chance and launched
an offense—and John Elway and Drew Brees with it

San Jose, Calif.
Spring 1979

Coaches find each other. They hang together and eat together and drink beer together—and they speak a language that nobody else really understands. It is their way of finding normalcy. But it's also a way of staying in the endless loop of innovation. Friends do not hide discoveries from each other.

In the spring of 1979 Joe Tiller and Jack Elway met up at a bar not far from the campus of San Jose State University, where Elway, then 47 years old, had recently been named football coach. Though 11 years apart in age, the two had become tight while working together in the early '70s on coach Jim Sweeney's staff at Washington State; Elway had gone on to a stop at Cal State–Northridge, Tiller took on a three-year stint as an defensive line coach for the Calgary Stampeders of the Canadian Football League and now was Calgary's assistant general manager. He was scouting college players in California, and that meant his trip to San Jose was a business expense, no small matter in those days.

"First thing I do is go watch Jack's team practice," recalls Tiller (who retired following the 2008 season after 12 seasons as a head coach at Purdue). "And he's got guys spread all over the place on offense. Now, when Jack and I had coached together at Washington State, we were a splitback veer team, triple option football, like a lot of teams were playing then. All of a sudden Jack is doing this one-back offense with people spread out all across the field.

"So after practice Jack and I went out for a couple of pops for medicinal purposes," Tiller says. "Someplace near the campus. Naturally, we're talking about football because that's what football coaches do. And I always thought Jack had a great football mind, so I'm curious about what I saw his team doing in practice when I'd been there. I say 'Jack, I'm really intrigued by what you're doing here. Where did you learn this stuff?' "

Elway had to be thinking that was a pretty funny question. The answer was something that Tiller couldn't have expected. "This is the stuff that John ran in high school," Elway told his friend. "I talked with John's coach a couple of years ago, and I decided this stuff might work at the college level. So I put it in."

Their conversation echoed one that Elway had had two years earlier when he'd gotten a phone call from Mike Price, who had also worked with Elway at Washington State and was still an assistant there. Price asked Elway what he was running. "Never mind what I'm doing," Elway said. "You should see the stuff my son is running. They're killing people, just killing 'em. I'm putting this stuff in next year."

John Elway, future Super Bowl winner and Hall of Fame quarterback with the Denver Broncos, was running a spread-out, pass-happy offense at Granada Hills High in L.A.'s San Fernando Valley. His coach was Jack Neumeier.

Neumeier was from the same generation as Tiger Ellison, a tough, old school football man. "Jack was a three-yards-and-a-cloud-of-dust guy," says Darryl Stroh, who was introduced to the coaching business by Neumeier in 1960, his first year at Granada Hills. "He was tough on kids. He believed in being tough on kids."

Stroh recalls a practice in which two Granada Hills players started fighting each other while still clad in full equipment. Neumeier whistled the scrap to a halt and then ordered the team to stand in a circle while the two combatants stripped off their helmets and pads before continuing with the fight. "Once kids realized they were going to have to settle their fights without pads and helmets," says Stroh, "we had a lot fewer fights."

Neumeier's strategic turning point came in 1969, when Granada Hills lost two close, low-scoring games in the regular season and failed to make the Los Angeles city playoffs. Granada Hills had a terrific defense and a steady offense, but that wasn't enough. Failure tore at Neumeier. "Jack was about ready to hang himself after that year, he was so distraught," says Stroh.

There would be a radical change. In the summer before the 1970 season Neumeier called a meeting with his returning starting quarterback, Dana Potter. "He told me he'd read a book by some high school coach in Ohio," says Potter. (That book was almost certainly Tiger Ellison's handbook on the run-and-shoot.)

"He said we were going to throw 35 passes a game. I had a hard time imagining that happening because at that time nobody was throwing the ball in Southern California. But sure enough, when the season started, we were throwing it like crazy. We were starting games in the two-minute drill. After a while we didn't even bother to look at film of the other team's defense."

Granada Hills won the city title with the wide-open spread game in 1970, and six years later John Elway arrived as a tall, skinny running back and switched positions. He would one day tell *The Denver Post*, "[Neumeier] was the guy who made me fall in love with football at the quarterback position."

Where Neumeier had once stressed physical dominance, he now became a tireless student of the passing game. In a 1990 interview with the *Los Angeles Times*, Neumeier explained his system: "Basically, my offense spreads the defense across the field," he said. "A lot of teams will spread the defense the depth of the field, like the Raiders for instance, but my idea is to spread them from sideline to sideline so you never get two defensive backs to cover one receiver. And when you catch the defense in a one-on-one, the receiver would go to an open spot and should get there before the defender because he knows where he's going."

Neumeier taught the system not only to John Elway but to Elway's father and to a coach named Dennis Erickson. During his time at

Granada Hills, Neumeier lived with his family in a house overlooking the San Fernando Valley. "So many times I would go up there to visit him," says Potter. "And he would be just sitting in the den, in the dark. His wife would let me in the house, and I'd walk into the den, and Jack would flip on the light and say, 'I was just thinking about something with the offense.' "

Neumeier was gravely ill with cancer when he attended John Elway's Hall of Fame induction on Aug. 8, 2004. "Jack was on his last legs, but on that trip he just came to life talking about football and memories," says Stroh. Less than a month later, on Sept. 1, 2004, Neumeier died at the age of 85. His football legacy would outlive him by decades.

The meeting at the bar between Tiller and Elway happened almost 20 years after Tiger Ellison had begun spreading the field in southwest Ohio but not long after Mouse Davis had installed the run-and-shoot at Portland State. The offenses were not identical: Neumeier's package often used a tight end, Davis's did not. But their systems unquestionably shared central themes influential to this day: Spread out the defense. Get favorable matchups in coverage. Create running lanes. Get the chalk last.

In five years at San Jose State, Jack Elway went 35-20-1, including three wins over nearby rival Stanford. But it was one of his assistants, Erickson, who would take Neumeier's offense nationwide. Erickson had been a feisty three-year starter at quarterback at Montana State (under the same Jim Sweeney, who would later mentor Elway, Price and Tiller at Washington State). Erickson joined Elway's San Jose State staff in 1979; a decade later he had won the first of two national championships at Miami.

On his way to Miami, Erickson took his offense—which came to be known as the "one-back spread" to Idaho and then to Wyoming. "There was a time when everybody was running the 'bone, and so people in Wyoming were happy with it," says Joe Tiller, who came to Laramie to work as an assistant in '87. "But Dennis came in and threw the ball all over the place, and people loved it." Erickson left for Washington State after just one season, but his offense he had brought stayed in place; when Tiller became head coach at Wyoming in '91, he did nothing to change it.

"I had no choice; they loved what Dennis had done," Tiller says. "People have asked me for years how I learned this offense. I tell them, 'Dennis left his playbook at Wyoming.' And that's absolutely the truth."

At Washington State, Erickson turned the Cougars around from 3-7-1 in 1987 to 9–3 in '88 and their first bowl bid in 56 years. In one game Erickson took the Cougars to Ann Arbor to play Michigan and trailed only 13–10 at the half before running out of gas and losing, 44–18. But Washington State happened to throw for 334 yards and completed 61% of its passes against the staid Wolverines. "I can't believe what you did with that gimmick offense," Michigan coach Bo Schembechler commented to Erickson after the game, a backhanded compliment if there ever was one.

Erickson remembers these years as a kind of free pass into the end zone for Neumeier's offense. "It was new, and nobody really knew how to cover you, so nobody did," says Erickson. "We'd motion a guy out of the backfield, and nobody would cover him, so we'd just throw him the ball, and he'd go 70 yards for a touchdown." His teams exploited matchups as few had done previously in college football. A college linebacker in the '80s couldn't cover a slot receiver or a running back in motion, and defenses weren't accustomed to trying.

Still, Erickson, like Mouse Davis, had to fight for respect. Says Tiller, "When he was at Idaho, people would say, 'That's just Division I-AA.' Then he goes to Wyoming and well, 'That's just the wacky WAC.' Then, 'Washington State is the Pac-10; they all throw it around out there.' I don't think the offense really had much credibility nationally until Dennis got to Miami. And then, wow."

The Hurricanes won national titles in Erickson's first season in Miami, 1989, again in '91, then lost the national title game in '92. Gino Torretta won the '92 Heisman Trophy operating the one-back. Not only did the Hurricanes throw, but they also ran. The one-back forced defenses into such wide formations that massive holes opened in the middle of the field. Coaching staffs from far and wide descended on the fields in Coral Gables to watch and learn. "One year we must have had 20 staffs on campus at the same time," says Erickson. "We shared everything."

Other Elway disciples, meanwhile, went forth with their own versions. Mike Price, in 1997, took quarterback Ryan Leaf and Washington State to the Rose Bowl. The statuesque Leaf (long since better known for dueling Tony Mandarich as the biggest NFL Draft bust in modern history) operated the spread one-back from a shotgun with no tight ends. Price recruited athletes for the team from all over the Los Angeles basin. He turned them into wideouts and then tested defenses with deeper throws than any coach had previously tried with this offense. Said Price, "I don't see anybody out X-ing and O-ing us. We might miss blocks, drop balls. But if the offense is run right, it can't be stopped."

Tiller had his chance in that same year, when Purdue hired him to bring the spread passing game to the Big Ten. It was an unqualified success. Nine times in 12 seasons the Boilermakers won at least seven games, and with future NFL star Drew Brees running the attack, they went to the Rose Bowl after the 2000 season.

In 1997 Tiller and his quarterbacks coach, Greg Olson, enhanced the Neumeier offense by adding what came to be known as the "bubble" screen. To run the bubble, there are three wide receivers flanked to one side; the two outside receivers run inside patterns, essentially either walling off their defenders or running them deep. The inside receiver slips back into the backfield to receive a short forward pass and take the ball upfield. Says Tiller, "It's not too complicated. The receiver kind a makes a little forward movement and then loops around backward, kind of like in the shape of a bubble. So we called it a bubble screen."

Defenses were ill-prepared against the bubble. Linebackers accustomed to stopping the ground game or blitzing would invariably overrun it; defensive backs were suckered away from the play by the deep receivers. The bubble screen would become one of the most popular and enduring innovations in the game.

Purdue's bubble made its debut on the second weekend of the Tiller era, which had begun with a loss at Toledo. Playing at home against Notre Dame and protecting a narrow lead in the fourth quarter, Purdue faced third-and-one near midfield. "Notre Dame is used to seeing Mike Alstott [the bruising Boilermakers fullback] bang over the A gap," says Tiller. "Instead of that, we decide to throw the bubble screen and Vinny Sutherland goes for about 30 yards. The stadium just erupted."

Purdue's win that day over the Fighting Irish helped shove the Big Ten into the modern era of wide-open football. Watching that game from the sideline was a Purdue freshman named Drew Brees would become the starting quarterback for the Boilermakers the following year. And there in West Lafayette, Ind., more than three decades after being designed by a desperate high school coach a half a continent away, the offense found its perfect triggerman.

OPEN 6

Spread offense aficionados Hal Mumme and Mike Leach made this a standard play, their variation on the "four verticals" espoused by Norm Chow at BYU in the mid-'80s. The quarterback sets up in the shotgun with four wideouts, two on each side, and one running back, in strictly for blitz pickup. At the snap, all four receivers work straight up the field, reading defenders. As the receivers are moving, the quarterback, on a three-step drop, is quickly reading the play either left to right (1 to 4) or right to left (4 to 1). If either of the safeties sits down on a route, the ball goes deep up the seam. If either of the cornerbacks plays soft, the ball immediately goes short. The play's effectiveness is based on the pressure continually put on the defensive backs to make decisions, with the quarterback then exploiting those decisions.

CHAPTER 14

BYU AIR RAID

An all-out, pass-happy system was born and raised in
Utah but then went flying into unexpected places

T HROUGH MUCH of the autumn of 2008, the eyes of the college football world turned to West Texas. Since the arrival in Lubbock of head coach and passing game provocateur Mike Leach in 2000, the Red Raiders of Texas Tech had used a four-wide shotgun attack to not only reconfigure the country's offensive statistics but also challenge longtime bullies Oklahoma and Texas for supremacy in the Big 12.

Behind quarterback Graham Harrell and wideout Michael Crabtree, Texas Tech won its first 10 games of the '08 season, including an epic 39–33 upset of Texas on the first Saturday night in November. That was the night football nation first truly understood the miracle that Leach had wrought in the plains of West Texas. Three weeks later the Raiders' national title hopes were snatched away by a very good Oklahoma team, but a statement had already been made. In the land where the wishbone was invented, where smashmouth football had long been worshipped on Saturday afternoons, a freewheeling, pass-crazy, scoreboard-popping offense had garnered not only success but also respect.

Texas Tech's invention was really a reinvention. Thirty-two years earlier, and 900 miles from Lubbock, the Cougars of Brigham Young had begun turning the passing game into an art form, forever altering the college game. Among the many young coaches watching was Mike Leach.

Brigham Young hired LaVell Edwards as coach in 1972, and before long he had assembled a staff in Provo perfectly suited to the needs of a pass-first offense. Norm Chow (who would later tutor Heisman Trophy winners Carson Palmer and Matt Leinart at USC, as well as Philip Rivers at North Carolina State) handled receivers and called plays beginning in '82. Roger French created clever blocking schemes. And Doug Scovil coached quarterbacks and oversaw the offensive operation from '76 until '80, when the Cougars' quarterbacks were Marc Wilson, Gifford Nielsen and Jim McMahon.

"Doug Scovil put it all together," says Robbie Bosco, who was BYU's starting quarterback in 1984 and '85 and coached under Edwards for 14 years after finishing his eligibility. "When I was being recruited [in '81], Doug had just gotten the head coaching job at San Diego State, so he was leaving BYU. I went there to visit, and he put his arm around me and he made it clear to me that it was his offense, and Coach Edwards never disputed that. Coach Scovil said to me, 'If you want to be like all those quarterbacks at BYU, you need to come here.' "

Among other coaches who passed through Provo were Brian Billick, Mike Holmgren and Andy Reid, all of whom would later excel as offensive coordinators and head coaches in the NFL. And all of them would run some form of the West Coast offense, making clear that permutations of the West Coast system were influenced by the Provo think tank. However, the wide-open spread passing game that Texas Tech had unleashed in Lubbock was a direct descendant of the offense born in Utah, and it had come to Mike Leach by way of a coach named Hal Mumme.

In the spring of 1986 Mumme became head coach at Copperas Cove High in Texas, 70 miles northwest of Austin, in the midst of some of the best high school football in the country. Mumme was 34 years old and at last he had his chance to be a head coach. So he would do it his way. "Back in 1982, when I was the offensive coordinator at UTEP," says Mumme, "we played BYU, and I just had tremendous admiration for everything they did on offense. I decided that if I ever got to be a head coach, I was going to do what they were doing up there. Some people, when they get to be a head coach, pick a little from this team and a little from that team. Not me. I was going to run BYU's stuff."

Mumme put himself on a shuttle between central Texas and northern Utah. "Hal was here *all...the...time*," says Bosco. "He was out at practice, he was in the film room." Mumme sat with Bosco, with Chow, with anybody on the BYU staff who would take time to explain to him the intricacies of the Cougars' offense. And it was a thing of beauty. Consider two of the basic plays:

Scat route In BYU parlance any form of this play was called "scat ball." It could be run from various formations but always keyed on releasing several receivers and a running back and then sending a flanker directly over the spot from which the ball had been snapped. "That way, says Bosco, "the quarterback would know exactly where the receiver was going to be. The short, quick pattern was dubbed a "scat" route. "When we were playing our best," Bosco says, "we completed that ball probably 90 or 95 percent of the time. And I'm talking over an extended number of years." Bosco would also see the play on Sundays. "The 49ers," he says, "ran that play thousands of times." The 49ers called it Flanker Drive, but the execution was very familiar.

Draw trap An enduring image of the BYU offense is of a steady succession of passes, followed by a draw play straight up the middle for huge yardage. "Our best running play, bar none," says Bosco. "Teams would come and watch us practice the draw trap, but that was our puppy. There were days when we would rep that play for 20 minutes straight. I'd get tired just from handing the ball off. But in games, if teams were blitzing us, sometimes I'd hand the ball off and look back, and I'd think, Man, that's a big hole."

Everything in the offense was run from a spread formation, with wide line splits. And Hal Mumme loved everything he saw. He took it back to Copperas Cove, installed it immediately and made a struggling program much better. "One day," Mumme recalls, "I was sitting in Norm Chow's office, and he says to me, 'Now, Coach, how do you run four verticals? I said, 'We don't run four verticals.' Chow says, 'Coach, if you're not going to run four verticals, you might as well not use the offense.' So we started running four verticals. Only we just called it '6.' Because what are you trying to do? You're trying to go get six points."

Mumme created a frenetic practice drill called Routes on Air, in which five quarterbacks were all throwing passes to five lines of wideouts (instead of the customary one quarterback throwing to one receiver, with all the others standing around waiting their turn). As an added twist, something he picked up from watching a 49ers practice on a visit west, Mumme would have every receiver run all the way to the end zone after catching the ball.

He moved up quickly, from Copperas Cove to Iowa Wesleyan to Valdosta State to Kentucky, where Mumme's system—by then called the Air Raid—got national exposure. The Wildcats won only 10 Southeastern Conference games in Mumme's four years there but beat LSU twice, scared everybody else and led the conference in passing for four consecutive seasons. Florida's Steve Spurrier had shaken the SEC to its conservative roots in 1990 when he brought his Fun 'n' Gun offense to Gainesville, but Mumme had taken it a step further with far less talent at his disposal.

At every stop where Mumme coached, one of his top assistants was Mike Leach, who had been a rugby player at BYU in the early '80s and had watched the same offense that Mumme so admired; but this was long before they met. Leach took a circuitous route to Mumme's side, a bizarre trail even by coaching standards: from BYU to law school at Pepperdine to the U.S. Sports Academy in Alabama to the College of the Desert in Palm Desert, Calif., to the European Football League in Finland. But as soon as he got a taste of the Air Raid offense, he became Mumme's enabler. "He was the guy who would walk up and down the sideline getting in my ear," says Mumme. "He was always saying, 'Keep attacking, keep attacking. Stay aggressive.' "

When Bob Stoops was hired as Oklahoma's head coach in 1999, he brought in Leach to run his offense, the first coach to bring the wide-open offensive philosophy to the Big 12. "Kentucky was hard to play against when I was at Florida," says Stoops. "I wanted to do that to other people." Under Leach, Oklahoma averaged nearly 37 points a game in '99, 20 more than in the previous season. When the Sooners won the national title a year later, Leach had already left for Texas Tech, where he put together everything that had been handed down to him—from Dutch Meyer to Tiger Ellison to Mouse Davis to Doug Scovil to Hal Mumme—and turned it into one of the most eccentric offenses the game has ever seen.

"Frankly," said Mumme in the fall of 2008 as Texas Tech rolled to its 10–0 start, "Mike is doing a better job with this than I ever did."

Leach's career has been fueled by a relentless curiosity, and he's always let his oddball instincts thrive. One example among many: On a summer evening in 1989 he was sitting in his apartment in Mount Pleasant, Iowa, watching NFL videotapes with other Iowa Wesleyan assistant coaches. Leach became obsessed with the 49ers' "smash" route, a high-low horizontal pass pattern in which two receivers essentially try to confuse a cornerback, and the quarterback reacts to the confusion.

Leach wanted to know what the indicators are for reading the play, so he jumped in his car and drove six hours to a Packers minicamp in Green Bay where he knew the offensive staff were keen to those routes. "I remember it really well because Tony Mandarich was there," says Leach. "Anyway, we wound up talking to Lindy Infante about the smash route, and he said he *thought* they picked it up from the 49ers, but wasn't sure. But he explained it, and we put it in at Iowa Wesleyan.

"And here's the thing," says Leach. "We would do the same thing if we saw a *high school* team with a good play. We'd go talk to them about it. I was a young coach, and I was excited about this stuff. Eighty-nine, that was the summer of love for the spread offense."

The Leach system makes no pretense of conventional balance. His Red Raiders passed the ball almost twice as often as they ran it. "To me," says Leach, "balance is making sure all your skill players touch the ball."

Texas Tech's Air Raid (a name co-opted from Mumme with sheer affection) was run out of a one-back set with five receivers. It advanced the Mouse and Mumme systems in its complete commitment to the forward pass, with routes based not on timing but rather on a simultaneous quarterback-receiver read. "Some teams like to go three-step drop and get rid of it," says Leach. "Our way is to have the receiver find a hole, and we'd tell him, 'We'll find you in that hole.'"

From Leach's arrival in 2000 through the '08 season (his tenure in Lubbock would end in discord at the end of the '09 season), Texas Tech won at least eight games a year with five quarterbacks and averaged more than 530 yards of offense a game. Perhaps the most telling measure of the Air Raid's efficiency is that none of those Red Raiders quarterbacks have been successful in the NFL. They were, in fact, made by the offense.

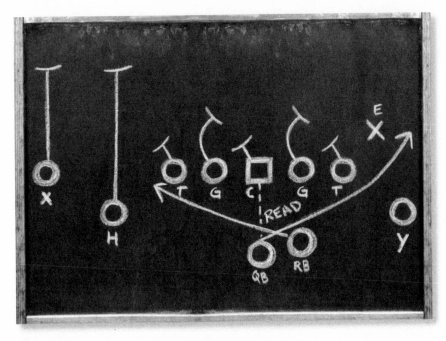

THE ZONE READ

The blending of the modern spread running game with the venerable read option is built on this core idea. The principle is the same as that of the late-'60s wishbone: It's easier to read a defender and run away from him than it is to block him. In the spread, though, that read is done behind zone blocking. In the zone read option, the quarterback lines up in the shotgun with one back next to him. Upon taking the snap, the QB puts the ball in the belly of the running back and then reads the backside defensive end. If the DE pinches down and runs parallel to the line of scrimmage to chase the RB, the QB keeps and runs to the corner vacated by the end. If the DE stays home, the QB gives the ball to the RB, who runs what is essentially a power off-tackle play the other way.

CHAPTER 15

THE SPREAD OPTION

The game changed on a bobbled ball by an obscure quarterback at a school you've never heard of

INNOVATION IS often accidental, and it certainly is so in football. In the spring of 1990 Rich Rodriguez was named head coach at Glenville State College, a National Association of Intercollegiate Athletics (NAIA) institution in Glenville, W.Va., halfway between Morgantown and Charleston. Rodriguez was just 27 in that first season but already a veteran of sorts; he had been only 24 when he was named head coach at Salem College. That school dropped its program after a 2–8 season. Glenville started no better in Rodriguez's first year, going 1-7-1.

During that same fall a young quarterback named Jed Drenning was trying to find someplace where he could settle and have a college football career. As a high school quarterback he had twice led Tucker County High in Davis (a town of 624) to the West Virginia Class A state championship. From there he had gone to Samford University in Birmingham to play for Terry Bowden.

Drenning transferred after two seasons and sat out the '90 season while awaiting clearance to restart his career at the University of West Virginia. Then came word that at Glenville, Rodriguez would be running the multiple I formation offense, a staple of the Bowden family of coaches and familiar and comfortable to Drenning, so he switched again and rolled on down to Glenville to play for Rodriguez in the fall of 1991.

There were more surprises ahead. "I get to campus for practice," says Drenning, "and the first day on campus I run into Dean Hood, who was our defensive coordinator. He says, 'Did you meet your offensive coordinator?' And he's smiling, and I ask what's so funny, and he says they're putting in the run-and-shoot."

Drenning was clueless as to how to operate the run-and-shoot, and predictably, it was not an immediate success in Glenville. Entering an October game against Wingate University in that first year, Glenville State was 1-3-1; worse, Wingate had beaten Glenville 63–0 the previous season. Even more ominous—in fact downright frightening—was that Drenning had been sacked 32 times in the previous two games. Fearing for his health, Drenning was constantly bugging Rodriguez to run from a shotgun formation, to at least give the quarterback an extra beat to find receivers and an extra step of safety from the ferocious pass rushes they were seeing.

On Monday before the Wingate game Rodriguez asked Drenning, "How often do you want to run out of the 'gun?" Drenning answered, "Coach, I'll run the clock out in the 'gun if you want." Glenville went to the shotgun for the entire game and narrowly missed pulling off the upset, losing 17–15.

They stayed in the 'gun for the rest of the year, finished 3–1 down the stretch and began shaping the offense that Rodriguez would so effectively run later as a coordinator at Tulane and Clemson and as head coach at West Virginia. "Whatever incarnation of Rich's offense exists today," says Drenning, "it was born that day when we played Wingate. And he turned the place around pretty quickly after that."

There would be one more major invention. Rodriguez was not the first offensive-minded coach to operate the run-and-shoot from a shotgun, but his next move was almost surely an original one.

It was the fall of '92, and Glenville was en route to a respectable 6–4 season while operating its run-and-shoot almost strictly from a one-back shotgun. (Mouse Davis, back in the day, had never used a shotgun.) Included in Glenville's offensive package was a series of running plays using zone blocking in which Drenning would receive the snap and stick the ball in the gut of a running back lined up next to him.

One afternoon Drenning bobbled a snap on one of these zone-blocked running plays. Unable to get the handoff delivered to the running back, Drenning tucked the ball himself and saw the backside defensive end crashing down the line of scrimmage to tackle the running back—who, in fact, did not have the ball but was behaving as if he did—from behind. On a broken play the quarterback customarily follows the running back into the assigned hole and tries to salvage yardage. But Drenning, seeing the end closing, instead ran wide into the area vacated by the end. "It was just an instantaneous reaction thing," says Drenning.

After the whistle, Rodriguez casually asked Drenning, "Why did you do that?"

"Do what?" said Drenning.

"Why did you run *that* way?" Rodriguez said.

"The end pinched," said Drenning.

Rodriguez nodded, as if to say, Oh, uh-huh. This, as best anyone can tell, was the birth of the modern "zone read," now a cornerstone play in any run-based or balanced spread offense. It is the play that essentially fulfilled Jack Elway's wish—to add an option run to a spread passing game. It is a play that, in effect, wed Tiger Ellison's run-and-shoot to the Texas wishbone, because the zone read is simply another version of the same read that triggers the wishbone triple option. In the wishbone the quarterback reads the defensive tackle; in the zone read he reads the backside defensive end, just as in Jed Drenning's accident.

Glenville State rode Rodriguez's offense to 32 wins in his last four years there, and then Rodriguez rode it into Division I—first at Tulane, where he was offensive coordinator under Tommy Bowden in 1997 and '98. The quarterback there was Shaun King, and the offense was made vastly more flexible and complex.

"It wasn't really a run-and-shoot because we were 50-50 run and pass," says King. "But in the passing game we had four wides, and we tried to challenge vertically as well as spread the field. There was a lot of two-by-two mirrored formation stuff [two wide receivers running mirrored patterns on each side of he field]. All of our runs had an automatic slot check; if the slot was uncovered on a running play, I would just throw it to the slot guy."

Rodriguez also tried to ramp up the zone read, but King, who was an accurate thrower and a better athlete than Drenning, wanted no part of it. "We put in the zone read," says King. "You don't block the weakside defensive end. The quarterback reads that guy. But I never wanted to keep the ball, because there was no blocker over there [to protect me]. I told Rich not to call running plays for me. I said that if nobody's open, *then* I'll run it, O.K.?" This happened often enough that in 1998, when Tulane went 12–0, King became the first quarterback in NCAA history to pass for 300 yards and run for 100 in the same game, a 49-35 win over Army.

But at Rodriguez's next stop, Clemson, where he went with Bowden in 1999, again as offensive coordinator, his quarterback was Woody Dantzler. While he was a less capable thrower than King or Drenning, he was a far superior runner. In 2001 Dantzler became the first college quarterback to pass for 2,000 yards and run for 1,000 yards in the same season.

By then Rodriguez had left for West Virginia to become head coach, and there, in 2005, a quicksilver freshman quarterback named Pat White proved to be the perfect pilot for the Rodriguez spread. In the '08 season (and once again Rodriguez had already moved on, this time to Michigan), White became the first quarterback in college football to pass for 5,000 yards and rush for 4,000; twice he had thrust West Virginia into the national championship race. "The genius of Rodriguez," says King, "is in the way he's used different quarterbacks. He did things one way with me and then another way with Dantzler and then another with Pat White."

Even as Rodriguez was busy reconfiguring offensive football, he had a shadow. Urban Meyer is a year younger than Rodriguez. Meyer was raised in Ohio, Rodriguez next door in West Virginia. But while Rodriguez was twice a head coach at obscure schools before turning 28, Meyer was taking a more traditional path, working as an assistant at Ohio State, Illinois State, Colorado State and, from 1996 through 2000, under Lou Holtz and Bob Davie at Notre Dame. He got his first head coaching job in 2001 at Bowling Green, the same year that Rodriguez got his third head job.

"When we got to Bowling Green, I felt like we were a little under-manned," says Meyer. "So we started asking each other, as a staff, 'How can we move the ball?' We tried to put together a combination quarterback-run, passing game, with our entire goal being to create numbers for the offense. Where can we get an advantage?"

The philosophy was not unlike Rodriguez's: Try to balance a sophisticated pass offense while making the quarterback a viable threat as a runner. Against conventional offenses, defenses essentially ignore the quarterback as a potential ballcarrier; if the quarterback becomes a running threat, a defensive player has to be assigned to track him, limiting that defender's freedom to move to any other point of attack. "If you can make the defense account for the quarterback," says Meyer, "that meant one guy you didn't have to block."

Meyer learned much of his attack from two sources. The passing game came from Louisville and offensive coordinator Scott Linehan (who had played at Idaho for Dennis Erickson and would later become head coach of the St. Louis Rams). Meyer had visited Linehan at Louisville. "We went down there with the intention of staying one day," he says, "but we stayed for about five days. We studied their whole passing game and the idea of spreading the field with five-man protection and no backs."

Meyer's quarterback-run game was copied in large part from Kansas State's offense of the '90s under coach Bill Snyder. When Snyder took over the Kansas State program in 1989, the Wildcats were infamously proclaimed by SPORTS ILLUSTRATED to be "The Worst Football Program in America." In less than a decade K-State would contend for the national championship.

The first steps in the climb came on defense, in which young assistants like Bob and Mike Stoops (later the head coaches at Oklahoma and Arizona, respectively) and Jim Leavitt (South Florida) put together an unorthodox, high-pressure package that was effective on Saturday but also all week long.

"They were very smart young guys, and they got us into what I thought was a very innovative defense," says Snyder. "They put a defender in every gap, rolled up the corners and got eight men in the box, and consequently, we were very, very good against the run. But as a result of that, when we practiced against ourselves during the week, we were not very good on offense. We had to get better.

"We had to create some running lanes, and the answer was pretty simple: Involve the quarterback in the running game. So essentially what we did was run every play that we had been using in the run game, but we gave ourselves the option of running it with the quarterback, which forced the defense to account for him as a ballcarrier. That took one man out of the box." The Wildcats had power plays and counter plays and trap plays and, eventually, the zone read. They had talented quarterbacks, most notably Michael Bishop, who led the Wildcats to the Big 12 championship game in 1998.

More than one football historian has argued that Snyder, Meyer, Rodriguez—and many others—were really running nothing more than a modernized version of the single wing. Pop in a couple of DVDs, watch both offenses at work, and it's clear that the argument holds a lot of water.

Meyer took the Louisville passing game, mixed it with the Kansas State run game, and won 39 of 47 games in four years at Bowling Green and Utah, taking the latter to a BCS bowl after the 2004 season and finishing the year ranked No. 4 in the nation. At Florida, with more talent than most of his opponents, Meyer won the '06 and '08 national titles, and in '07 quarterback Tim Tebow won the Heisman Trophy after throwing for 32 touchdowns and running for 23 more, a statistic that eloquently speaks to the balance of the attack.

Tiger Ellison would have loved those numbers, illustrative of where his original master plan has taken the game. The question that follows logically—and is routinely dismissed by coaches and pundits alike—is whether the NFL will soon employ a spread game similar to the one that prevails in college football, and whether quarterback runs would be part of the system.

Many NFL systems are already rooted in the spread passing attack. The New England Patriots went unbeaten in the 2007 regular season, with Tom Brady often running out of a five-wide, empty-backfield set and isolating Wes Welker—the ultimate version of Mouse Davis's pissants— on linebackers who couldn't hope to cover him.

But Brady wasn't running the ball. "At the NFL level you invest an awful lot of money in the quarterback," says Linehan. "And if you're going to run that college stuff, you're putting him in harm's way. But somebody is going to come in and do it effectively. The Falcons did it some with Vick. The Titans with Vince Young. NFL teams don't spend a lot of time preparing to defend the option, so you're going to wreak havoc with coordinators. And the team that incorporates the option effectively at the NFL level, well, all bets are off."

TAMPA TWO

Popularized in the late '90s by the Tampa Bay Buccaneers under coach Tony Dungy and defensive coordinator Monte Kiffin, the Tampa Two is a full-defense (11-man) extension of the Cover Two secondary defense (a four-man pass coverage "shell") that teams had used for more than two decades. The Tampa version is the ultimate bend-don't-break defense, designed to eliminate big plays and force the offense to methodically drive the length of the field. Two deep safeties share the deep zones. (The name "Cover Two" derives from these two deep safety zones.) The cornerbacks disrupt wideouts at the line of scrimmage. The most demanding position is middle linebacker; he is forced to drop as much as 30 yards into the middle to prevent completions on deep crossing routes.

CHAPTER 16

THE COVER TWO

As the long passing game began to run amok in the NFL, frantic defensive coaches needed help; this was it

St. Louis, Mo.
Jan. 23, 2000

H ERE ARE dates on which the NFL felt a seismic shift, momentous days when the league changed course. Jan. 12, 1969: Super Bowl III, Jets over Colts, establishing sudden legitimacy for the American Football League. Jan. 10, 1982: Dwight Clark and the Catch marks the beginning of the Bill Walsh dynasty in San Francisco. Those are among the obvious ones. But Jan. 23, 2000, would appear on very few lists of such dates. Obscure as it may seem, though, it was a watershed evening in the history of the league, a day on which defensive ingenuity and execution stymied the celebrated offensive revolution, in the process expanding the lexicon of the sport. And the defense did all that without even winning the game.

The St. Louis Rams had seized the NFL by its throat during the 1999 season. Offensive coordinator Mike Martz had stretched the boundaries of Don Coryell's daring vertical passing game (Chapter 6) and rung up a league-high 526 points while winning 13 games, even after a preseason injury to designated starting quarterback Trent Green. His replacement, an obscure 28-year-old quarterback named Kurt Warner, became the league's MVP. The Rams had scored 49 points on the Minnesota Vikings in the divisional playoffs and on this January day would face the Tampa Bay Buccaneers for the right to represent the NFC in Super Bowl XXXIV.

"There was a sense around the league that the Rams were pretty much unstoppable," recalls Tony Dungy, who was then in his fifth year as the Bucs' head coach. "And there was a real respect there. Not just among the fans but among coaches, too. That was a very good offense."

The Bucs had a defense that was very good too. Dungy knew it, and his defensive coordinator, 60-year-old Monte Kiffin, knew it. The Bucs had yielded more than 20 points in a game just four times. They had become dominant, but offense sells. The Rams were expected to roll, favored by two touchdowns.

They played a time warp game that night in the Trans World Dome in St. Louis. Warner needed 43 attempts to complete 26 passes for 258 yards (in the regular season he had needed only 31 attempts on average to get more than 270 yards in a game). He was intercepted by the Bucs three times. Warner had to settle for short completions, and the Bucs ran to the ball in swarms, gang-tackling and reducing damage. St. Louis drives stalled for lack of a big play. Nevertheless, the Rams won when Warner squeezed a late-fourth-quarter touchdown pass to Ricky Proehl into a tiny seam in the Tampa Bay coverage. The final score was 11–6. The Rams went to the Super Bowl.

The Bucs went into a different kind of history. "That day we just played the same defense we'd been playing all season," says Dungy. "And we did a pretty darn good job of keeping them out of the end zone. This is a copycat league. People saw that game and started doing what we were doing."

Six years later the copycat evolution of that Bucs defense looked like this: Late in the first quarter of a Sunday-night regular-season game early in the 2006 NFL season, the Bears led the Seahawks, who faced third-and-14 on their own 39-yard line. Seattle lined up in a four-wide offensive set. The Bears' defense countered in a 4–3 set with two deep safeties. It would defend the play in the conservative "Cover Two" hybrid scheme now known as Tampa Two, so named because it took hold with Dungy's Buccaneers. It had become the single-most-popular defense in the NFL, a bend-but-don't-break system that forces offenses to execute the length of the field five yards at a time. After a season-opening shutout loss to Chicago, venerable Packers quarterback Brett Favre had said, "I think the Bears are the best that's ever played that style."

In simplest terms, Tampa Two is a zone defense with two deep safeties playing Cover Two (each is responsible for half the width of the field), two cornerbacks jamming wide receivers at the line of scrimmage, two outside linebackers patrolling the short zones and a middle linebacker roaming from the line of scrimmage to as much as 30 yards downfield, and four pass rushers. By the 2006 season the defense was at the peak of its popularity. Jim Schwartz, then the respected defensive coordinator of the Tennessee Titans, said at the time, "I'll bet you 30 out of 32 teams in the league play it." Those teams that most relied on the Tampa Two would employ it on as many as 40% of their defensive plays.

On the play in that 2006 game, Seattle quarterback Matt Hasselbeck took a five-step drop and threw toward slot wideout Bobby Engram in the curl zone 10 yards downfield, slightly to the right of center. The ball, Engram, Bears nickelback Ricky Manning Jr. and linebacker Lance Briggs arrived simultaneously. The pass bounced off Engram's hands as he was taken down by Manning and Briggs. The Seahawks punted and lost the game, 37–6. It was a classic Tampa Two stop, with the Bears' defense functioning precisely as designed. "From now on we're calling it Bear Two," said Chicago's All-Pro linebacker Brian Urlacher later that week. "Best thing about this defense? It works, man."

It works, man, because it is the cumulative result of more than three decades' worth of defensive progression. Follow along.

In the midsummer training-camp heat of that same season, Bears head coach Lovie Smith stood on a practice field between two-a-day sessions. He is one of the devotees of the Dungy-Kiffin system—he was a member of that Tampa Bay staff during its run of defensive dominance, and he took the Tampa Two with him to Chicago from St. Louis, his intermediate stop. Smith knew as well as anyone that this was one of those football innovations that may have seemed to arrive suddenly but has roots deep in the game.

"I played Cover Two when I was in high school back in Texas in the 1970s," Smith says. "And they were playing Cover Two long before I got there."

Early Cover Two was straightforward. Two safeties split the field, far from the line of scrimmage. It was the simplest way to defend the deep zone in case the cornerbacks got beat, or in case the offense used more than two receivers, which, until the 1970s, they seldom did at any level of the game. Cover Two was uncomplicated and safe.

But as with any zone defense, there were holes: between the safeties and outside the safeties. Generally, Cover Two allowed wide receivers to roam relatively freely in the secondary. Defensive coaches began concocting ways to fill those holes. One was to roll the cornerbacks up close to the wide receivers, disrupting them at the line to throw off the timing of pass routes and allow the safeties more time to react. First to try it?

"Late 1960s, I was a quarterback with the 49ers, and we're playing the Cleveland Browns," says longtime college head coach (and briefly the Redskins' coach) Steve Spurrier. "John Brodie was the starter, and he used to love to throw the quick out. Five yards, zip it right in there. If the cornerback rolled up on one side, John would throw it the other way. So in this game, John sees one corner rolled up, looks the other way, and that corner is rolled up too. He comes over to the sideline and says, 'They can't do that!' I said, 'Well, they just did.' "

Former Michigan State head coach George Perles does Spurrier one better: "In 1967, I was at Michigan State working under Duffy Daugherty. We played Houston in the first game of the season. Bill Yeoman was the coach there. They played Cover Two and rolled up the corners. Beat us 37–7."

The great leap forward was initiated in the early 1970s by Bud Carson, a slight man among the giants of the NFL. Like so many coaches who impacted the game, Carson was born in steel country near Pittsburgh. He played high school football and then at North Carolina. In '67, at the age of 37, Carson succeeded the legendary Bobby Dodd as head coach at Georgia Tech but lasted just five years, losing as many games as he won (27–27). For the '72 season he was hired by Chuck Noll to be the Steelers' defensive coordinator. Carson could not have known that he stood on the cusp of something big.

Noll was in his fourth year coaching the hapless Steelers, a franchise known for being scrappy, but usually in defeat. They had improved from 1–13 in 1969 to 6–8 in '71, slowly clawing at respectability. As they climbed, the pieces of a legendary defense were coming together: Defensive tackle "Mean" Joe Greene was selected No. 4 overall in '69, cornerback Mel Blount in the third round in '70, linebacker Jack Ham and defensive end Dwight White in '71. On this foundation Carson installed a basic Cover Two scheme, and then he tweaked it.

Capitalizing on the power of the 6' 3", 205-pound Blount (he was really as much a linebacker as he was a defensive back), Carson pushed the corners up to the line of scrimmage and instructed them to jam wide receivers. The safeties—Mike Wagner and Glen Edwards (or, when Edwards was hurt, Ralph Anderson)—were assigned to cover deep zones behind the jamming corners. Outside linebackers Ham and Andy Russell would cover vast space from hash mark to sideline, and middle linebacker Henry Davis, a journeyman keeping the seat warm for the Hall of Famer to come, would be required to drop deep in the middle zone, sometimes 25, even 35 yards deep. Using linebackers in deep coverage was a radical scheme, but its liberation of the rest of the defense would serve as a viable counterattack to the short-throw, possession-passing systems that were beginning to proliferate, particularly Bill Walsh's so-called West Coast offense (Chapter 8).

"Bud came in one day, I think it was early in the season," as Wagner recalls, "and just drew it on a chalkboard. It was different, but I think everybody in the room could see the potential right away. We went out to practice that same day and started running it. And we loved it."

Ham, then just a year out of Penn State, says, "We actually played a lot of Cover Two in college, but this was different. And obviously Bud could see that we had the right people to play it."

Russell loved the concept and loved playing for the coach who gave it to them, telling SPORTS ILLUSTRATED, "He's like a mad scientist, looking for a formula and changing it every day."

The Steelers went 21–7 over the next two seasons, losing twice in the playoffs. But they continued to add the right people to play Carson's cover two. Cornerback J.T. Thomas was taken out of Florida State with the first pick of the '73 draft; he was 6' 2", 196 pounds, only slightly smaller than Blount and just as inclined to play a physical game. A year later the Steelers used their second-round pick to take a skinny 6' 4" middle linebacker out of Kent State named Jack Lambert. He was freakishly skilled and also ferocious, and he proved to be the perfect Cover Two linebacker: He had the speed to make the deep drops and the instincts to know when to get there.

Carson's core philosophy was to force an offense to settle for short gains on underneath dump-off passes, requiring the offense to show sustained execution, clock consumption and, perhaps most significant, patience. "There are not a lot of big plays out there against this defense," says former NFL quarterback Rich Gannon, who played from 1987 through 2004, in the heart of the Tampa Two resurgence. "You have to be patient and take four-, five-, six-yard plays and work your way up the field. That's something coordinators and quarterbacks don't always enjoy doing."

Think of these as the Five Commandments of Tampa Two:

1) The front four must be able to rush the quarterback, allowing the linebackers freedom. "If you get four men who can rush the passer, you can play cover two, Tampa Two all day," says Ham. "But you can't play it without a pass rush, because it's a zone defense, and there are lots of holes if the quarterback can sit back and wait." The Steelers made their pass rush effective with Joe Greene and L.C. Greenwood, the Buccaneers with Warren Sapp and Simeon Rice and the 2006 Bears—all the way to the Super Bowl—with Tommie Harris and Alex Brown as part of an eight-deep posse of solid defensive linemen moving in and out of the game.

2) The middle linebacker must be able, and willing, to frequently drop as deep as 30 yards, filling the deep crossing zone between the safeties, and leaving many of the glamour plays—helmet-popping tackles, interceptions—to the outside linebackers and the safeties. "My primary purpose in that defense is to run back to the huddle and congratulate somebody for making a play while I was running down the field with the tight end," says Brian Urlacher, who went on to become

an All-Pro playing Tampa Two middle linebacker in the mid-2000s. Urlacher refined the position played by Lambert. At 6' 4", 258 pounds with running back speed, Urlacher could sit on the line longer than most Tampa Two middle linebackers, allowing him to read running plays before bailing out, yet still able to drop into 25-yard pass plays and disrupt them. "He's a freak," said Bears quarterback Rex Grossman in 2006. "Trust me. I play against him every day, and I test him. You can't throw over him in the middle."

3) The outside linebackers have to be smart enough and athletic enough to not only cover receivers in the middle zone but also to rally to runs at the line of scrimmage. "You're not looking for your old-fashioned linebacker who makes tackles in a phone booth," says Dungy. "You're looking for an open-field tackler and athlete." Think nickelback Ronde Barber with vintage Tampa Bay teams or linebacker Lance Briggs with the mid-2000s Bears. The outside 'backers also have to jam tight ends and slot receivers to keep them from releasing into the middle zone vacated by the dropping middle linebacker. In 2006 the woeful Detroit Lions hired Rod Marinelli from Tampa Bay as their head coach, and Marinelli then drafted lightning-quick 230-pound middle linebacker Ernie Sims from Florida State to play the Lambert-Urlacher role with the Lions.

4) The cornerbacks must be physical enough to jam wideouts at the line of scrimmage and also to tackle ballcarriers. In Tampa Two they are not expected to run down the field with receivers but merely disrupt them and pass them along to the safeties. "I think one of the big reasons Tampa Two developed was to take pressure off the corners in terms of coverage," says former NFL quarterback and *Monday Night Football* analyst Ron Jaworski. Yet the initial disruption is vital. "Our job is to get our hands on the receiver and knock him off his route," says Charles Tillman, who played on the Bears Super Bowl team in 2006. "That little bit of a bump can change the whole play." Blount was the prototype in 1972 and, all these years later, it is hard to imagine a more ideal Tampa Two corner.

5) The safeties must be smart enough to break properly on balls in the air and physical enough to create, and survive, the violent collisions with wide receivers that happen when the safety has run

25 yards from his deep starting position. "This defense is the reason you see so many penalties on safeties," says Ham. "They're out there to create collisions."

CARSON'S 1974 Steelers played the first true, modern Cover Two defense. It would be known far and wide as the Steel Curtain. While the Steeler offense during the '70s dynasty was no slouch (Bradshaw, Harris, Swann, Stallworth, Webster), it was the defense that was the heart of a franchise that won four Super Bowls in six years. In 1976 (a non–Super Bowl year), the Steelers gave up 28 points over the last nine regular-season games and pitched five shutouts.

The front four of Greene, White, L.C. Greenwood and Ernie Holmes was almost unblockable even without blitz help from linebackers. Ham, Lambert and Russell were as good as any trio of linebackers that has ever played together. Thomas and Blount were perfect Cover Two corners, Wagner a cerebral yet reckless safety. "The amazing thing," says Woody Widenhofer, a defensive assistant with the Steel Curtain Steelers (as was Perles), "is that Bud had played a lot of two-man zone, but he looked at our personnel and just adapted everything to it."

After the 1977 season Carson left Pittsburgh to join the Los Angeles Rams. He would work as the defensive coordinator for the Rams for four seasons, helping get them to the '79 Super Bowl. In '89 he was finally given his own team, the Cleveland Browns, but lasted just a season and a half as head coach before being fired in the middle of a 3–13 year.

Yet Carson not only earned an important place in coaching history but was also a vital link in a coaching chain. Before the 1977 season, the Steelers had signed University of Minnesota quarterback Tony Dungy as a free agent and then converted him first into a wide receiver and then a safety. He played two years for the Steelers, including the season of their '78 Super Bowl championship. He also paid close attention. Dungy would become one of the most successful coordinators, then head coaches, in league history. At every turn Carson was in his head. "Everything we do now," Dungy said in the fall of 2006, with his Colts en route to winning the Super Bowl, "you can find in my Pittsburgh Steelers playbook. I did keep it all those years."

Dungy left the Steelers after two seasons, but by 1981, at the age of 25, he was back in Pittsburgh as an assistant coach. He was the Steelers' coordinator from '84 through '88 and assumed the same position with the Vikings in '92, where he met up with Monte Kiffin, then a 52-year-old Nebraska native and coaching journeyman with a jones for defense and some of the same ideas that Dungy was carrying around in his old Steelers playbook. Offenses were getting better, faster, more sophisticated; defenses needed an answer.

Like the best coaches, Kiffin enjoyed finding answers. He was raised on Cornhuskers football in Lexington, Neb., in the south-central part of the state between Kearney and North Platte. He took his game to Lincoln in 1959 as a two-way tackle and returned in '66 as a defensive assistant coach under Bob Devaney. The Huskers won national championships in '70 and '71, and a tradition of defensive excellence—starters wore black shirts in practice and became known as the Blackshirts even before Kiffin arrived—was established.

Kiffin worked at Nebraska for 11 years, under both Devaney and his successor, Tom Osborne. Then he did a typical coach's tour: six stops in 15 years, including a 16–17 record in three years (1980–82) at North Carolina State, his only head coaching job, before landing back in Minnesota. Dungy's arrival led to a marriage of like minds. Together he and Kiffin modified Carson's old system, putting Jack Del Rio in the crucial middle linebacker spot and rolling up the corners aggressively. The Vikings made the playoffs for three straight years and in '94 led the NFL in total defense.

When Dungy was hired as head coach of the Tampa Bay Buccaneers in 1996, he brought Kiffin aboard to run his defense. Together they refined the Cover Two into a defensive force. "Tony and I had both used a lot of the theories that became what everybody calls Tampa Two," says Kiffin. "He had learned some things with the Steelers, and I had been playing some of it when I was coaching in college. We sort of put them together." Their defensive mission was to close the traditional holes in the Cover Two. All defenses have holes on paper, and theirs was no exception.

They worked primarily at two things: One was finding the perfect personnel, like tackle Sapp and outside linebacker Derrick Brooks, whose ability to cover flat zones and rally to ballcarriers was crucial to the Tampa Two—and almost unmatched in the NFL during Brooks's prime. Second was improving the Cover Two against the run on a consistent basis.

"And that's exactly what Monte did," says former USC coach Pete Carroll, a lifelong friend of Kiffin's. "He made it awesome against the run. What Monte and Tony did in Tampa was almost revolutionize defense. They took a good, simple system and made it very, very precise."

For years, Cover Two was played with an "under" front four. *Under* signifies a shift to the weak (non-tight end) side of the offensive formation. At Tampa Bay, Kiffin completed a transition to an "over" front alignment, meaning that the defensive front four is shifted to the strong (tight end) side of the offensive formation. "In the over defense you play your linebackers more off the line of scrimmage," says Kiffin. "That puts more emphasis on your seam droppers [outside linebackers and nickelbacks] to get into the flat zones. We had Derrick Brooks and Ronde Barber playing those positions."

If the Tampa Two reached its peak with Tampa Bay's Super Bowl victory following the 2002 season, it remained a force with the Bears' Super Bowl appearance in '06. Predictably, receivers evolved, becoming better skilled at beating the essential jams at the line of scrimmage; at the same time, officials became more diligent in calling penalties on hand-chucks at the line.

Offenses began to find new holes to exploit. "There's a sweet spot against the Tampa Two," Jaworski said in 2006. "Eighteen or 19 yards on the sideline. But any less than 18, 19 yards, and the receiver is still jammed; and any more, and the receiver is in the hospital because the safety came over to hit him. And it takes a great throw."

Quarterbacks became more adept at making that great throw. Receivers got better at making the catch and getting to the ground before the concussive hit was delivered. "The biggest thing," says Kiffin, "was that it got harder to catch teams off balance with the scheme. They had a chance to study it."

In the spring of 2009 Kiffin suddenly left the NFL to return to the college ranks as defensive coach at Tennessee, where his son, Lane, had become head coach. A year later Lane moved on, together with his father, to L.A. to become head coach at USC—taking the place of Pete Carroll, who has suddenly returned to the NFL to coach the Seahawks. In the coaching world, these were seismic changes. But one thing remained the same: both Kiffin and Carroll would still be coaching the Tampa Two.

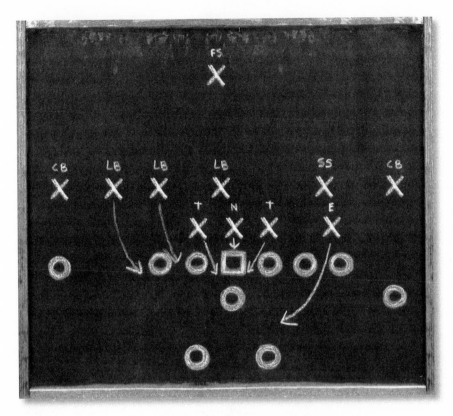

THE 46 DEFENSE

Out of desperation over the mediocre defensive personnel of the early-'80s Chicago Bears, Buddy Ryan concocted the 46 defense (so-named by Ryan spontaneously for strong safety Doug Plank, whose jersey number was 46). It is effective largely because it "covers" head-on the three interior offensive linemen with defenders, dramatically reducing the protection packages available to the offense because the center and both guards had to block one-on-one and could not move or help in another manner. Ryan also overloaded one side of the defense close behind the line, further confusing the offense as to which defenders might blitz. It is a high-risk defense, with as many as eight defenders in the box and just a single high free safety.

CHAPTER 17

THE RYAN FAMILY DEFENSE

How Buddy Ryan invented the 46, dominated a Super Bowl with it, then passed his wisdom to his sons Rex and Rob

THE SCENE was remarkable not just because it was poignant but also because it was so unusual. The 1985 Chicago Bears had just finished off a 46–10 deconstruction of the overmatched New England Patriots to win Super Bowl XX in the Louisiana Superdome, and the giddy celebrations had begun on the field. Chicago coach Mike Ditka, beloved by these Bears, was lifted onto the shoulders of some of his players—this came as no surprise. But then the strangest thing happened: Suddenly there was Bears defensive coordinator Buddy Ryan being hoisted by linebacker Otis Wilson and defensive end Richard Dent, Ryan's right leg over Wilson's left shoulder pad and his left leg on Dent's right pad, both men laughing, while the rumpled old coach, stuffed into his Bears sweater, awkwardly tried to keep his balance. A defensive coordinator getting a victory ride?

Only once in the intervening years has a Super Bowl title been as convincingly built on defense (in 2000, by the Baltimore Ravens). But the '85 Bears were more than their defense. They had become a pop cultural phenomenon, with a celebrity coach, Ditka; a celebrity quarterback, Jim McMahon; and a celebrity nosetackle turned tail-back, William (the Refrigerator) Perry. They had released a kitschy, funky video—*The Super Bowl Shuffle*—that was recorded long before the championship game and had become a ubiquitous hit. And, to balance the scales of fame against the frivolous, the Bears also had the seriously gifted Walter Payton, maybe the best running back in the history of the game.

Still, what pulled it all together into winning football was a defense that redefined every essential element: strategy, speed and size, along with intimidation. The '85 Bears went 15–1 in the regular season, losing only to the Miami Dolphins on the first Monday night in December. Eleven times in 16 regular-season games they held opponents to 10 points or less. Statistics tell only a part of the story; these Bear defenders were scary-good, putting real fright into opposing players. In the postseason they proved even more intimidating. The Bears shut out the New York Giants (21–0) and the Los Angeles Rams (24–0) on consecutive frigid, windswept weekends at Soldier Field. The Giants and Rams combined for a total of 311 offensive yards in eight quarters, with four turnovers to the Bears' one. It was a display of domination seldom seen at the highest levels of any major sport, and it matched perfectly the city of Chicago's hard-ass self-image.

Behind this success was a 51-year-old football lifer whose only break from playing and coaching the game he learned growing up in Oklahoma was to serve as a master sergeant in the Army during the Korean War. James David (Buddy) Ryan had been coaching football since he latched on at Gainesville (Texas) High in 1957, but almost three decades later in Chicago he created the perfect amalgam of coach, system and personnel. Ryan had been hired by Bears head coach Neil Armstrong in 1978, and he so inspired his defensive players that when Armstrong was fired after three seasons, they successfully petitioned owner George Halas to keep Ryan in place.

The single most important factor in Ryan's rise in Chicago came early in his tenure there, while he was in the throes of frustration with the way his unit was performing. Ryan devised a defense that moved balls-out safety Doug Plank to middle linebacker. Ryan called it the "46" because that was

Plank's jersey number, and it would challenge evolving NFL offenses like as no defense had before.

On the night before the Super Bowl in the Bears' team hotel in New Orleans, the defense gathered, as it would on the eve of every game, for the ritual viewing of one reel of inspirational game film. First Ryan gave a speech; the players were well aware of the rumors that Ryan would be leaving the team after the game (which he did, to become head coach of the Philadelphia Eagles). "Quivering lip, tears, pretty emotional," recalls Gary Fencik, the team's veteran safety and defensive captain.

The reel chosen by Ryan was film of a midseason game in which the New York Jets were trying to play the Bears' 46 defense, having poached the basic concepts from Bears tape. The Jets version was a poor imitation of the real thing. Bears defensive end Dan Hampton jumped from his chair. "I'm sick of watching the fucking New York Jets try to run our defense!" Steve McMichael, the tackle who played inside Hampton, took up the cause by heaving a folding chair so hard that it became impaled in the chalkboard. "Then," says Fencik, "we went next door and ate milk and cookies."

Less than 24 hours later they crushed the Patriots. And scored the karmic total of 46 points.

Shelbyville, Ky.
April 2009

IT HAS been spring for a month on the calendar, but there is winter in the air in the horse country of central Kentucky. A dark overcast sky spits out periodic snow flurries. The Kentucky Derby will be run in less than two weeks, but warm sunshine, fancy hats and mint juleps seem impossibly distant. Late in the afternoon Buddy Ryan pulls up in a dust-covered pickup truck alongside a horse barn where he rents stall space. He owns 16 horses—four broodmares, four yearlings born just this spring and eight colts. They are not the type of horses bred to win the Triple Crown, but they keep a man busy just the same. Ryan is wearing a Jets windbreaker (in honor of his son Rex's recent hiring as head coach—as well as his own first job in the NFL) and shuffling with a limp because a horse stepped on his right foot a few days earlier. As he fills plastic feed tubs, he stops to point out a January foal he's unofficially named Jetty.

Buddy moved here with his second wife, Joanie, in 1996, after the Cardinals fired him from what would be his last coaching job, but retirement hasn't been all easy. Joanie was diagnosed with Alzheimer's disease in 2001, and two years later Buddy moved her to an assisted living facility in Louisville. "She's not doing good," says Buddy on this day. "But we go to mass every Sunday, and she seems to like that, so it's O.K." In the winter of 2005 Buddy fought off a case of encephalitis. (Rex came down to Louisville and raised hell with the hospital staff, telling them, "This ain't Johnny Bumfuck you're treating here.") The illness left some holes in Buddy's memory, but not when it comes to football.

It was a long journey that had brought Ryan to that evening in New Orleans, sitting atop his players' shoulders, the most famous defensive coordinator in football, and then carried him to this barn smack in the middle of Kentucky's horse industry. The wind blows harder as Ryan moves from stall to stall, filling the feed tubs and making sure the horses have water, using a black rubber hose to fill up the pails.

The horses' names tell the story of Ryan's life. One broodmare is named Bayside Girl, for Joanie, who was born and raised in Bayside, Queens. Another mare is Fired for Winning, which happened when Ryan was dismissed as coach of the Eagles following the 1990 season. One colt, still actively racing at the time, is named Forty-Six Blitz. That one makes Ryan smile. Buddy always wanted to raise horses, so when his coaching career finally ended, he brought Joanie to the green hills and bought some stock.

After the horses are fed and watered—"put up," in the parlance of the business—Ryan drops onto a couch in a cluttered tack room just off the shedrow. Two wary cats scurry to cuddle at his feet. "So what do you want to know about the 46?" he asks. "There wasn't all that much to it at first." He laughs, because of course there was a lot more by the end.

Raised in the Oklahoma panhandle town of Frederick, Ryan was a lineman on the local high school team, but after graduation, instead of taking his game to college, he enlisted in the National Guard. "I went in when I was 16," Ryan told SPORTS ILLUSTRATED in 1986. "No one had much money back in Frederick, so a bunch of us joined the National Guard to get that extra $40 a month. Then the sumbitches went and mobilized us." At 18 he was a master sergeant, leading a platoon in Korea.

Ryan was back home before his 19th birthday, a grown man, and a lineman at Oklahoma A&M, which would later become Oklahoma State. "I was more mature than most of the other players," he says. "You would expect that." There he met his future wife, Doris, the homecoming queen, and they were married while still in college. Buddy became a coach, first in high school and then in college, 12 years at six different addresses.

RYAN'S FIRST NFL job was with the 1968 New York Jets. Weeb Ewbank had three assistant coaches on that team, and Ryan ran the defense that would eventually shut down the Colts 16–7 in Super Bowl III, shocking the football world. "We really weren't very creative on defense with that team," says Ryan. "We played a straight 4–3 and tried to gap teams a little bit. Offset some. Get off the ball quick." This would become a Ryan signature, using linemen who were too quick off the ball to be easily blocked to disrupt offenses trying to control the line of scrimmage. On that Jets team, Ryan did it with defensive end Gerry Philbin and tackle John Elliott.

"We had a great defense on that team," says Ryan, "but the coaches didn't call nothin'. [Middle linebacker] Larry Grantham called all the defenses. But there wasn't a whole lot to it. Like I said, we weren't creative, but we were pretty good. Everybody found out in that Super Bowl."

Ryan stayed in New York for eight seasons before Bud Grant hired him in 1976 to run the Minnesota Vikings' defense. The Vikings made the Super Bowl in Ryan's first season with Grant but were beaten by the Oakland Raiders 32–14 in a game that was never close. "We got beat clean," says Ryan. When reminded that Hall of Fame wideout Fred Biletnikoff had a good game against his defense, Ryan sniffs. "Shit, everybody had a good game."

Ryan spent just one more season in Minnesota before Neill Armstrong brought him to Chicago as defensive coordinator. "That," Ryan says, "was the first time I was a true defensive coordinator." It was not necessarily an enviable job. The proud Bears possessed eight NFL titles, but none since 1963 and just one since 1946. They had gone 9–5 in the previous year under Jack Pardee, and that had been the team's first winning season in a decade. Ryan assessed his hand quickly. "When I got there," he says, "we didn't have many good players."

History will hold that Ryan was a genius—in that generous way the noun is applied to coaches—both as a motivator and strategist. It will less likely declare him a thoughtful, engaged, defensive scientist who loved nothing more than to doodle formations on a chalkboard, an inveterate tinkerer. But that indeed was Buddy Ryan. Some of those chalkboard creations were modest, variants on the standard; others were outlandish. Many would never find their way into a game. But throughout his career Ryan loved to play with schemes. In his early years with the Bears, as the team struggled to build an identity with marginal players, Buddy's blackboard got a workout. The team went 7–9 in 1978, Armstrong's, and Ryan's, first season, and were 4–5 through October of the '79 season, preparing for a home game against Detroit, when Ryan drew up the 46 during a defensive team meeting.

Doug Plank was then a fifth-year pro from Ohio State, an undersized hit man (listed at 6 feet, 200 pounds, but smaller in reality) who, as starting free safety, would throw his body recklessly around the field. (Plank would later explain his style: "I had to play a certain way," he said in a 2009 interview. "And once I started playing that way, I developed a reputation for playing that way, and I had to protect that reputation." He admitted to often experiencing foggy memory now.)

Plank sat in every one of Ryan's defensive meetings in 1978 and '79. "In those years, and even beyond," says Plank, "Buddy was very creative. Every week he would come up with some sort of new defense. He was always trying new things. Most of them didn't last very long. So this one day he puts this defense up on the board where I move up from free safety to middle linebacker, along with some other shifts and changes. We're getting ready to leave the room, and one of the guys says, 'What are we going to call this one?' Well, Buddy was always drawing up packages but never drew them up with peoples' names or with X's and O's. He would always just write numbers."

Ryan circled Plank's number 46 several times, over and over, and then said, "We'll call it '46.' "

"Now, at this point," says Plank, "a marching band did not come into the room and start playing music because of the invention of the 46 defense. At that point none of us knew if the 46 was going to be around any longer than some of the others, and that might be one game or one quarter or one snap.

But it turns out that the 46 worked a little better than some of the others."

Ryan says, "I was just trying to screw up teams' blocking schemes until we got some better players. In '79, when I first started messing with the 46, it wasn't really a scheme at all, it was just something we tried. We had to do something. And it did mess up some of their blocking patterns. Then we got better at it. And then we got real good at it when the players were better."

Sitting in the tack room of the horse barn in Kentucky, Ryan grabs a writer's notebook and draws up the 46, narrating as he scribbles. Now he writes X's and O's, not numbers—after all, he has no team, no jerseys. But the task is so familiar that it takes just a few seconds. Like any good defensive coach, the last thing he does is count the symbols, making sure there are 11, which there are.

The 46 was a 4–3 defense, the base alignment Ryan liked best. But it was much more than a 4–3. The 46 was the first defense in modern football in which three interior linemen covered the center and two offensive guards, forcing the offensive linemen to block one-on-one and thus limiting their ability to move or help elsewhere. (Customarily, in a 4–3 defense, the center is uncovered and free to assist in double-team blocks or picking up blitzers. In a 3–4 defense, the defensive ends are usually lined up over the offensive tackles, leaving the guards uncovered.) Those first three Bears linemen, in 1979, were Alan Page (who had spent most of his career in Minnesota and would land in the Hall of Fame), Jim Osborne and Dan Hampton. The fourth defensive lineman, effectively the weakside defensive end, would line up outside the tackle assigned to block him. Behind the front four Ryan moved two linebackers to the tight end side and brought one safety—Plank—up as a fourth linebacker. That was the 46. "Now they call it 'eight in the box,' " says Ryan.

The 46, even in its infancy, had two primary goals: One, stop the run. Eight in the box (four linemen, three linebackers, one safety) will do that. Two was to position the defense to bring more pressure on the quarterback than the offense can block. As the scheme evolved, that aspect would become more effective. "Eventually," says Bruce Coslet, who coached against Ryan as defensive coordinator for Cincinnati through the mid- and late-1980s, "the 46 became a fucking nightmare to coach against. It was something nobody had seen and nobody knew how to prepare for it. Buddy changed football with that defense."

On Nov. 4, 1979, the Bears beat Detroit, 35–7. They won five of the next six games to finish the regular season with a 10–6 record; two days before Christmas they lost to the Philadelphia Eagles in the first round of the play-offs. A year later they slipped to 7–9 and in 1981 they went 6–10 after losing 10 of their first 13 games. Armstrong was finished, and the players knew it, but the defense felt that Ryan was building something special. "We played San Diego in 1981," says Fencik. "We had gotten off to a lousy start [the Bears were 1–6], and they had Dan Fouts and Kellen Winslow. And we beat them 20–17 at home, and the 46 was great that day. We had them confused, and everything just clicked."

There was a bond forming, emotionally and schematically. "Neil Armstrong was a true gentleman," says Fencik. "But I really don't think he appreciated how young we were. He had come from the Purple People Eaters, and those guys were so mature." The Bears' defense began growing up with Ryan. In late December '81, Fencik and Page drafted a letter to Halas, asking that Ryan be retained when Armstrong was inevitably canned. "Alan and I wrote the letter, and to cover our asses we had the whole defense sign it," says Fencik. "So George Halas shows up one day while we're practicing indoors on concrete floors at the Great Lakes Naval Training Center because it's snowing like crazy outside. That was the day he dismissed Neil Armstrong. He rides over to the defense in his golf cart and points at us and says in this gruff, old voice, 'I got your letter. *Your* coaches will be retained.' And that's how Mike Ditka wound up inheriting Buddy Ryan."

More important than Ryan's retention, even he would admit now, were the additions made to the roster. Linebacker Otis Wilson was drafted in 1980 and middle linebacker Mike Singletary a year later. Defensive tackle Steve McMichael was signed as a free agent before the '80 season. Pass rush end Richard Dent would join in '83 and linebacker Wilber Marshall in '84. Piece by piece the Bears got better. "It was a great scheme," says Ryan. "People called me a genius back then. When you get great players, you can be a genius."

The Bears who took the field in '85 were exquisitely suited to Ryan's system. The inside three linemen—McMichael, Hampton and either Refrigerator Perry or Mike Hartenstine—had the brute strength to occupy the inside of the offensive line and often put pressure on passers without blitz help. Dent, an eighth-round draft pick who came into the NFL at 230 pounds, much too small for a defensive end, grew to 260 and became an edge-rushing force. The clogged middle forced teams to try to run outside, where regular linebackers Marshall, Singletary and Wilson were fast enough to pursue. Plank, who retired following the 1982 season after suffering a spinal concussion, was replaced first by Todd Bell, and then by Dave Duerson. "The whole thing started with covering the center and both guards," says Ryan. "Nobody had really ever done it before. It was hard to run against it. And with the guys we had in the middle, and Richard Dent, it was hard to pass against it too. Not to sound arrogant, but for a while there nobody really gave us any problems."

The great potential weakness of the 46 is that cornerbacks can often be left in one-on-one coverage. Ryan's hope was always that the quarterback wouldn't have time to exploit it. Or wouldn't be able to recognize quickly enough how to exploit it. Despite its reputation as a scheme of relentless, one-dimensional pressure, the 46 is, in fact, a complex combination of fronts and blitzes. "The scheme forced people to make quick decisions," says Fencik. "And some teams just couldn't adjust. Buddy set up this system within the 46 where we would audible fronts and coverage based on what the offense showed. It required a lot of coordination. But very few offenses were prepared to audible two times, and once we would show something and then audible, well, it just made you very confident that you would rarely be in a bad position." As an added benefit, the multiple fronts forced teams to eat up practice time preparing for the Bears' 46, limiting their ability to game-plan a diverse offense.

On a much different level, Ryan connected emotionally with his players. This facet is often now muddied by episodes that would taint Ryan's legacy later in his career. In 1989 as coach of the Eagles, Ryan was accused by the Dallas Cowboys of putting "bounties" on kicker Luis Zendejas and quarterback Troy Aikman, promising rewards to players who could knock either man out of the game, charges Ryan has always denied. Four years later, as defensive coordinator of the Houston Oilers, he was captured on national television slugging offensive coordinator Kevin Gilbride after criticizing Gilbride's run-and-shoot offense, which Ryan felt left his defensive players on the field too often and too long.

But in 1985 Ryan's fire burned all to the good. He was rough on some players. "I hated him," Singletary told *The New York Times* in '85. "He was always picking on me. When I first came into camp, he referred to me as 'the little, short, fat guy' and always 'Number 50.' He never called me by my name." (Gary Fencik, it seems, takes it a little differently: "When I see Buddy to this day, or call him up, he calls me '45.' And I would be offended if he called me anything else.") But Fencik does recall the treatment of Singletary. "The first training camp," he says, "Mike Singletary couldn't finish the 10-minute run, and Buddy was merciless with him for a long time after that. Buddy was a sergeant in the Korean War. You had to earn his respect."

And most players wanted to earn that respect. "Buddy was a one-of-a-kind individual," Fencik continues. "You did not want to fail him. There were times when I was playing for Buddy, and out on the field if something was going wrong, all I could think was that I didn't want to disappoint my coach or my teammates. How is this going to look when they play the game film on Monday? It became a very emotional situation. Buddy created a unit mentality. We're all in this together. And this was a very big part of the success of the Bears' defense in that era. When you combine that with the encyclopedia of defenses that our opponents had to prepare for, it just set us up very well."

Ryan routinely allowed his players to tweak his defensive schemes. Fencik, the defensive captain, would approach Ryan on the sideline with a message from Marshall or Dent asking for freedom to run a certain stunt. Ryan would grumble, "Who's running this defense, anyway?" but then he would grant permission with the caveat that if something didn't work, it would be shelved for the rest of the day.

The Bears' defense was brilliant in 1984, leading the NFL in overall defense, rushing defense and sacks. By the time '85 arrived, Chicago often had teams beat before the first snap.

"Say a team had first-and-10," recalls Fencik. "They know they can't run the ball, so they call a pass play and go to max protect, keeping both backs in and helping with a tight end. But we're not blitzing at this point; we rush four and drop seven, and they're looking at throwing into that with two receivers. No chance. So it's second-and-10. Now it comes down to tendencies, and maybe we blitz and get them in third-and-long, and then all the advantage goes to Buddy.

"We had one series where we would blitz inside our own 20-yard line," says Fencik. "But then teams would recognize that and start calling an audible if we looked like we were showing blitz, and we would back off and double both wideouts. It was just a period in time where not only did we have superior talent, but we had a superior system."

Ryan took the 46 to Philadelphia and went 43-38-1 in five seasons before he was fired. He would have less success in Arizona, where he was head coach of the Cardinals for two seasons. As with all innovations, Ryan's 46 forced adaptation on the league. Passing offense grew more sophisticated, finding ways to put more pressure on the vulnerable cornerbacks and the single high free safety. Yet defensive coaches continued to rely on creative pressure packages to disrupt timed pass routes, none more than one Rex Ryan in Baltimore. "I'm not the only one," he said in the fall of 2008. "Every time you see some team moving people around to get pressure, you should think of my father. He influenced every one of them."

Florham Park, N.J.
May 2009

AS COACH of the New York Jets, Rex Ryan has a huge office, but he fills it nonetheless. He fills it with a big body: tree-trunk legs stretching massive mesh shorts and a gargantuan torso draped in a green Jets golf shirt. But more than with his bulk, he fills the room with his personality, a self-confidence that borders on bravado, driven by a sense of having been denied too long. There is a good deal of Buddy in Rex, and Rex likes to hear that. "Dad was a hell of a football coach," says Rex. "He knew what he was doing."

Buddy was a hell of a football coach in Buffalo, traveling on a recruiting trip in December of 1962 when his wife, Doris, gave birth to twin boys back in Oklahoma. The news of their birth reached Buddy slowly. "He found out about it the next day," says Doris. "Or maybe it was two days." Rex and Rob the twins were named. They had an older brother, Jim. All three were in the stadium in Miami for Super Bowl III and again in New Orleans for Super Bowl XX. Rex and Rob would become coaches. (Jim is a lawyer.) The family now has a combined five Super

Bowl rings: Buddy's two with the Jets and Bears, Rob's two while working as a defensive assistant under Bill Belichick with the Patriots and Rex's with the 2000 Ravens.

Should anyone doubt the Ryan boys' bona fides as football coaches, consider this: Both Rex and Rob played football as fourth-graders living in Toronto but were thrown off the team for hitting a player too hard. Doris marched onto the field and said, "This is a contact sport where I come from."

Banned from football, the Ryan boys played baseball and hockey. (Rex was an all-star goalie.) In the fall of 1977 Doris sent the boys, then 14 years old, to live with Buddy, who was beginning his second season under Bud Grant with the Vikings. "It was time for them to be with their father," says Doris (by then, she and Buddy were divorced). They lived with Buddy and Joanie for a year in Minnesota and four years in Chicago. Rex and Rob were ball boys for the Bears. Walter Payton was their best friend. They soaked up football every day. Buddy knew firsthand what coaching could do to a man's personal life, and as Rex and Rob moved on through college, he tried to steer them away from it. But they persisted, and in the spring of '87, while he was coach of the Eagles, Buddy traveled to Oklahoma, rented a hotel conference room and taught his sons the 46 on a paper easel with a black marker. And they gave as good as they got. "They knew plenty," says Buddy. "So I told 'em to go get some jobs."

Rex went from Eastern Kentucky to New Mexico Highlands to Morehead State—"the big time," he says—before joining his dad and brother on the staff of the Arizona Cardinals in the fall of 1994. Both were defensive assistants. "Best ones I had," says Buddy. "People said it was nepotism. *Bullllllshit.*" The Cardinals went 8–8 in the Ryans' first year and ranked No. 3 in the NFL in defense but slipped to 4–12 and last in scoring defense in '95. That got Buddy fired.

Rex didn't get a single job offer from an NFL team. So he took a job as the defensive coordinator at the University of Cincinnati under coach Rick Minter. I'm gonna punish people now, Ryan thought to himself. I'm going back to the college game, and I'm gonna punish people. Early in two-a-days in the summer of 1996, Minter called for a nine-on-seven inside running game drill, in which the two defensive safeties are on the field essentially as props and not intended to tackle or be blocked. "On the first rep Rex calls for a free safety blitz up the A gap," says Minter. "He just stones the running back. I say, 'Rex, my gosh, it's a nine-on-seven drill.' Rex says, 'Coach, we've got to set the tone around here.'"

Rex coached for two years at Cincinnati, where he built a defense that was indeed punishing. In '98 he spent a year as defensive line coach at Oklahoma, and then, in '99, Brian Billick hired him as a defensive assistant with the Ravens, bringing him back into the NFL. He immediately connected with players. "Coaches are mostly pains in the ass," says Rob Burnett, who was a nine-year veteran defensive tackle when Ryan came to the Ravens in '99. "Rex has a humanity to him that most coaches don't have. It's rare for guys to want to win for their coach in this league. But we would have jumped on a grenade for that guy."

In 2002 defensive coordinator Marvin Lewis left the Ravens, and Billick promoted Mike Nolan to defensive coordinator. "I was pissed because, basically I got fucked," says Rex. "Brian never knew me. Maybe I never fit his image. But it was a crock of shit." (Billick's take: "When Marvin left, I had Mike Nolan on my staff, and I felt we needed a more veteran presence. But I knew Rex had coordinator capabilities. You don't spend five minutes around Rex Ryan and not see his passion.")

Three more years under Nolan. Three more years waiting for a chance. Finally, when Nolan left to become head coach of the 49ers in 2005, Ryan was promoted to defensive coordinator. For four years he would be a key figure in accelerating the defensive evolution in the NFL.

For starters Rex installed the Ryan family attitude, which, at its core, meant the intimidation of opponents, achieved primarily by hitting and hitting hard, right up to the edge of what the rules allow (and sometimes beyond). "It starts with a common mind-set," says Plank. "And without that mind-set, the playbook the Ryan family has used for 30 years is irrelevant." Then Rex went to work on his schemes.

Dick LeBeau and Dom Capers had changed the pressure paradigm with the zone blitz (Chapter 18). Rex used many of their ideas, mixed with two cornerstone principles. One: Stop the run. "Say what you want about me," says Ryan, "but if I want to, I'll stop your run." Two: Knock the quarterback on his back, for the simple reason best expressed by Rob Ryan (who in 2009 was Eric Mangini's defensive coordinator with the Browns). "The more you hit the quarterback," Rob says, "the better you're going to do."

LeBeau's zone scheme is characterized by unpredictability within a fairly static 3–4 formation. Rex took the next step, dramatically altering the placement of players on the field. It became common to see the Ravens line up with only one player in a three-point stance and five or six other linemen and linebackers strolling around in the tackle box, waiting for the offense to call an audible before deciding where to attack from, or whether to attack at all. While his base alignment is a 3–4, Ryan's willingness to move players around to anywhere on the field freed him to conceive almost limitless schemes.

Jim Fassell, who has coached both with and against Ryan, says, "Rex started doing things that nobody had ever done before. He would start out with seven or eight guys in the box, and then walk five of them out of the box right before the snap. He really caused a lot of consternation to offenses."

"Rex has an immense defensive package," says former Oakland and Tampa Bay head coach Jon Gruden. "I've seen him do almost everything imaginable. He was one of the first guys to major in what I call 'designer blitzes,' which are blitzes that are dialed up just for a particular game or a particular situation."

Ryan's defenses clearly dovetailed neatly with the changing profile of the modern athlete. No longer is a professional defense made up of cookie-cutter positional players. Defensive ends are faster than some running backs. Linebackers are stronger than some offensive tackles. Safeties are capable of rushing the passer from 10 yards off the line of scrimmage, bringing speed and power to the blitz from the deep third of the field. "Look at the collection of athletes we had in Baltimore," says Adalius Thomas, who played under Ryan with the Ravens. "There were a bunch of versatile guys out there, and some of them are going to the Hall of Fame." Since all 11 of Ryan's defenders were capable of blitzing, he disguised his pressures by making it seem as if they might all blitz.

Thomas was among the most versatile. At 6' 2", 270 pounds, he played every position on the defense except cornerback. There were other transcendent athletes: safety Ed Reed, linebackers Ray Lewis and Terrell Suggs and interior space-eaters Tony Siragusa and Haloti Ngata.

The 2006 Ravens led the NFL by allowing an average of just 12.1 points per game and held Peyton Manning's Indianapolis Colts to just five field goals in a 15–6 playoff loss.

Rex Ryan's defense has no name to put alongside his father's 46, but it is invoked in every NFL game on every weekend. Scrambling, amorphous defensive looks have become common. Hybrid players have become standard. The blitzing of quarterbacks has never been more at a premium. That is the influence of Rex Ryan's unnamed defense, a link in the chain between his father and the future.

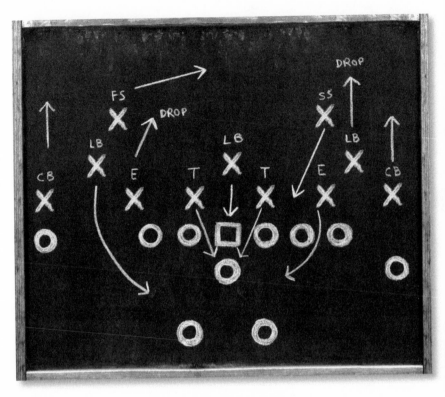

4–3 ZONE DOG

As first conceived, at least in part, by Bill Arnsparger in Miami with the early '70s Dolphins and later brought to full force by the Pittsburgh Steelers' defenses of the '90s, the zone blitz is designed to leave an offense uncertain as to where pressure on the quarterback might be coming from and to provide disguised zone pass coverage in those areas that would typically be left vacant by blitzers. On this play, from a 4–3 set, a linebacker blitzes from the right defensive edge. The middle linebacker also blitzes, along with the strong safety. But the defensive end drops back into the short curl zone, taking away the most obvious "hot read" from the quarterback.

CHAPTER 18

THE ZONE BLITZ

In 1983 Dick LeBeau and the Cincinnati Bengals hit on a defensive ploy that really worked. It still does

Tampa, Fla.
Feb. 1, 2009

I N ONE of the most important plays of the most important game of the NFL's 89th season, a 242-pound, shot put–shaped linebacker intercepted a pass on the final snap of the first half and returned it 100 yards for a touchdown. The play was a bizarre sight, as the Steelers' James Harrison staggered the final 10 yards into the end zone where he collapsed and lay exhausted from the effort of lugging his dense, powerful body the entire length of the field, a body clearly not designed for such work. But it was the beginning, not the end, of this long, operatic play that fits more significantly into football history.

The situation: With just over two minutes remaining in the first half of Super Bowl XLIII at Raymond James Stadium in Tampa, with the favored Steelers leading the Arizona Cardinals 10–7, Cards linebacker Karlos Dansby intercepted a Ben Roethlisberger pass and returned it to the Steelers' 34. In seven plays Arizona quarterback Kurt Warner moved the Cards to a first-and-goal at the Steelers' one-yard line with 18 seconds to play. It seemed a virtual certainty that the Cardinals would go into the halftime dressing room with a lead.

On first down the Cardinals lined up with Pro Bowl receivers Larry Fitzgerald and Anquan Boldin (who between them had caught passes for 42 touchdowns over the 2007 and '08 regular seasons), both to the left side of the formation, both split, with Boldin outside Fitzgerald. The Steelers had six men on the line of scrimmage—four standing and only two with a hand on the ground; but just before the snap three other defenders moved up close, into gaps, as if preparing for an all-out blitz. At the snap, from a stand-up right defensive end position, Harrison took a step forward.

In fact, Harrison was baiting Warner, giving the impression that he was blitzing, when he was actually planning to drop off into the middle of the field in a form of zone pass defense. The tactic is called a "zone blitz," a catchall phrase for any defense that blitzes from one area while dropping players—linemen, linebackers or defensive backs—into zone coverage in another area. These defenses are also called "zone dogs" (as in "red dogs," an old school name for blitzes) or "fire zones."

Kurt Warner, of course, knew all about them, and he knew that the Steelers and 71-year-old defensive coordinator Dick LeBeau loved them. "Pittsburgh lives off zone dogs," Warner had said in the spring before that season. "You see zone dogs everywhere, but Pittsburgh is so athletic and so skilled, they've really made it a part of their package. Against them, you're going to see it four, six, eight times a game. Against a lot of other teams, you might see it once."

In nearly 30 minutes of the Super Bowl the Steelers had not yet used a zone blitz. Warner took the snap, and the Steelers brought five rushers, not nine. But Warner was already convinced that he was going to be pressured heavily—he expected Harrison to rush—and needed to unload quickly. To Warner's left, Fitzgerald slipped outside and set a pick on Steelers' corner Deshea Townsend, allowing Boldin to cut inside, where he looked momentarily free at the goal line. "Your instinct in those situations is to throw hot," Warner had said earlier, meaning to throw quickly to a receiver in an area theoretically vacated by a blitzer. Following this instinct, Warner looked for Boldin running into the area from which Harrison had blitzed.

Except Harrison hadn't blitzed. He had turned his hips to the outside and rotated out of the box and into the curl-slant area. "I never saw him," Warner would say after the game. He delivered the ball toward Boldin. but instead it hit Harrison directly in the hands, and 15 painful seconds later, the Steelers had a 16–7 lead and Harrison had made what LeBeau later called "the greatest play in Super Bowl history." (The Steelers would need another great play—a toe-tapping catch by Santonio Holmes in the back corner of the end zone with just 35 seconds to play in the game—to secure a 27–23 victory and their record sixth Super Bowl championship.)

LeBeau, more than anyone, could appreciate Harrison's zone dog. The seeds of that play had been planted more than quarter-century earlier, when LeBeau embarked on a professional odyssey that would lead to a reinvention of defensive football.

March 2008

A PHONE rings, and the writer answers. A voice on the other end says, "This is Coach LeBeau. You want to talk about the zone blitz?" It was hard to tell if there was a question mark at the end of the sentence. Maybe his words were a statement rather than a query, but the topic on the table was, indeed, the zone blitz. A request had been made through the Steelers' media-relations department. There had been e-mails and phone calls. All declined. LeBeau didn't want to talk about himself. Finally, there had been a letter—old school—sent to LeBeau's office. It was the letter that prompted the phone call.

"I felt like I should get back to you," says LeBeau. "The problem is, I want to write my own book someday, and I'm afraid I won't have anecdotes left." That was amusing, and a little poignant too. If anybody has a football book in him, no matter how many stories he's already told, it's Dick LeBeau.

He continued, "Plimpton took all my good anecdotes." Of course he had. George Plimpton, the iconic journalist-author, essentially invented the genre of participatory sports journalism with *Paper Lion*, published in 1965. It was a brilliant, funny, self-deprecating account of Plimpton's experience as a "quarterback" at the Detroit Lions' '63 training camp. More than the personal recollection of an erudite, Harvard-educated writer, *Paper Lion* drew back the curtain on the world of the professional football player. While far less scandalous than Jim Bouton's *Ball Four*, the bawdy baseball memoir published in '70, it was every bit as insightful. When Plimpton arrived at the Lions' camp in 1963, LeBeau was already established as one of the best defensive backs in the NFL, a 6' 1", 185-pound starting right cornerback (a position he would hold for 171 consecutive games, from '59 to '71). He was a part of a Lions team that had gone 11–3 the previous year and finished second to Vince Lombardi's Packers in the Western Conference of the premerger NFL. LeBeau was also part of a truly outstanding defense that included future Pro Football Hall of Famers Joe Schmidt at linebacker, Dick (Night Train) Lane at cornerback and Yale Lary at safety, along with multi-time Pro Bowlers Alex Karras and Roger Brown (tackles), Wayne Walker (linebacker) and LeBeau himself.

LeBeau had come to Detroit from London, Ohio, by way of the Ohio State Buckeyes, where he started on Woody Hayes's 1957 national championship team. He was also just a little different from the average professional football player, as Plimpton observed in *Paper Lion*:

> LeBeau was from Ohio, with a pronounced midwestern twang, nasal and slow, which made the songs he put to his guitar quite incomprehensible, though fetching: gentle songs full of melancholy and poverty, one supposed, and love unrequited. He himself had a lady-killer reputation. Thin-hipped, built like a high school basketball player, his hair worn longer than most of the others', he was called Ricky, less a diminutive of Richard than derived from a crop of teenage movie stars and singers of the time, all of that name, whose manner and attitude he seemed to cultivate.

LEBEAU WAS different on the field too. He played at the opposite corner from Lane, one of the greatest and most instinctive defensive backs in the history of the game, whose 14 interceptions in his rookie year of 1952 as a member of the Los Angeles Rams still stands as an NFL single-season record (what is more remarkable is that Lane did it in 12 games). LeBeau, meanwhile, was more of a thinker, analyzing offenses and offensive players long before he began coaching against them. Plimpton described interviewing Lane about LeBeau's propensity for reading the strides of long-legged receivers and quoted Lane's response: "Well, that's Dickie-Bird for you. He's complex. He confirms and thinks on it about reading the receivers."

THAT REPUTATION for cerebral play was validated in LeBeau's first year of retirement, when Mike McCormack, head coach of the Eagles, hired LeBeau, 36, to coach special teams. He spent three years in that role before moving to Green Bay in 1976 under Bart Starr to coach defensive backs and then to Cincinnati under Forrest Gregg in '80 in the same capacity. The Bengals of the early '80s were a premier franchise, losing in the Super Bowl at the end of the '81 season to the 49ers 26–21 and then winning seven more games in the strike-abbreviated '82 season.

But LeBeau saw change coming. Here, a brief bit of history is in order. Throughout most of the 20th century, pass defense was man-to-man, with occasional double coverage. Zone defenses became prominent in the 1950s; Bill Walsh's short-passing, possession-based West Coast offense, born in '70 and cultivated through the ensuing decade, was the first air attack to exploit the moving voids and seams in the zone defense.

It was also one of the first offenses to use "hot reads," in which quarterbacks—like Kurt Warner a quarter century later—were conditioned to throw quickly to preassigned receivers when the defense blitzed or to exploit man-to-man single coverage. "The one thing you knew," says Steve Spurrier, who played quarterback in the NFL from 1967 through '76, "was that if you saw a blitz, you were getting man-to-man defense behind it. That didn't mean it was easy to deal with the blitz, but at least you knew what coverage you were going to get."

By the time Walsh's 49ers beat the Bengals in that Super Bowl at the end of the '81 season, it was obvious to football insiders that defenses would have to somehow adapt to match the Walsh offense—and quickly, or the blitz would be neutered.

LeBeau believed in pressure. It was in his DNA. (One of LeBeau's good friends, basketball coach Bob Knight, was a pal from their days at Ohio State. They often talked about ball pressure in their respective sports.) Says LeBeau, "When I was with the Lions, we ran an 11-up blitz, all 11 guys on the line of scrimmage. Wayne Walker was one of the best blitzers I've ever seen." But by the time he reached Cincinnati, LeBeau could see the new challenge. "At that point, around 1982 or '83, we were really looking for a way to get to the quarterback," he recalls. "But with some of the offenses that were being developed at that time, the quarterbacks were getting pretty good at throwing quickly when you blitzed."

LeBeau had already begun tinkering with new ways to attack the quarterback. He had all the support he needed from defensive coordinator Hank Bullough, a 3–4 defense pioneer who had fiddled around with elements of the zone blitz when he was with the Patriots from 1973 through '79. In '78 Bullough had used Mike Hawkins, a versatile 6' 2", 232-pound rookie linebacker, as the focal point of several zone blitz–type schemes. He was more than happy to let LeBeau try to work up some new schemes.

Before the 1983 season, LeBeau put in a coverage package in which the Bengals would show blitz, encouraging the quarterback to read man-to-man in the secondary. But instead of manning up his corners on the outside in straight one-on-one coverage, LeBeau had 14-year veteran corner Ken Riley "sit down" (hold his ground) and rotated a safety into zone coverage behind him. Before long, this would become a standard coverage, but at the time it was highly unusual. As soon as a quarterback read blitz, his assumption would be that Riley would be backpedaling to avoid getting beat deep, prompting the QB to throw quick and short, into Riley's short zone.

LeBeau happily recalls that first experimental zone blitz. "So there was this exhibition game and we just decided to try it. We ran the zone blitz and the quarterback just threw the ball straight to Ken Riley," he says at a Steelers training camp practice in the summer of 2009. "And I thought, hey, we might have something here." He smiles broadly. "Turns out we did."

LeBeau continued to play with the scheme throughout the Bengals' 7–9 season in '83. In the off-season, Forrest Gregg left the Bengals to become head coach at Green Bay and took Bullough with him. New Bengals head coach Sam Wyche gave LeBeau his first shot as defensive coordinator, and LeBeau made the zone blitz his top priority. First stop: Baton Rouge, where longtime NFL defensive guru Bill Arnsparger, 57, had taken the head coaching job at LSU.

LeBeau picks up the story. "I got off the airplane, drove straight over to Bill's office, walked in and started asking questions. I knew he had done some stuff in the past that was similar to what I thinking about."

And he was correct. Arnsparger, raised in Paris, Ky., had played his college football at Miami (Ohio), long known as a "coaching cradle" for the many coaches who were nurtured there; he took his first job at Ohio State, leaving two years before LeBeau arrived there in the fall of 1955. And now, almost 30 years later, LeBeau had come to LSU seeking Arnsparger's advice. "I remember the day Dick visited me like it was yesterday," says Arnsparger. "We were two guys talking football on a beautiful day in Baton Rouge. What could be better than that?"

Arnsparger's coaching history made him a perfect resource for LeBeau. While working at Kentucky from 1954 through '61, one of Arnsparger's colleagues had been Don Shula, who would become coach of the Baltimore Colts in '63. A year later, Shula hired Arnsparger as his defensive-line coach, and in '70, when Shula took over the Miami Dolphins, he took Arnsparger with him.

In '71, Arnsparger began using Dolphins linebacker Bob Matheson, a 6' 4" 238-pounder, as a defensive end who would sometimes drop off into pass coverage. The scheme left the Dolphins in a de facto 3–4 defense and also enabled them to zone-blitz by rushing the likes of Nick Buoniconti and Doug Swift from one side, along with three down linemen, while dropping Matheson into coverage.

"With Bob there, with linebacking skills," says Arnsparger, "we were able to rush five guys and cover with six. That's what you need to run a zone blitz. We could usually drop a linebacker into that slot zone, and that gave people a lot of problems." Arnsparger became progressively more creative, at times running double blitzes from the outside and dropping tackle Manny Fernandez, a brilliant athlete, into coverage. A year later the Dolphins went 17–0, winning the Super Bowl, and the following season won another.

Arnsparger wasn't finished. After spending three years as coach of the New York Giants from 1974 to '76, he went back to Miami for another eight years and built another solid Dolphins defense, known as the Killer B's for employing as many as seven starters whose last name began with B. Those Dolphins played in two more Super Bowls, though they lost both.

What had drawn LeBeau to Louisiana was the chance to tap Arnsparger's thinking behind the zone blitz. Two words stayed in his head. "Bill's catchphrase was that he wanted to get 'safe pressure,' on the quarterback," says LeBeau. "And that expression stuck with me because that was a very succinct way to summarize exactly what I was looking for. Safe pressure. I walked out the door saying those words to myself."

When he got back to Cincinnati, LeBeau made the zone blitz central to the Bengals' defensive philosophy. But it wasn't until 1986 that it truly took off, and it happened when the Bengals drafted 6' 3", 228-pound safety David Fulcher out of Arizona State.

"David Fulcher was a unique athlete," says LeBeau. "Very big for his position, but also very talented. Blitzing with him was one of the ways we expanded the possibilities of the fire zone, and it was very effective." In a play that LeBeau called Fulcher Two Stay, he had Fulcher, at strong safety, jump into the scrimmage box and blitz while the free safety slid into a two deep zone with a cornerback, and at least two other linebackers dropped off in coverage. In effect, Fulcher was a fifth linebacker in the Bengals' 3–4 scheme.

In 1988, Fulcher's third season and LeBeau's fifth as coordinator, the Bengals went back to the Super Bowl and again battled Walsh's 49ers to the final possession before losing 20–16.

By then, in the course of eight seasons, the offense-defense paradigm had been reversed; now it was offenses that needed to adapt, to counter the effectiveness of LeBeau's zone. "I always felt that we contributed greatly to the development of the run-and-shoot offense," says LeBeau. "Teams were just looking for quicker and quicker ways to attack, to the point where it might not even matter where the pressure was coming from. We showed teams the holes in their protection with what we were doing."

IN THE decade following the success of that Bengals' defense, other teams around the NFL, of course, began to install pieces of the zone blitz, including the New Orleans Saints of the late '80s. One of the Saints' defensive assistants in 1986 was 36-year-old Dom Capers. Like LeBeau, Capers was an Ohioan to his marrow: born in Cambridge, Ohio, grew up in Buffalo, Ohio, and played safety and linebacker at Mount Union in the state. (His roommate there was Larry Kehres, who would later become the coach at their alma mater and lead it to 10 national championships through 2008.)

Capers had coached 12 years at seven colleges before he joined head coach Jim Mora in 1984 as a defensive assistant with the Philadelphia Stars (who the next season became the Baltimore Stars) of the soon-to-be-defunct United States Football League. Mora left after two seasons and in '86 took Capers with him to New Orleans. Capers had experimented with elements of zone blitz schemes in the USFL, but in New Orleans, he discovered, the schemes themselves were often less critical—because the talent itself was so outstanding.

"During the time we were there," says Capers, "we had some of the best front-seven players in the NFL. Look at our linebackers: Pat Swilling and Rickey Jackson on the outside, Sam Mills and Vaughan Johnson inside. Two of our up-front pass rushers were Frank Warren and Jumpy Geathers. With those guys we could beat people one-on-one, and we did. We didn't have to get real creative."

Those Saints went to the playoffs after the '87, '90 and '91 seasons and averaged just under 10 wins a year from '86 to '91. In '92, Kansas City Chiefs defensive coordinator Bill Cowher was brought to Pittsburgh as head coach, and Cowher hired Capers as his defensive coordinator and then brought in none other than Dick LeBeau to coach his secondary, after LeBeau had been ousted in Cincinnati with head coach Wyche.

The two Buckeyes, Capers and LeBeau, put their heads and their experience together. "Dick had done more zone blitzing than I had," recalls Capers. "But I had done some too. We started talking, and it was really pretty exciting."

Less exciting was the Steelers' personnel. Pittsburgh had gone 7–9 the previous year. "Our pass rushers were not nearly as good as what we had in New Orleans," says Capers. "Three quarters of the way through that first season, we only had 19 sacks. We just weren't getting to the quarterback enough. It reached the point, late in that season, where Dick and I just said to each other, 'We've got to do something X's and O's–wise because our front seven guys are just not beating people one-on-one.'

"If you looked at our secondary," Capers continues, "we had some pretty good guys back there—Rod Woodson, Carnell Lake. So in the latter part of the season we started mixing in some zone pressures and getting more pressure on the quarterback. The secondary responded well, and the guys up front loved it because it was aggressive." The Steelers improved so significantly down the stretch that year, en route to an 11–5 record, that they finished No. 2 in the league in scoring defense.

In the off-season Capers and LeBeau committed totally to the zone blitz, hence giving birth to the nickname Blitz-burgh Steelers. The Steelers also added outside linebacker Kevin Greene and inside linebacker Chad Brown, upgrading their front seven.

Says Capers, "That second year we ended up doing a lot of zone pressuring. We started doing things like having a lineman step forward to occupy a blocker and then dropping back into coverage. And we found that offenses started to play us differently. Their linemen couldn't be as aggressive because they just didn't know if our guys were coming. So much of football is mental, and if you can make an offensive line passive, that's half the battle. Then if you can confuse them by dropping guys out into pass coverage when they think they're going to pass-rush, that's another big part of it."

Those seasons in the early '90s established the Steelers' defensive reputation that has lived on for nearly two decades. As a team the Steelers ascended through the postseason, from a playoff loss in the '93 season to a conference championship loss to the Chargers in '94 to a Super Bowl loss to the Cowboys ending the '95 season. "We jumped off the diving board with the zone blitz in Pittsburgh," says LeBeau. "And it turns out we could swim pretty well."

Capers moved on in 1995 when he was named head coach of the expansion Carolina Panthers. There he built his defense around veterans with experience in the zone blitz package. He brought in 36-year-old linebacker Sam Mills from New Orleans and, in his second season, Kevin Greene, then 34 years old, from Pittsburgh.

Success came quickly. The Panthers went 12–4 in '96, finishing second in the NFL in scoring defense and reaching the NFC Championship Game, where they ran into Brett Favre's Green Bay Packers and lost 30–13. The zone blitz had propelled them deeper into the postseason than any previous expansion team in the league's history.

"The newness of the scheme was what really made it fun in those years, with Pittsburgh and Carolina," says Capers. "Teams weren't ready for it. There were very good teams that had a lot of trouble with it. Miami had real problems, because Dan Marino had become so accustomed to making man-to-man reads that the fire zones really seemed to confuse him." LeBeau recalls talking to Marino after a game and asking him what reads he was making: "He said, 'I had no idea what I was reading.' "

Capers is a coach's coach, with 15 stops in his 38-year career—so far. His latest stop is Green Bay, where he became defensive coordinator in

2009. The zone blitz also rewarded LeBeau with a head coaching job, back with the Bengals in 2000. It didn't go well. Under LeBeau, the Bengals went 12–33 in three seasons. He was fired and spent a year in Buffalo before returning to Pittsburgh in 2004 as defensive coordinator, and there he has remained.

The Steelers have since won two Super Bowls and only once finished out of the NFL's top five teams in total defense. Eighteen years after first arriving in Pittsburgh, LeBeau is considered something of an icon as a defensive strategist. (He's also much loved by his players, to whom he recites *The Night Before Christmas*, from memory, every year in the locker room.)

Yet he remains too humble to talk freely about himself, and is fully humbled by success. "Everybody does it now," he says of his zone blitz. "And really, it's a joy to see how popular it is. Anybody who was around those teams in Cincinnati would feel the same way. And you'll never hear me say I was the first guy to do it. All I can say is that at the time, it was a pretty good idea."

It remains a pretty good idea, a staple of the game, undiminished by time or opposition.

THE TCU 4-2-5

The TCU Horned Frogs, once among the nation's football elite in the '30s and '40s under the revered Dutch Meyer, have returned to the upper ranks over the past decade largely on the strength of coach Gary Patterson's 4-2-5 defense. The scheme uses the extra defensive speed gained by replacing a linebacker with a fifth back. The quintessential fifth back is a strong safety–type who can be as effective in run support as in pass defense, giving the defense, in effect, two strong safeties that can attack forward or drop back, providing better and faster overall pursuit—critical in the modern game. At TCU, it is more than an occasional scheme; it is run on every defensive snap.

CHAPTER 19

SPREAD STOPPERS

Joe Lee Dunn uses a 3-3-5 defense, Gary Patterson uses a 4-2-5, both for the same reason: dread of the spread

Los Angeles, Calif.
Sept. 2, 1991

IT'S NOT unusual for college football coaches to use the spring of the year to pay visits to their peers. They are a notoriously generous lot, these coaches, and spring is their giving season, as they freely open their playbooks and film rooms to others who might line up against them in future years, all in the name of collegial courtesy. But when 44-year-old Joe Lee Dunn boarded a plane from Memphis to Los Angeles in the spring of 1991, his motivations were entirely different. He was scouting for the coming fall, and he was scared to death.

Dunn was beginning his third season at Memphis State under head coach Chuck Stobart, and the upcoming season's schedule included an opening game against Southern Cal on Labor Day afternoon in the storied L.A. Coliseum. It would be the first—and to this day the only—meeting between these two schools, one a foot soldier in the weekly college football wars, the other a titan.

Any national attention was focused on the fact that Memphis State was taking the matchup—or mis-matchup—largely for the $300,000 guarantee that USC was paying the Tigers for making the trip. But Dunn, the defensive coordinator, only wanted to know one thing: What the hell was his undermanned defense getting into? So he visited USC's spring workouts.

The team he saw on the practice field was not the USC of O.J. Simpson, Charles White and Marcus Allen. Nor was it Pete Carroll's USC, which would take off more than a decade later. Larry Smith was preparing for his fifth season as coach of the Trojans. He had relieved Ted Tollner, who won 26 games in four seasons—not good enough on the heels of the John McKay–John Robinson dynasties that had produced five national championships from 1962 through '78.

Smith had, so far, been better. His Trojans won 27 games in his first three seasons and went to three consecutive Rose Bowls. In 1990 they finished 8-4-1, including a loss to Michigan State in the John Hancock Bowl in the last game of the turbulent, two-year Todd Marinovich quarterback era.

That loss, and that season, were a harbinger of struggles ahead. But that mattered little to Dunn, who was accustomed to watching his players at Memphis State; to his eye, there was still plenty of talent out on that field in Los Angeles. "I was there for a few days," says Dunn, "and I saw those USC guys walking around, up close. They were even scarier that way than they were on film. Big, good-lookin' guys and all that. Mighty impressive. I went back to Memphis and told everybody, 'There's no way in the world we're going to beat those guys.' "

Dunn grew even more certain when he started game-planning for the Trojans with his own defense at Memphis. He had been a football coach for 21 years and had always played a five-man defensive front, usually in a 5-3-3 alignment: five linemen, three linebackers, three defensive backs. But Dunn looked at USC and saw too much speed to defend with five bulky defensive linemen; he just had too many slow-footed players and too few fast ones.

In his moment of need, he was struck by an idea. "I didn't think we could just line up and play against USC," recalls Dunn. "But I thought maybe we could run something that would confuse them. So here's what we did: We backed up the two defensive ends about seven yards off the line of scrimmage and about three yards outside the tight end, or wherever the tight end would normally be. We put those guys in space. Once I had the idea, it was a pretty easy transition to make."

In fact, it was jarring, a sea change in defensive scheming. But some minds accept risk more readily than others. Two decades earlier Dunn had coached a season of high school football in Georgia with a coach named Bob Nellums. "He did all kinds of crazy things," says Dunn. "He'd stand the whole defensive line up. Nobody with a hand on the ground. He was creative and changeable. I always remembered that."

Moving the defensive ends back and outside turned Memphis State's 5-3-3 into a 3-3-5, with those defensive ends acting essentially as hybrid linebacker–strong safeties. In the post-Marinovich era, USC was attempting to run some option football with quarterback Reggie Perry. Memphis State's alignment brought defenders in closer to the edge at the snap and filled open space on the field. It was not an immediate success. Before a half-full Coliseum, USC took a 10–3 halftime lead; Trojans tailback Mazio Royster rushed for 97 yards on 20 carries in the first 30 minutes.

But Memphis State owned the second half. USC failed to score again, making just three first downs in the first 20 minutes as Memphis took control. The Tigers put up 21 consecutive points to win 24–10. The upset reverberated through the college football world. There had always been upsets, but in the fall of 1991, college football was still a game of haves and have-nots. The day after the defeat USC coach Smith would call the loss "perhaps the biggest upset, disappointment and embarrassment this university and football program has ever had."

For Dunn, it was, of course, equally shocking. "Really a remarkable victory," he says, nearly two decades later, still amazed by what took place that afternoon in Los Angeles. But it was something more than an upset. It was a small window into the future of the college game, where long-held principles would give way to a new set of rules. Nevertheless, the next weekend in Memphis, the Tigers played host to Mississippi and Memphis State went back to Joe Lee Dunn's 5-3-3 defense. "But I didn't forget about that USC game," says Dunn. "I put that 3-3-5 in the back of my mind."

Abilene, Texas
November 2009

MAYBE THIS is the last stop for Joe Lee Dunn. It is a Wednesday in November, and another season is coming to a close, his 39th as a football coach. He has landed as defensive coordinator at tiny NCAA Division III

McMurry University (enrollment: 1,500) in Abilene, where Hal Mumme is now the coach. In 2007, when Mumme, the erstwhile pioneer of the spread passing game, was named head coach at New Mexico State he felt himself slipping down the coaching ladder he'd once climbed. Dunn had just been fired a year before back at Memphis after three seasons under coach Tommy West. So Mumme, once bedeviled at Kentucky by Dunn's varied and relentless blitzes at Mississippi State, had hired Dunn to run the Aggies' defense.

After four years at New Mexico State, Mumme was fired, and now had dropped another rung, to McMurry. On this day there is but a sliver of hope for a successful end to the season: McMurry had begun the campaign with four consecutive losses then turned it around with four consecutive wins before falling at home to Hardin-Simmons 21–10. In a few days the season would end 489 miles to the east in Pineville, La., against a very good team at Louisiana College. "I think we've got a chance to win," Dunn says, "but I'm afraid the guys are kind of deflated after last week, losing at home to our rival and all. So I don't know . . ."

It's a grueling bus ride, nearly eight hours each way, across Texas and over the border into Louisiana. And, sure enough, McMurry gets pasted, 55–13. For much of the long, quiet ride home, Dunn will settle in and read a book, but he takes a little time to reflect on all the years gone by. "I started out this way," he says. "I guess maybe I'll end up this way."

He had been a high school quarterback and defensive back in the mid-1960s at Columbus (Ga.) High, where he played under former Auburn All-America Jim Pyburn. "You talk about mean as a snake, that was Coach Pyburn," says Dunn. "But he was a heck of a football coach." Dunn played in college at Chattanooga, then coached at several high schools before starting his long college career with a nine-year run (1971–79) back at his alma mater, Chattanooga.

Dunn coached low-down, nasty defense at every level. He pushed bodies up to the line of scrimmage, filling the box with tacklers. He blitzed like crazy. "But I got to be honest with you," he says. "People didn't throw it around all that much, didn't spread out all those wide receivers." From 1980 through '86, he coached at the University of New Mexico, the last four seasons as head coach. Every year the Lobos played Brigham Young. And there Dunn saw how different the game could be. Brigham Young did throw it around and did spread out all those wide receivers. And Dunn decided he would not sit back and watch. The '80 Lobos beat BYU 25–21 and pounded Jim McMahon. "By the end of the game," says Dunn, "Jim was throwing the ball at his linemen's feet just to get rid of it." New Mexico lost to Brigham Young in each of the subsequent six years, sometimes by huge margins (66–21 in 1983), sometimes by very small margins (31–30 in '86). But Dunn never stopped bringing the heat. "Joe Lee Dunn was a blitzing guy," says Robbie Bosco, the Brigham Young starting quarterback during three of those seasons, from '83 through '85. "You knew what you were going to get, and you knew you were going to get it all day."

Dunn began to understand that creativity and speed were going to be the new keys to defensive survival.

He was not alone in reaching this revelation. When little-known Oklahoma State head coach Jimmy Johnson took over at the University of Miami in 1984 (in the season immediately after Howard Schnellenberger had guided the Hurricanes to a stunning upset of Nebraska in the '83 Orange Bowl to win the national title), he took a good look around and promptly reached into the deep well of speed and athletic talent in Florida's high schools. Stressing speed over size in his recruiting, Johnson began changing the way positions were deployed, shrinking the acreage of the field.

"We took safeties and made them linebackers; we took linebackers and made them defensive linemen," says Butch Davis, who came to Miami with Johnson from Oklahoma State as the 'Canes defensive-line coach. "Jimmy wanted to make every position faster. It was all about speed." It was a philosophy that helped Johnson win a national title in the 1987 season, and when it worked for Johnson at Miami, every college coach in the country, it seemed, tried to follow suit.

Dunn, meanwhile, kept moving: Two years at South Carolina in 1987–88 (it was there that his best friend, head coach and former New York Giants flanker Joe Morrison, died of a heart attack; Dunn found him on the floor of the locker room shower). He went on to Memphis and that epic upset of USC, then to Mississippi (where the Rebels led the nation in defense in '93), then to Arkansas for a single year, in '95. He landed at Mississippi State in the spring of 1996 and would spend seven years in Starkville under coach Jackie Sherrill. There Dunn finally went fully back to the 3-3-5 for the first time since that Labor Day in L.A. in 1991. He did it because, like Jimmy Johnson, he wanted to put fast people in space. But he also did it because he just couldn't find enough big defensive linemen to play a 4–3 or a 5-3-3.

"About the time I got to Mississippi State," says Dunn, "it started to be where there were not a lot of schools in the country that could get big ol' defensive linemen. It's hard to find those big guys that are really good. And if you're at Mississippi State and you do find one of them, Florida is probably going to come in and take him away from you. Or Texas. Or somebody like that. But if you're willing to go to a 3-3-5, look, you can get good people on the field. When you're out recruiting, everybody's got linebackers. Everybody's got strong safeties. Put those guys out there and let them make plays for you."

Dunn helped turn Starkville, Miss., into every other SEC team's worst nightmare. In 1996 the Bulldogs beat No. 8 Alabama, and a year later they knocked off No. 11 Auburn. By '98 Mississippi State was a big dog, advancing to the SEC title game and a loss to Tennessee in the Georgia Dome. In 1999 Dunn's defense led the nation, giving up a paltry 222 yards a game. All of this Dunn did with his bold 3-3-5, using five defensive backs—two corners, two strong safeties and a free safety.

Dunn worked his scheme relentlessly. He spent one off-season learning how to pressure with a three-man front, getting schooled on slants and stunts by Michigan head coach Gary Moeller, who had been Bo Schembechler's defensive coordinator. He worked to recruit free safeties who could tackle; in the 3-3-5, the free safety is the often the first man to the ball.

It was serendipitous that while Dunn was going all-in with the 3-3-5 on his side of the ball, spread formations were proliferating throughout college football on the offensive side. The 3-3-5, it turns out, is well-suited to defending the modern spread. In the 3-3-5, the down linemen almost always slant left or right, and behind them—often "stacked" directly behind them—the linebackers fill gaps left by the slanting linemen. Consequently, offensive linemen are forced to push deep downfield to block in the running game, often tipping off the direction of the play with their movements in space long after the snap.

The two outside defensive backs act as conventional corners, but the three other DBs can play either zone against four wideouts or straight man-to-man against five wides. (Typically, if Dunn sees five wides, he's blitzing six defenders against five blockers and gambling that he can get to the quarterback before one of those five wides beats somebody.)

It would be an exaggeration to say that the 3-3-5 can *shut down* the modern spread. From 1991, when Dunn first put those linemen in space, through 2007, passing yardage increased in major college football by more than 43 yards a game and scoring by nearly five points a game. The 3-3-5 is a defensive answer, but not a solution. "In the last 10 or 12 years, somebody decided that fans like scoring," says Dunn. "They let offensive players hold now. They don't let defensive backs hit receivers after they release. I don't like all of that, but I suppose it's good for the game. We're just doing the best we can."

And Dunn's phone never stops ringing. "You wouldn't believe how much it rings," he says. "People calling and asking about the 3-3-5. I just tell 'em what I know."

Fort Worth, Texas
November 2009

A CAR trolls the Dallas/Ft. Worth Metroplex; TCU head coach Gary Patterson is at the wheel. Patterson, too, is just doing the best he can, and that's mighty good in the autumn of 2009. He is three days away from a regular-season-ending 51–10 trouncing of New Mexico, which will leave his Horned Frogs with a 12–0 record and their first perfect season in 71 years. "We can play with anybody," Patterson will say after that game. He has put TCU into the middle of the BCS discussion, and as messy and convoluted as that discussion can be, it's important that the boundaries of the system be tested by schools once regarded as outsiders. Like TCU.

As Patterson guided TCU onto that hallowed ground, he was 49 years old. At the same time that Joe Lee Dunn, 14 years Patterson's elder, was contemplating a 500-mile bus ride across Texas and Louisiana and the approaching end of his career, Patterson's name was surfacing in connection with the soon-to-be-vacant coaching job at Notre

Dame. Different men in very different stages of their careers, yet they came from a similar place in the small world of football coaching.

In Patterson's tenure as defensive coordinator and head coach (following the departure of his mentor, Dennis Franchione), the Horned Frogs have won 103 regular season games in twelve years; they won four consecutive bowl games from 2005 through '08 and crashed the party of college football royalty; they have won with Texas talent and with all the organizational efficiency and passion any rising program must have. They have also won with the 4-2-5 defense. It is but a distant cousin to Dunn's 3-3-5, but it was founded on similar principles.

Patterson, like so many of his peers, has risen unglamorously through the coaching ranks: Before landing at TCU, he made 10 stops in 16 years at the likes of Tennessee Tech and Cal Lutheran. He even coached a few months in 1992 in the quickly defunct Professional Spring Football League with the Oregon Lightning Bolts. He is a small-town football junkie from Rozel, Kans. (pop. 156), divorced with three sons, now remarried. He plays a mean guitar. He also earned his football degree on a tough road, playing two years of strong safety and linebacker in junior college and two years as a walk-on at Kansas State in '80 and '81 on teams that won six games in those two seasons.

Here is a good example of how coaching alliances tend to form: During Patterson's junior year at Kansas State, Dennis Franchione was a member of coach Jim Dickey's staff; Dick Bumpas would join the staff in '81. Both Bumpas and Patterson would work with Franchione at Tennessee Tech in '83 and '84. In '88 Franchione hired Patterson to coach linebackers at Pittsburg State University. Four years later, in the fall of 1992, Patterson landed at Utah State, along with Bumpas.

The Aggies then played in the Big West Conference with the likes of New Mexico State and UNLV. They played Brigham Young and Utah out of the conference. In any given season they were going to see far more passes than runs. Like Joe Lee Dunn nearly a decade earlier, Patterson and Bumpas had to figure out how to stop the passing game.

"We had to develop, we had to change," says Patterson. "The passing game was changing everything. When Coach Bump and I got to Utah State with Charlie Weatherbie, that's when we really started doing things differently." In the 4-4-3 Patterson and Bumpas used two cornerbacks and one deep safety. In the Big West they went more often to what would become the 4-2-5, with five defensive backs instead of three. As with Dunn's defense, three were strong-safety types, two were corners. As with Jimmy Johnson's defense, the 4-2-5 put more speedy athletes on the field, the better to play in space and attack the passing game.

In Patterson's second year at Utah State the Aggies rebounded from a 1–5 start to finish 7–5. After Utah State slipped to 3–8 the following season, Patterson followed Weatherbie to Navy for a season. Franchione then hired Patterson at New Mexico for '96 and '97 before getting the TCU job and handing the defense to Patterson. Three years later coach Fran was gone, and Patterson was in charge. In 2004 he brought Dick Bumpas back as his coordinator. The Patterson-Bumpas alliance was rejoined, and for the greater good of the Horned Frogs.

Patterson-has run the 4-2-5 for 12 years in Forth Worth. "It fits with five-receiver offenses," says Patterson, "because you've already got five defensive backs in the game." But it has endured its growing pains. In 2004 Patterson's fourth year as head coach, Texas Tech, with Mike Leach's precision spread, beat the Frogs 70–35 in Lubbock. Two years later Tech returned the game in Fort Worth, and TCU held the high-flying Red Raiders without a touchdown in a 12–3 victory. Patterson and Bumpas aggressively zone-blitzed Tech out of the 4-2-5 and just as aggressively mixed coverages behind the blitzes.

"Let me put it this way," says Leach. "I wasn't real impressed with Patterson's 4-2-5 when we put 70 points on 'em. But I was pretty impressed when they held us to three points. That doesn't happen too often."

It should be noted that the TCU team that gave up 70 points was a 5–6 team; the team that gave up three points was a much more talented 11–2 team. Both played the 4-2-5, but the better team played a more evolved version. As any coach will remind you, the quality of the athletes deeply influences the effectiveness of the system.

"A lot of people play the 4-2-5 now," says Patterson. "But nobody runs it like we do. Over the years we've made changes. Our answer to any offense used to be: We'll just blitz one more [defender] than you can block. That's not our only answer anymore. We've evolved. We can zone-blitz you out of a two-deep shell. We can zone-blitz you out of a three-deep shell. We'll never leave ourselves in a single high free safety. And we will always play with great leverage and speed."

Leverage is a vital word in the lexicon of modern defense and essential to the Patterson-Bumpas philosophy. Patterson explains leverage in simple terms: "If [a TCU defender] starts deeper than [an offensive player], you don't ever let him get deeper than you. If you start outside someone, you don't let him get outside you. If you start inside, you don't let him get inside you."

When Texas Tech scored those 10 touchdowns on TCU in '04, Patterson says his defense was unprepared for yet another leap of offensive evolution. "The passing game changed again," Patterson says. "They weren't just throwing it a lot and spreading you out, but everybody went to a three-step passing game. Three steps, pump fake, throw." Offensive plays were suddenly unfolding more quickly. Filling space was no longer sufficient in the 4-2-5; TCU had to close down that space quickly and make sure tackles on receivers, or the yards-after-catch would accrue like high interest. "We had to sit down [cover tightly] on some routes; we had to zone-blitz a little more," says Patterson. "We went out on the road in the spring and learned from other teams, and we added everything. You've got to do that. You've got to leave your ego at the door. Look, all of us as defensive coaches would like to just get in our base defense and be better than the other team's offense. But offenses are just too good.

"Here's the way I figure it," says Patterson. "Let's say an offense runs 60 plays, which is about average for a game. You're gonna need a better call than them on about 30 of those plays. That takes a lot of work, a lot of preparation, and every offense is different. Texas Tech plays the spread; Air Force runs the option."

There is another factor. A common axiom in recruiting (and drafting) is that teams select the best athletes and find a way to use them. Patterson dismisses that thinking. He and Bumpas have been running the 4-2-5 for nearly two decades and know what it takes to play each position in the scheme and play them well. They look for certain key qualities, including versatility. For instance, 6' 3", 257-pound All-America defensive end Jerry Hughes, a senior in 2009, had been a high school tailback, quick and agile. "You recruit to fill a certain role," says Patterson. "You can't just grab athletes and hope they fit."

Modern defense is a game of survival. It is rare to win by shutting down an opponent, inconceivable to win by shutting down a dozen. As a defensive coach, especially when, like Patterson, you're bouncing to a new job almost every year, you learn to understand the realities. "All you're trying to do is get the offense back in the huddle," says Patterson. "Not kicking off."

DOUBLE A BLITZ VS. SLIDE PROTECT RIGHT

Popularized in the mid-2000s by the Philadelphia Eagles, the Double A Gap blitz puts extraordinary pressure on the offensive line and forces protection adjustments that limit offensive possibilities. Two inside linebackers line up on either side of the offensive center (in the "A gaps"), both as if preparing to blitz. Whether they actually blitz or not, the offense must call a protection change to block them, which can open up other holes for blitzers from other angles. In this diagram the offensive line opts for a "slide protection" to its right to cover the two linebackers, but it leaves itself vulnerable to the backside defensive end who gets a free run at the quarterback.

CHAPTER 20

DOUBLE A GAP BLITZ

All the late nights in Jim Johnson's office paid off in what may be the ultimate defensive weapon—so far

East Rutherford, N.J.
Sept. 30, 2007

THE 2007 New York Giants had risen from the dead. They had opened the season with consecutive losses to Dallas and Green Bay, games in which their defense gave up a total of 80 points. In Week 3 they had trailed Washington 17–3 at halftime, only to rally to a desperate 24–17 victory that, in essence, kept their season viable, given that the long-term prognosis for NFL teams opening 0–3 is exceptionally poor. But it was a week later in creaky Giants Stadium that the team's season—which would climax with an upset win over the unbeaten New England Patriots in Super Bowl XLII—truly turned.

Their opponents that Sunday night were the Philadelphia Eagles, who had also recovered from an 0–2 start with a 56–21 destruction of the Detroit Lions. The core of the Eagles' 2004 NFC championship team was still in place, Donovan McNabb still the quarterback. The Eagles could not have imagined that they would enter the NFL record book that evening, but when the night was over, the Giants had tied an NFL record with 12 quarterback sacks, including a team-record six by fifth-year defensive end Osi Umenyiora. "And it wasn't just the six sacks he got," Giants linebacker Antonio Pierce said that day. "He probably caused the other six sacks too."

In the short view, perhaps, it was just one man's incredible performance. But in the longer view, the last day of September 2007 was one of those moments when football evolution, generally a gradual unfolding of innovation and change, reaches critical mass and surges forward.

The Giants defense that took down McNabb 12 times was coached by first-year defensive coordinator Steve Spagnuolo, who dialed up an endless array of blitzes to confuse the Eagles' offensive line, including, among the victims, substitute left tackle Winston Justice, who was playing for the injured Tra Thomas that day. Justice, who would become a starter, remembers the game all too painfully. "It seemed like they came from everywhere that day," he says. "It wasn't one guy or one blitz."

But it was one scheme that set the tone: the Double A Gap Blitz, in which two linebackers blitz—or threaten to blitz—the quarterback from positions on the left and right shoulders of the offensive center (the "A" gaps), trying to get immediate pressure via the shortest route and forcing the offense into a series of quick and potentially dangerous decisions. "We ran it a bunch of times in that game, with Antonio Pierce and Kawika Mitchell in the A gaps," recalls Spagnuolo. "It presented some problems for the Eagles, obviously."

The Giants' defensive game plan had been devised just that week, but the foundation was laid eight years earlier when Spagnuolo was hired as a defensive quality control assistant—the bottom of the coaching food chain—for the Eagles. The head coach was Andy Reid. The defensive coordinator was 57-year-old Jim Johnson. It was Johnson who would teach Spagnuolo defense, and influence the entire league in the first decade of the new century.

Columbia, Mo.
September 1959

THE DOUBLE A Gap is a product of many elements in the sport that came before it, but it was crystallized in one man's brainstorm.

Upon his arrival at the University of Missouri in the fall of 1959, coming from his home in Maywood, Ill., Jim Johnson played both ways—quarterback and safety—on a good freshman team, then joined the varsity under coach Dan Devine for the best three-year run in school history.

The Tigers went 11–0 in 1960, won the Big Eight title and beat Navy 21–14 in the Orange Bowl to finish ranked No. 5 in the nation; Johnson was a sophomore safety and backup quarterback. A year later he started at safety on a 7-2-1 team whose two losses were by a combined total of eight points; as a senior he was the starting quarterback when Mizzou went 8-1-2 and beat Georgia Tech in the Bluebonnet Bowl. In that senior year of '62, Johnson played in a backfield that included future NFL personnel executive Bill Tobin (Johnson's best friend) and future pro players Andy Russell (who would star at linebacker for the Pittsburgh Steelers) and Johnny Roland (who played eight years at running back in the NFL with the Cardinals and the Giants).

That team pounded opponents by running out of the Delaware Wing T. "We ran the power sweep all day," says Tobin. Johnson attempted a mere 33 passes in his entire senior season, completing 12. Tobin was the Tigers' leading receiver, with three catches. But because Johnson had been a defensive player the year before, he had seen football both from the deep secondary and from the offensive backfield, leaving him ideally qualified to understand certain nuances of the sport. "He was always very observant," says Tobin. "He understood everything he was seeing out there."

After two years fighting unsuccessfully for a spot in the NFL, Johnson was named the first head coach at Missouri Southern State College, building the program in 1967 and fielding its first team in '68. He subsequently spent four years at Drake, four years at Indiana and seven at Notre Dame, where Devine was the head coach. Johnson's first NFL job was from 1986 to '93 with the Cardinals, where his mentor was the respected but conservative Fritz Shurmur. When Johnson went to the Indianapolis Colts in the mid-'90s, his defensive philosophy took a sharp turn. Frustrated at getting nickel-and-dimed on long drives by the evolving West Coast offense, Johnson began conceiving unorthodox blitzes.

On Nov. 16, 1997, the 0–10 Colts, struggling with injuries, knocked off the defending Super Bowl champion Packers 41–38 at the RCA Dome in Indianapolis. Johnson blitzed all day, and his defense gave up 441 yards in offense but also sacked Brett Favre three times, intercepted two passes and left a lasting impression on Green Bay assistant coach Andy Reid. "We scored a lot of points that day, but Jim destroyed our protections with his blitzes," says Reid. "I told myself that day, If I'm ever lucky enough to get a head coaching job in this league, that guy is going to be my defensive coordinator."

Two years later Reid was hired to coach the Eagles and made good on his promise, hiring Johnson, then 57, as defensive coordinator. They would work together for a decade, an eternity in the high-pressure, high-turnover NFL. Johnson would die in July of 2009 of complications from melanoma; by then he and Reid had made the playoffs seven times, and reached the Super Bowl at the end of the 2004 season.

On a December morning in 2009, Reid sat in an office at the Eagles' headquarters and recalled his friend and colleague. "The first time I met Jim was in Hawaii at the Pro Bowl, and it was before that game in Indianapolis," said Reid. "We were at the pool at the hotel and our families were there, and I just went up and introduced myself.

"Right from the beginning," says Reid, "Jim was real. From a coaching standpoint, I didn't want to get in the way of his creativity. Jim was a brilliant guy. And for me, as a young coach [Reid was 40 when he took the job], Jim supported everything I was doing. It was never about offense versus defense. It was always about us. I probably did some things that Jim was thinking, Holy Toledo, what's this guy doing? But he never said anything like that."

Johnson installed multiple blitzes as soon as he arrived. He focused most of his pregame preparation on an opponents' pass protections and designing blitzes to exploit their weaknesses. "Jim wasn't worried about what teams did in the running game or how they ran pass routes," says Spagnuolo. "Instead, he studied protections and attacked them." Johnson's peers chided him about his blitz-crazy schemes. They told him it was his "retirement defense," saying that because he was getting up in age, he didn't mind taking risks—he'd be retiring soon anyway.

He spent time talking to offensive line coaches and struck up a particular friendship with Eagles O-line coach Juan Castillo. "Jim and Juan would get together all the time and talk about pass protections," says Reid, "and then Jim would go back down to his office and create the blitz."

On the practice field Johnson was tough on players. He despised mental errors. "My first minicamp as a rookie, I was supposed to blitz on this particular play," says Eagles strong safety Quintin Mikell, who arrived in Philly in 2003. "Well, I'm trying to learn the city and my teammates and the defensive system, and I didn't blitz. I figured it would be O.K. It was not O.K. Jim came up to me, yelling and cursing me out: 'Don't you know what you're supposed to be doing there? You're supposed to be on a fucking blitz!' Man, he gave it to me. But I'll tell you what else: If you got beat because the offense made a great play, he would not take you down. He understood that sometimes the offense makes a play."

Says Spagnuolo, who worked under Johnson, "He was hard on players and hard on coaches, but he had a heart bigger than you can imagine. He was tough on everybody because he was trying to get us ready for what we were going to face on Sunday."

The Double A Gap came in 2001. It was Johnson's ultra-aggressive extension of everything he'd been doing, first conjured when Johnson asked himself this question: Instead of a single blitzer on the edge or a single blitzer in the middle, why not load up the middle of the formation? The first time Johnson called it in a game, Eagles defensive tackle Darwin Walker came unblocked for a sack. From 2000 to '08 the Eagles had 390 sacks, second in the NFL. In '07 Spagnuolo moved on to the Giants as defensive coordinator and built on the Double A, using it as a foundation for the pressure defense that would sack Tom Brady five times and keep him under siege all night in the Giants' 17–14 upset win in Super Bowl XLII.

"The thing about the Double A," says Eagles linebacker Jeremiah Trotter, who was with the team when Johnson installed the scheme and rejoined them in '09 for his third tour, "is that it doesn't really have a major weakness."

JIM JOHNSON was gone before the 2009 season began, having passed away shortly before the Eagles broke training camp in Bethlehem, Pa. But his legacy was firmly established. NFL defense had become a game not of whether to blitz, but of which blitz to use. "Right now, in the NFL, it's blitzkrieg," said Washington Redskins offensive line coach Joe Bugel, a 35-year league coaching veteran, in the fall of 2009. "If you're going to have your quarterback throw out of seven-step drop, you better have about 12 offensive linemen."

The Double A Gap Blitz is one of the most popular among many blitz options for aggressive defenses (which now means *all* defenses). It usually begins with the defense in "nickel personnel," or five defensive backs. There are also usually four down linemen and two linebackers in a 4-2-5 configuration (although it can be run from various other sets). As the offense reaches the line of scrimmage, the two linebackers move menacingly into the two A gaps. If the quarterback is under center, the 'backers can probably smell his breath, and he theirs. "At that point it's mental gymnastics," says former Raiders and Bucs head coach Jon Gruden. "There's no doubt there's going to be some penetration in the middle if they blitz, and it's going to mess with your blocking schemes."

The offense has several options, none of them ideal.

• Gap (or squeeze) protection, in which both guards block down inside, putting three big bodies on the two blitzing linebackers. This, however, forces the offensive tackles to block down as well, in order to pick up the two defensive tackles, and it leaves some combination of running backs and tight ends to deal with edge-rushing defensive ends like Dwight Freeney, Jared Allen or Elvis Dumervil. "They're trying to create a negative one-on-one matchup with your halfback," says Broncos quarterback Kyle Orton.

• Slide protection, in which the entire offensive line slides one way, with the center picking up one blitzer and one guard picking up the other. The same problem results with one defensive end left rushing against a running back or, at best, a tight end or H-back.

• Straight protection, in which the center takes one blitzer, and the other one is allowed a free release to the running back, who must make a key block in the quarterback's lap. "This blitz has changed what you need in a running back," says Bugel. "He's got to be able to pass-block, or you really can't have him on the field."

Even if the back stops the blitzing linebacker, his involvement in that block prevents him from helping out on any other pass rusher. "You like to have your running back chip the defensive end, stick an elbow in the guy's ribs off the edge," says Gruden. "But if the defense shows a Double A Gap, that running back is going to be too late to chip, so you're one-on-one with Dumervil or Freeney on the outside."

Another consideration: It's perilous to leave the quarterback under center. "It's imperative that you get into the shotgun, to give the quarterback some breathing room," says former Giants head coach and Ravens offensive coordinator Jim Fassel. "But you really need to know what situations you might see it in, because it's hard to check to the 'gun."

The most devilish aspect of the Double A is that the linebackers don't even need to blitz in order to make the play effective. "And you can't be sure," says Gruden. "Defenses aren't stupid. Those linebackers will get up there in the A gaps, but they won't have blinking red lights on their helmets with signs saying, 'I'm coming.' " Because the Double A threatens to bring pressure so close to the quarterback and so quickly, the offense must adjust to one of the above protections on the assumption that the A gap rushers are going to blitz.

"Once those two linebackers are down inside, [the offense has] got to deal with them and tip their hand," says Mikell. "That's the whole thing with the Double A, make them adjust and then attack." Empty backfield sets, with five wide receivers, make it difficult to adjust, and so are clearly impractical against teams that favor the Double A.

There are numerous other variations of this blitz. In '07, Spagnuolo rotated defensive ends Justin Tuck and Umenyiora into the A gaps and linebackers Pierce and Mitchell to the edge, creating an even more daunting mismatch—Tuck or Umenyiora on a running back or center—on the inside. The Giants called that combination Bombs. Other teams have dropped both 'backers into coverage and rushed a safety late, after the offense has committed to countering the A gap rushers.

The best way to exploit the Double A is to effectively block it, a difficult proposition. Or, says Gruden, "If you're using it against a CEO-type quarterback, like a Peyton Manning or Drew Brees, who understands how to pick up blitzes, you can have problems because you're short of personnel in coverage and they'll get rid of the ball quickly."

Says Trotter, "Teams run quick screens, slants, things like that, because normal pass routes take too long and the pressure is right on the quarterback. Jim Johnson always told us, 'You take away great receivers by getting in the quarterback's face.'"

THEY ECHO his messages like that in Philadelphia. Around the league they copy his plays. Johnson would appreciate that. During game week he could always be found in his office long after practice, working the coordinator's customary hours, searching for seams in somebody's offense. "He brought an energy and an enthusiasm to figuring things out," says Reid. "The players couldn't wait to hear how Jim was going gash 'em this week."

POWER RUN RIGHT (NO HUDDLE)
VS. DIME DEFENSE

The '80s Cincinnati Bengals used the no-huddle more often and more effectively than any team before or since. Coach Sam Wyche says he had great success by going to a quick snap on a power run immediately after converting a third-and-long against a dime (six defensive backs) defense. The ploy here is to quickly run two tight ends onto the field and remove two wide receivers (from the previous play), then line up in a two–tight end formation (though any power running formation could be used) before the defense can change personnel. The defense is still stuck with six DBs and just one linebacker, a weak alignment against a power run.

CHAPTER 21

THE NO-HUDDLE OFFENSE

Wicky Wacky Wyche took the two-minute offense and told Boomer to use it *every* minute

New York, N.Y.
Dec. 28, 1958

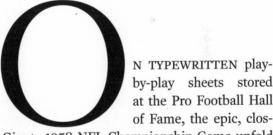

ON TYPEWRITTEN play-by-play sheets stored at the Pro Football Hall of Fame, the epic, closing minutes of the Colts-Giants 1958 NFL Championship Game unfold bloodlessly in a series of brief descriptions. Beginning here, on the third play of Baltimore's 86-yard, game-tying, fourth-quarter drive:

BALTIMORE

3-10-C14 (third-and-10 at the Colts' 14) Unitas hits Moore over center for 11.

1-10-C25 Unitas misses Dupre on long pass.

2-10-C25 Unitas passes to Berry, who runs for 25. 1:04 left.

1-10-50 Unitas passes to Berry on left sideline for 15.

1-10-G35 Unitas passes to Berry on left side for 22.

1-10-G13 Myhra kicks 20 yd FG with 07 seconds left.

BALTIMORE 17, NEW YORK 17

Reichichar kicks off tok [sic] Maynard in end zone, returns 18.

NEW YORK

I-IO-GI8 Conerly sneaks for no gain. End of Regulation game.

SUDDEN DEATH PLAYOFF PERIOD

THIS GAME, which the Colts would win in overtime 23–17, has long been described as the event that propelled pro football into its place as an all-consuming entertainment industry in the 21st century. It was a perfect confluence of sport, drama and television, portending the formula that would make football such ideal mass-market programming in the years that followed.

It is likely that professional football would have arrived where it lives today regardless of what took place on that afternoon and early evening on the hard ground of Yankee Stadium. The path might have been more circuitous, and taken longer, but in all certainty the NFL would have eventually captured America and America would have eventually become enraptured by the NFL.

Still, the process was helped significantly on that night in New York by the remarkable performance of Baltimore quarterback John Unitas and by his execution of the Colts' hurry-up offense—as it was called even back then—over Baltimore's last five plays from scrimmage in regulation time. Old-school NFL players will tell you that the two-minute drill, in which teams attempt to move quickly down the field, running a maximum number of plays in a minimum amount of time (often without huddling), had been a part of the game long before Unitas displayed it in the nation's living rooms.

"Bobby Layne was in the NFL when I came into the league in 1959," says Dick LeBeau, who played in the NFL from '59 through '72 before becoming one of the league's most respected coaches. "He was a master of the comeback, using the clock in the fourth quarter. Otto Graham [the Hall of Fame QB who retired after the '55 season] was the same way; I remember watching him when I was in college and hearing about him from other players in the league. Y.A. Tittle [who retired in '64 after a 17-year career] could also take a team down the field at the end of the game."

But it was Unitas who turned the no-huddle, two-minute offense into theater, and he did it most dramatically in the '58 championship game. Twice during the final drive Unitas called two plays in the huddle, and twice the Colts lined up immediately after completions and ran another play without calling time out. It was standard procedure for any football team trying to rally at the end of a game with little time left, but it was Unitas's cool and precision in such a big event in such a grand venue that thrilled the audience tuning in on TV.

Here was football played with breathtaking urgency. Baseball, the undisputed national pastime, couldn't be played this way: A tie game in the ninth proceeds with essentially the same tempo as any other inning. In the fourth-quarter hurry-up comeback, football had come upon something fascinating—a better version of itself. Yet nearly three decades would pass before a team and a coach would ask why that intensive pace had never been employed over the course of an entire game.

Cincinnati, 1984

THE GAME'S spider web of innovation reaches to all corners of the country, yet it seems that a distinctly disproportionate amount of football genius has lived and worked in this Midwestern city. It was here in 1970 that Bill Walsh invented the West Coast offense. It was here in '83 that LeBeau first tinkered with the defensive pressure packages that would come to be known as the zone blitz. It was here in '86 that Jim McNally (who, in geographical fairness, borrowed from the experiments of Howard Mudd not far away in Cleveland) became one of the first professional coaches to fully commit to a zone blocking scheme.

And it was here, in 1984, that a quirky coach named Sam Wyche became the first NFL coach—and most assuredly one of the first at any level of the game—to transform the two-minute drill into the 60-minute drill. Or, as Wyche puts it demurely, "We did everything on offense that we had always done. We just gave up the privacy of the huddle and let the defense listen in."

(A footnote: Use of the huddle dates to the earliest days of football, but the implementation of organized, every-play huddling is widely credited to H.W. (Bill) Hargiss at Oregon State in 1918. Interestingly, in his '27 coaching manual, Pop Warner referenced not only the huddle but also the no-huddle, writing, "If the huddle system is not used, the field general should give his signals in such a tone of voice and in such a manner that they will be easily heard and understood.")

Wyche was raised in Atlanta, the older brother of Bubba Wyche. Bubba was a brilliant athlete who once struck out every opposing batter in a Little League game, won All-State honors in three high school sports and went on to play quarterback at Tennessee. That wasn't Sam. "I was just a guy on the club," he told SPORTS ILLUSTRATED in 1989. "A worker, a classic overachiever." Sam never started a high school football game but walked on at Furman and became the starting quarterback as a sophomore. In '68 he networked his way onto the Bengals' taxi squad and spent seven years in the NFL with four teams, starting just nine games.

After Wyche retired as a player, the first coach to hire him as an assistant was Walsh, in 1979 with the 49ers. (Walsh had been Wyche's quarterback coach a decade earlier in Cincinnati.) Wyche aided in the refinement of the West Coast offense, then in the hands of Joe Montana. Before the '84 season, he was hired to replace Forrest Gregg as the Bengals' head coach.

Wyche would spend a dozen seasons as a head coach in the NFL, eight with the Bengals (including a Super Bowl appearance in 1988) and four with the Tampa Bay Buccaneers. He would lose more games (107) than he would win (84) and would be better known for veering from conventional sideline behavior than for his record. Example: During a Bengals home game near the end of the '89 season, the Cincinnati fans grew upset with the game officials and began heaving snowballs onto the field. Wyche, irate, found a microphone and chastised them over the public-address system by saying, "You don't live in Cleveland; you live in Cincinnati."

Wyche was a truly different sort of coach. While so many football coaches fit into a box—do it this way, do it that way, do it my way—Wyche had no box. He probably wouldn't acknowledge a box's existence.

From a strategic perspective, nothing Wyche did was further from the norm than his decision in 1984—his first as head coach—to attempt running a no-huddle offense for an entire game. It was something that Wyche had thought about for years. He had once discussed with it Hank Stram, who had been the innovative coach of the Kansas City Chiefs in the '60s and '70s. "Neither one of us could figure out why nobody had tried it," says Wyche. "That really motivated me to use it someday."

Wyche had never believed in obedience to historical practices. He liked to try different things. He had watched Walsh substitute the short passing game for running the ball, he had watched Montana—who was of average size and didn't have a powerful arm—control the game, and he concluded that you could beat opponents with your mind. "You can't go into every game saying, 'We'll just damn well outplay you,'" Wyche told SI in '89. "You're looking for the two-percent edge, the surprise of a safety blitz, the surprise of having fourth-and-12 on your own 25 and going for it. These things are *sound*. They work."

For Wyche, the basic idea of the no-huddle, which was installed with the help of offensive coordinator (and former teammate) Bruce Coslet, was to turn what is often a desperate circumstance—the two-minute offense—into an aggressive one. "A big part of the thinking behind the no-huddle," says Wyche, "was saying to your opponent, 'We're going to take away your normal recovery time. By the end of the game, you're going to be too tired to compete.' Teams couldn't fully prepare to play us in a week, because they couldn't re-create the tempo we were using."

It was, ultimately, an all-or-nothing proposition. In Wyche's mind there would ideally be no occasional use of the huddle. Wyche and Coslet reworked the entire playbook to be run in no-huddle fashion. But the process of reaching that goal would take two full seasons to shake itself out. In the first year the starting quarterback was 14-year veteran Ken Anderson, who had taken the Bengals to the Super Bowl after the 1981 season. But in '84 the Bengals opened the season with five consecutive losses. Wyche decided to take a shot with a rookie.

Norman Julius (Boomer) Esiason had been the first quarterback selected in the 1984 NFL draft, a 6' 4", 210-pound lefthander who had thrown for more than 6,000 yards in three years as the starter at Maryland. He was taken in the second round with the 38th overall pick (in stark contrast to the draft a year earlier when six quarterbacks were selected in the first 27 picks, three of whom—John Elway, Jim Kelly and Dan Marino—are now in the Hall of Fame).

But Wyche and the Bengals were thrilled to get Esiason, who was accurate and cerebral. Esiason was given a start on Oct. 7, and the Bengals finally got a win, 13–3 over the Houston Oilers. Esiason would start three more games that season, which the Bengals finished at 8–8. He would become the full-time starter early in the '85 campaign and almost immediately clicked with the no-huddle. "My rookie year, I had to figure out what the hell I was doing as an NFL quarterback," says Esiason, "so Sam couldn't fully commit to the no-huddle with me. In the next year, when I was the starter, we did a lot more of it, and then in '86 we went to it from the first day of training camp. And I'll tell you what: I loved every minute of it."

The Bengals' no-huddle was designed to do more than just take a defense out of its rhythm. Most important, it made it very difficult for defenses to use situational substitutions, whether simple packages like a nickel defense or more complex arrangements. The Bengals would run players onto the field so quickly that it was almost impossible for a defense to identify the Bengals' personnel and counter with the appropriate bodies. Opponents were often forced to play with whatever people they had on the field, leaving linebackers to cover wideouts or safeties to play in run support.

The mid- and late-'80s Bengals were a collection of exceptionally bright players, including Hall of Fame left tackle Anthony Muñoz and future broadcaster Cris Collinsworth. But the heaviest intellectual load, by far, fell on Esiason. "What Sam and Bruce demanded of me was that I know every formation and every personnel group and which plays would work with which personnel groups and which formations. I had to be extremely well-prepared to do all of this at the line of scrimmage."

Each play was literally a fresh start, without a huddle. Esiason explains the sequence:

As soon as the previous play ended, Sam would send the next personnel group onto the field, and then he would signal to me with one hand to let me know what the personnel group was that was coming into the game. Then he would signal me with one hand for the play.

Say he gives me "regular" personnel: halfback, fullback, tight end, two wide receivers, and we're running a play called 28 Grace, which is the halfback to the strong side. He would give me a hand signal for the play. I would have to know which formations we could use for that play—pro right, far double wing right, hum short, trips right—and then I would choose the formation I wanted to run and communicate that to everybody on the field. This would all happen in the first five seconds after the referee spots the ball.

So then I yell, "Regular! Regular! Regular!" That's so the people who are not in the regular personnel group know to get off the field. Then I would yell the formation. Next was the play. In a huddle I would have said, "28 Grace," but even though defensive players are stupid, almost anybody who has ever played football knows that even numbers mean a run to the right. So we needed code words.

Our code words for the "2" back were Raider, Oakland and Millen, because Matt Millen was playing for the Raiders at the time. Then I had to call right. Our right words were Denver, Trigger and Orange. Our left words were Dallas, Bullet and Black. The blocking scheme was Grace, so I could just say Grace or sometimes I would say Bible or Jesus.

So we're getting lined up, and I would say, "Hum Raider Denver Bible!" Then I would throw out a dummy call, like "399 Fly," that meant absolutely nothing. Then the snap count, which was also words. That was back when Bo Jackson was doing all those Nike commercials, so our code was A (snap on one hut) Bo (snap on two) Can (three) Do It (four). So I'm yelling, "Hum Raider Denver Bible! 399 Fly! Do It Do It Do It! Hut Hut Hut Hut!"

ESIASON NOT only had to communicate all of this, he had to do it while reading the defense and quickly contemplating an audible. There were shortcuts. If a running back was uncertain of the play call, Esiason could quickly turn around and simply tell him the play, because his back was to the defense. "The whole exercise was football at such a high intellectual level," says Esiason. "Every week was a final exam. But the thing it did best was create indecision in the defense. And any indecision on their side of the ball was to our advantage."

In 1986 the Bengals went 10–6, and Esiason passed for 3,959 yards, a team record that stood until 2006, when Carson Palmer went over 4,000. But a year later, in the strike-interrupted '87 season, the Bengals stumbled backward to a 4–11 season (1–2 in replacement games), and Wyche's no-huddle came under intense heat. Local media called him Wicky Wacky Wyche; and worse, they called for his head.

One year later, however, everything clicked. Esiason ran the no-huddle beautifully, and McNally's zone blocking scheme turned Ickey Woods, James Brooks and Stanley Wilson loose in the run game. The Bengals opened with six consecutive wins, finished 12–4 in the regular season and went to Super Bowl XXIII in Miami, losing 20–16 to Walsh's Niners on Montana's touchdown pass to John Taylor with 34 seconds left.

The season validated Wyche's madness, and it also spawned an unlikely imitator in an unlikely fashion. During the 1988 season Buffalo Bills coach Marv Levy accused the Bengals of skirting the "spirit" of the rules of football in their use—or nonuse—of the huddle. Most specifically, Levy pointed to the Bengals' habit of keeping 12 or 13 players on the field as Esiason began calling plays. The Bengals argued that there were more than 11 players on the field because they were exchanging personnel—some leaving the field, some entering the field; and what's more, NFL rules only prohibit more than 11 players in the *huddle*.

The issue came to a head on Jan. 8, 1989, when the Bengals played the Bills in the AFC Championship Game at Riverfront Stadium in Cincinnati. According to Wyche, a representative of NFL commissioner Pete Rozelle, who would retire 11 months later, was sent to the Bengals' locker room. Wyche picks up the story:

"The commissioner sent a league representative into my office one hour and 55 minutes before kickoff. [Bengals assistant G.M./legal counsel] Mike Brown was with me, and we tape-recorded the entire conversation. The guy tells us Marv Levy is planning to have his players fake injuries to counteract our no-huddle. The commissioner is worried that this will make a farce of the game and maybe we shouldn't run the no-huddle offense. So I told this guy, 'You go back and tell Pete Rozelle that he's tampering with the competitive balance of the AFC Championship Game less than two hours before kickoff. How are you going to explain that to all the bookies and gamblers who bet on this game?' The guy walked out of the room, came back in 30 seconds and said, 'You can run the no-huddle.' "

As it turned out, the Bengals, as a matter of strategy, ran fewer no-huddle snaps than normal but still won the game.

The bizarre conclusion to this episode unfolded a season later, when Levy, offensive coordinator Ted Marchibroda and quarterback Jim Kelly installed their own version of the no-huddle offense with Kelly operating from the shotgun. Appropriately, it was called the K-Gun. Marchibroda installed the K-Gun in training camp but used it only sparingly in the regular season. It became the Bills' go-to offense only on Jan. 6, 1990, in a 34–30 divisional playoff loss to the Cleveland Browns. Kelly ran almost exclusively from the no-huddle and threw 54 passes, completing 28 for four touchdowns. It was the birth of an offense that the Bills would ride to four consecutive Super Bowls, from '90 through '93.

It was also a sweet match of quarterback and system. Kelly had been a high school star in Pennsylvania and the first in what would become a line of accomplished quarterbacks at the University of Miami in the 1980s. But it was not until Kelly joined the renegade United States Football League in the fall of '83 that he really matured as a quarterback. He first played with the Houston Gamblers, whose offensive coordinator was run-and-shoot offense impresario Mouse Davis. Davis quickened Kelly's release and taught him how to read defenses on the fly. All of these would be vital skills in the K-Gun.

"We were always pretty good in the no-huddle at the end of games," Kelly recalls in the summer of 2009. "And we were pretty good going into half-time. Ted and Marv both decided it made sense to try it for a whole game."

There was a fundamental difference between the Bengals' no-huddle and the K-Gun: Esiason did not call plays; Kelly did (and is regarded as the last pro quarterback to truly call all of his own plays—as opposed to simply choosing from among a small number of plays at the line of scrimmage). In the K-Gun, the Bills streamlined their offense each week down to 20 plays, and sometimes fewer than that.

"We probably had a total of 35 or 40 plays in the playbook," says Kelly. "We would narrow that down every week. We used different formations, but it was always three wide receivers, one tight end, one running back [who happened to be the great Thurman Thomas].

"For me," Kelly continues, "it was all about quickness and feel. Everything had to be so quick. As soon as a guy gets tackled, you're thinking about the down and distance and field position and you've got to call that next play. Then you call the protection. Then you look at the defense and see if they're in man or zone." There were certain keys to simplify Kelly's job at the line: If the defense had seven men in the box, he would give the ball to Thomas and run it. If there were eight in the box (an extra safety dropped down in run support), he would get man-to-man coverage and throw it, often to Andre Reed.

Like the Bengals who preceded them in the no-huddle, the Bills had smart players. Reed was a clever, intuitive wide receiver. Center Kent Hull read defenses as skillfully as Kelly. "Kent did all the line calls," says Kelly.

"There were a lot of times when I would call a running play and Kent would just yell, 'Get out of it!' And I would get out of it."

Kelly recalls that, again like the Bengals, the Bills had code words for plays, formations and snap counts. For instance, a snap count of "on three" was "Louisville," because left tackle Will Wolford wore number 73 early in his career and was born and raised in Louisville, Ky. Occasionally a player would be traded and take his knowledge of the Bills' signals with him. Fred Smerlas played with the Bills in 1989 but later played against them as a New England Patriot. "Freddy knew our signals," says Kelly. "So on the sideline I told the offense, we're calling on two, so I'm going to call 'Noah!' " (That was the Bills signal for 'on two' because Noah had two of each kind of animal on the ark; in this case, though, it was a dummy call.) "I told everybody, 'Watch Freddy jump.' Sure enough on the second hut, Freddy ran across the line and was standing right next to Thurman."

The effect of the K-Gun on defenses was palpable. "It wore them out," says Kelly. "The pass rush would diminish as the game went on. And they couldn't disguise coverages because they couldn't substitute. They had to show what coverage they were in. Defenses hate that. I was really fortunate as a quarterback that Marv Levy and Ted Marchibroda let me run this offense."

History records that the Bills lost four consecutive Super Bowls, the last three by a combined 65 points. But it's unfair to dismiss the 49 regular-season victories and four AFC titles earned with the no-huddle. "There was this feeling," says Kelly. "You just knew what plays were going to work, and you didn't have to think. It just came to me and we went right down the field. It was a pretty special time."

IN THE summer of 2009, 64-year-old Sam Wyche is raking rocks off a practice football field in Pickens, S.C. (pop. 3,026), where he lives, coaches high school football and contemplates changing the world. He won a seat on the Pickens City Council with 80% of the vote, and on this day, he is considering a run for the U.S. House of Representatives. "There are some people who want me to do it," he says. But he's hesitant. "The people up there in Washington," says Wyche, "I'm not sure I'd have the patience to work in that system."

Perhaps not. Patience was clearly not a facet of his no-huddle system. But risk most certainly was, and risk is the chief reason why no NFL teams since Wyche's Bengals and Kelly's Bills have installed a full-on no-huddle offense, and why no NFL coach is letting his quarterback call all his own plays. Clearly the increasing complexity of the modern game makes it a huge gamble to entrust an entire playbook to a quarterback at the line of scrimmage.

The closest relative of the no-huddle in use during the 2009 season was the Peyton Manning machine in Indianapolis. But even that was not a no-huddle in the purest sense, because it makes no attempt at increasing the tempo of the game. The Colts' entire offense loiters near the line of scrimmage while Manning receives play calls—at least three options on every play—from offensive coordinator Tom Moore. Wyche calls this arrangement a sugar huddle, "because it's short and sweet."

The Colts' version brings Manning nearer to Esiason than to Kelly because he is running plays relayed from the sideline (albeit to his helmet by transmitter, not with hand signals), and although he has the option to change a run to a pass or a pass to a run and adjust routes on the fly, he is not actually calling the plays. Nor is he hurrying to exhaust the defense.

Those concepts are gone for now, reduced to museum pieces, awaiting the next coach who will roll the dice and bet his livelihood that his quarterback can be Unitas for 60 minutes.

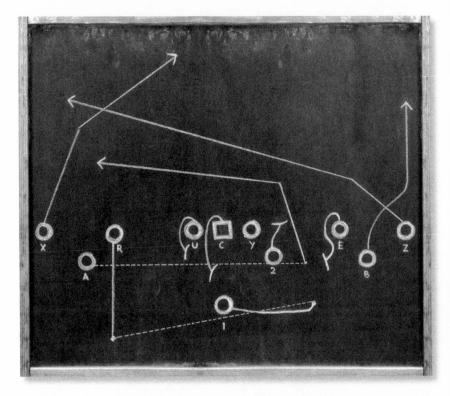

BASE (A) ZOOM 18 CIRCUS

Daring even by the edgy standards of the radical A-11 offense, the Circus play begins with a shotgun snap to the quarterback, who rolls right and sets up at the right hash mark. An ineligible receiver (R, a reserve quarterback wearing a "legal" lineman number, like 74) runs into the backfield and takes a backward pass—by the rules a lateral—from the QB. The four receivers work various routes downfield, including a "zoom motion" shallow cross by the A receiver. The "new" quarterback delivers the pass to any one of them depending on coverage. If the play is run properly, the defense is likely not only to chase the rollout (the original QB) but also to ignore the "ineligible" quarterback until it's too late.

CHAPTER 22

A-11 AND BEYOND

When two California high school coaches found a loophole in the rule book, they may have seen the future

San Francisco, Calif.
January 2007

THEY WERE in the long limbo between high school football seasons when Kurt Bryan and Steve Humphries met at Humphries' apartment to begin planning the 2007 campaign for Piedmont High, located in the East Bay hills outside Oakland. It would prove to be a fateful evening.

Bryan, then 42, was starting the second year of his second tour as head coach at his alma mater. Humphries, another Piedmont alumnus, whose father, Michael, had been the Highlanders' freshman coach for decades, was the director of football operations, in his third year on the staff.

Like so many high school coaches, they shared a passion for a job they perform tirelessly over long hours and for minimal pay. Bryan had played at Piedmont in the early '80s, was named offensive coordinator there in 1987 at age 23 and head coach six seasons later. He does more than coach football; he's a full-time insurance salesman and a novelist who has written two football-themed suspense books.

Humphries's route was different—he was a receiver and safety at Piedmont, played rugby at Cal, then went first into baseball coaching—but it landed him back in the game of football at Piedmont. "Sometimes," he says, "it takes a little while to realize what you love."

That doesn't make the job easy. In 2006, Bryan's first season back on the sideline at Piedmont, the Highlanders went 5–5. They played conventional football, trying to win physical battles along the line of scrimmage, establish a running game and tackle well on the other side. But Piedmont happens to be one of the smaller schools in its conference, and that means its players are smaller too. Most are less than 200 pounds. In the first round of the playoffs, the Highlanders played Miramonte High, a bigger school from nearby Orinda. Piedmont played well but lost 13–6. That's not what Bryan remembers about the game.

"It was a brutally physical game," recalls Bryan. "We actually played pretty well, but we just didn't hold up, physically. We'd spent a lot of time working that game out on paper. We had stuff that should have worked if we executed. But when it came time to play the game, we just couldn't do it. We weren't big enough or strong enough. That was very frustrating to me, and I felt bad for our players."

His story is as old as the game itself. In the end, many football games—especially at the high school level, where most of the football in America is played—come down to pure physical superiority.

Take running backs, for example. Says New England Patriots coach Bill Belichick, "At the lower levels of the game, in high school and sometimes even in college, the best running backs are just faster than everybody else. They get to the outside, and then they outrun everybody to the goal." But the same simple formula applies across all positions. A faster defensive end will beat an offensive tackle to the edge. A huge offensive guard will overwhelm a smaller defensive lineman. And so on.

At the core, every offensive and defensive system ever created was devised for one of two reasons: To *enable* a physical mismatch to take place or to *avoid* being on the wrong end of a physical mismatch. Put another way: In football, if you are the windshield, you seek out the bug. If you are the bug, you try to avoid the windshield.

Bryan felt like the bug. "I went to Steve's apartment one of those nights," he says, "and we had books and tapes and whiteboards out. At one point Steve said to me, 'I want to show you something.' He had this Emory and Henry–type formation."

(A brief explanation: When Steve Spurrier was coaching a highly successful Florida program in the mid- and late-'90s, he occasionally ran plays from a bizarre formation with only three interior linemen and two sets of three wideouts, not all of whom were eligible receivers. Spurrier called the formation Emory & Henry, for a small liberal arts college in southwestern Virginia that had used the formation when he was growing up in Johnson City, Tenn.)

The Emory & Henry look fascinated Bryan. "A lot of teams have 'light' formations of some sort," Bryan said. "The Emory and Henry is a light formation with a lot of vertical passing routes. But I was wondering if there might be something more we could do with it. I scoured the rule book for about two days nonstop." And then he found something.

"Kurt put the book in front of me and said, 'Look at this,'" says Humphries. "I give him full credit. He found it."

What Bryan found inside the national high school rule book was the exception to the scrimmage kick definition, intended for punts, which stipulates that if the player taking the snap from center is at least seven yards behind the line of scrimmage (slightly farther than a conventional shotgun snap), then the usual uniform-number rules do not apply (i.e., the rule that at least five players must wear "lineman numbers" 50 through 79).

Thus, Bryan realized, as long as the quarterback sets up in a deep shotgun, a team could legally break the huddle with 11 players wearing uniform numbers which allowed them to line up as eligible receivers. Once lined up, some players would be rendered ineligible by formation, but until the formation was set, any offensive player on the field represented an eligible pass receiver.

While the rule was clearly written for the punting game, Bryan envisioned something else altogether—a scrimmage scheme in which every player in the huddle was an offensive threat and the entire field was in play. The confusion it would obviously create for the defense was tantalizing.

"Pretty unique idea," says Humphries.

The two coaches decided that night to implement the offense, which they would call the A-11, because "all 11" players are potentially eligible. Its root concept was not out of line with current trends at other levels of football—spread offenses were overtaking the college game and evolved passing games and offense-friendly rules changes (the five-yard no-chuck rule, among others) were altering the NFL. For Bryan and Humphries, the operative word was *space*, and they were taking that concept to its extreme.

They conceived a playbook in which the base formation was Emory & Henry—a center flanked by two "guards," a quarterback in shotgun with a running back nearby and two "bunches" of three wide receivers on each side of the field. All 11 of these players wore the jersey numbers of eligible receivers, meaning, again, that when they broke the huddle any of them could legally catch a pass.

Football rules, however, mandate that even in "scrimmage kick formation," seven players must be on the line of scrimmage when the ball is snapped, with four players in the backfield. Of the seven on the line, only the two on the outside (the "ends") are eligible to run downfield and receive a pass, along with three of the four backs, excluding the passer.

Yet, because the A-11 breaks the huddle with 11 potential receivers and relies on last-second shifts before revealing the final alignment of the formation, the defense is challenged to quickly identify the eligible receivers on any given play. The offense was instantly successful; Piedmont went 7–4 in 2007 and 8–3 in 2008. Defenses were predictably befuddled, and Piedmont piled up points.

More surprising were two other developments. According to Humphries, despite their offense having the appearance of Ultimate Frisbee, Piedmont had a nearly 50-50 split between the run and the pass. Much like the one-back spread offense from the 1980s, the spread A-11 opened up massive running lanes for ballcarriers.

Secondly, says Humphries, "we had hardly any injuries." Intuitively, this would seem to owe to a reduction of fierce interior line battles. However, the offense also leads to more open-field tackles, and open-field tackling produces high-speed collisions. Despite the paradox, the evidence of fewer injuries in the A-11 made the offense worthy of consideration at a time when football is racked by injury concerns, particularly head trauma.

Instead, the offense was nearly killed.

Indianapolis, Ind.
February 2009

PIEDMONT'S A-11 generated intense interest. *The New York Times* and ESPN were among the many media outlets that seized upon its quirky genius and made countercultural football celebrities out of Bryan and

Humphries. *Scientific American*, in a relentlessly quoted article, calculated that the A-11 had 16,632 possible postsnap play possibilities, whereas conventional formations had only 36.

On a rainy fall Saturday at the time, a Connecticut high school coach named Deron Bayer, whose team was running the single wing, pulled a writer aside and began sketching the A-11. "This is the next thing," he said, almost conspiratorially. "We might use it next year. All our big guys are graduating."

Hundreds of other high school coaches were thinking the same thing. Bryan and Humphries said they had to change their cellphone numbers because so many coaches were calling, seeking holy water for their programs. But there was another side to the story. As much cheerleading as there was for the novel attack, there was also vehement criticism.

The college football rule offered only a more restrictive scrimmage kick option and the NFL has no such rule. Since there was no obvious A-11 loophole to exploit at those levels, detractors said that this renegade offense had no place in the higher strata of football. The Piedmont geniuses were accused of corrupting the spirit of the game by contorting what is clearly designed as an old punt rule to enable more players to run down the field in passing routes as an every-down offense.

Technically, the critics were right: That's exactly what Bryan and Humphries were doing. But that doesn't mean it wasn't good for football to be exposed to such radical thinking. After all, if Pop Warner hadn't thought up the single wing, football might have died before 1910, the victim of too much violence.

However, the National Federation of State High School Associations, the organization responsible for the rule book, didn't see it that way. In February 2009, the NFHS changed the scrimmage kick formation rule, mandating that only the center—the long snapper—could wear an eligible jersey number (though, at the center position, he would be ineligible), while the other four interior linemen must wear jersey numbers from 50 to 79. Word rippled through the football world: THE A-11 IS DEAD.

But not to Bryan and Humphries. "All [the Federation] did," says Bryan, "is make it so that you can't throw a forward pass to those guys. But those guys can still throw a pass. They can still take a handoff. They can receive a pass thrown *backward*." So for the 2009 season the two men got even more crafty. "And the offense, if anything," says Humphries, "got even more deadly."

So, undaunted, the two coaches created a new term: anchors. In their new version of the A-11, the anchors are the "linemen" assigned to wear jersey numbers from 50 to 79. But they are not linemen in the traditional sense. Often they are hybrid athletes capable of playing several positions.

On Sept. 8, *Oakland Tribune* columnist Carl Steward covered the first Piedmont game of what was supposed to be the post-A-11 era and wrote the following sentence with considerable wonder: "On the Highlanders' second play of the 2009 season Friday night against Drake of San Anselmo, a Piedmont player wearing No. 77, George Fullerton, took an end-around from quarterback Cormac Craigie for a seven-yard gain, out of a Statue of Liberty handoff."

Bryan explains: "Just think about it. Just because a guy is wearing number 68, doesn't mean he can't be a fast, explosive player. Think of a 4.4 [40-yard dash] guy in that anchor position, who can receive a lateral." Under the new rules, Bryan and Humphries could no longer present to the defense 11 potential receivers coming out of the huddle. But they would continue to move players into positions and roles not normally associated with their jersey numbers. And they would still use myriad formations and shifts. "This year I think we had 331 different formations," says Humphries. "Before the rule changed, we had 232. All it did was push us to be more creative and push out even more new formations."

The offense began to seep into other levels of football. As it turned out, the college rule book does, in effect, allow an A-11-type offense when "it is obvious that a kick may be attempted." In the 2009 season Boise State, which would finish 14–0, twice ran plays from an A-11 formation. On an NFL Monday-night game in December '09, the Washington Redskins lined up with just a snapper and a nearby flanker in the middle of the field on an apparent field goal attempt in a game against the New York Giants. The play led only to an ugly interception, but A-11 devotees across the country jumped from their seats.

Traditionalists laughed, of course. Football is forever in a state of dynamic tension, staunchly resisting change while desperately demanding it. Every innovation in the history of the game carried risk, challenged norms and put the creators' jobs at stake. Darrell Royal and Emory Bellard would have been laughed out of Austin if their funky wishbone hadn't worked. But it did. Bill Walsh would never have become the revered coach of the champion 49ers if that weird offense of his hadn't panned out in Cincinnati. But it did.

As you read these words, some sleep-deprived coach in some window-less room is doodling on a whiteboard or pushing his computer mouse, trying to come up with something that's never been tried. Some coach is on the verge of losing his job, desperate enough to try something crazy. Some coach has just looked at his roster and realized he can't win in the ordinary way with what he's got. One of these coaches will conjure a vi-sion and take the leap. And the game of football will change again.

ACKNOWLEDGMENTS

IN THE fall of 2006 Mark Mravic, the senior editor who handles the NFL for SPORTS ILLUSTRATED, suggested we write a piece on the ubiquitous Cover Two (or Tampa Two) defense. I got the assignment. The story appeared in the Nov. 27, 2006, issue of SI, under Mravic's headline, *Two Tough*. It was a good story. People seemed to like having America's most popular game explained to them in terms they could understand. Besides looking at the mechanics of the Cover Two, I had also tried to explore its lineage: Who started it? Who popularized it? Why did they do it? What were the stories behind those coaches? People liked that, too.

Not long after the story appeared, I received an e-mail from Jud Laghi, a literary agent in New York. Jud thought maybe the story could be the foundation for a book. The idea was instantly appealing to me, and we went from there. Mravic to Laghi to Layden. That's the creative chain.

The process took more than two years from first phone call to last keystroke. I interviewed 145 people, but that number does not tell all, because in a very real sense the book was informed by every coach or player I've come across since I first picked up a football in upstate New York.

Dozens of people helped in the completion of this book, including many at SPORTS ILLUSTRATED, where I've worked for the last 16 years. That list starts with Terry McDonell, Editor of the Sports Illustrated Group, who supported the project and gave me the time I needed to finish it. Executive editor Mike Bevans has been a friend and confidant since he helped hire me at *Newsday* 22 years ago; he offered comforting advice when I was ready to panic. David Bauer was the book's editor, and there is nobody better. He was ably assisted at all times by Stefanie Kaufman, who kept the project on the rails and tolerated my long silent periods. Kelvin Bias and Elizabeth McGarr doggedly fact-checked the manuscript, saving me from myself. Jill Jaroff and Kevin Kerr painstakingly copyedited every sentence. Designer Stephen Skalocky turned my crude X and O drawings into chalkboard illustrations and Chris Hercik created the cover. Others just listened to my nonsense and sometimes gave it back, most notably Mark Bechtel, Steve Cannella and Mark Beech, but also others to whom I apologize in advance for absentmindedly leaving out.

SI librarians Joy Birdsong and Natasha Simon helped with research early in the project, when there was no light, only a tunnel. Peter King, truly the king of all modern-day NFL writers, a media machine if ever there was one, was always ready with a phone number or an e-mail when I needed it, which was often. He is the man.

Over the course of the last 56 years SI has done towering work on the sport of football, often revealing teams, coaches or players to the public for the first time. Many of the stories are quoted here, and many others were read and cataloged. The work of Paul (Dr. Z) Zimmerman is particularly noteworthy. In the last decade Z has become known for his hard-core football analysis and pithy SI.com columns. But for nearly two decades Zimmerman turned out a stream of long, thoughtful pieces on some of the central figures in the game. I read most of them when I was younger and reread many of them in the last two years.

My good friend Kenny Moore, known to so many as the best chronicler of track and field and distance running the sport has ever known, wrote terrific SI pieces on the great Bill Walsh, and on Mouse Davis and Sam Wyche, as well. I borrowed from all three stories and am thrilled to credit Kenny accordingly. Rick Telander's 1982 SI story on single wing coach Keith Piper at Denison University was also very helpful.

The conceit of this book is that across the history of football, certain men were moved by some flicker of inspiration to change the game. But some of them lived at the vortex of multiple changes. Hence, I leaned heavily on my interviews with the remarkable Don Coryell; with Anthony Muñoz, who was arguably the best offensive lineman in history, but also a central part of three different revolutionary offensive systems; and Bill Yeoman, the legendary University of Houston coach.

Just as important to me were several books. Glenn Scobey (Pop) Warner's *Football for Coaches & Players*, written in 1927, provides eloquent evidence of Warner's genius in turning the game away from the mass-momentum scrum of the late 19th century. It's not an easy read, but any football fan should make the effort.

Former TCU coach L.R. (Dutch) Meyer's *Spread Formation Football*, written in 1952, clearly influenced the generation of coaches that followed by teaching them to use the entire breadth of the field. Glenn (Tiger) Ellison's *Run and Shoot Football: Offense of the Future*, published in 1965, reveals the primal roots of the modern wide-open passing game. Ellison is without question one of the great minds in the history of the game but is little known and underappreciated. (A valuable aid to my work was a deeply personal biography of Tiger Ellison written in 2007 by his oldest daughter, Carolyn J. Ellison, revealing not just a remarkable football coach, but an educator of extraordinary principle and reach.)

Building a Champion, written by Bill Walsh with Glenn Dickey in 1990, is an engaging story of the West Coast offense and the 49ers dynasty. It was an indispensable road map through interviews with several coaches who learned under Walsh. And I was honored to borrow from the incomparable George Plimpton's *Paper Lion*.

On a fall day in 2008 I returned to my alma mater, Williams College in Williamstown, Mass., where retired football coach Dick Farley, an old and good friend, sat me down in his office and taught me some football. He drew formations, filled, then erased, then filled again a whiteboard, and at the end of our session showed me how he used to jam Lance Alworth at the line of scrimmage when Dick played for the San Diego Chargers in the mid-1960s. As a coach, Dick went 114-19-3 (.849) in 17 years at Williams before retiring in 2003, and many, many players will never forget him. It's easy to understand why.

In the same fall Dennis Daly gave me a similar tutorial at Westminster School in Connecticut, and it was so helpful that I'll forgive him for having graduated from Amherst.

It would have been impossible to reach many of the primary sources interviewed for this work if not for the assistance of numerous college sports information directors and NFL team media-relations officials.

College contacts included: John Bianco and Bill Little (Texas), Wade Branner (Virginia Military Institute), Dean Buchan (Georgia Tech), Mark Brand (Arizona State), Art Chase (Duke), Mark Cohen (TCU), Chris Cook (Texas Tech), Tina Dechausay (Florida State), Steve Fink (South

Carolina), Troy Garnhart (Air Force), Mike Lund (Portland State), Steve McClain (Florida), Kenny Mossman (Oklahoma), Brett Pyne (Brigham Young), Greg Remington (New Mexico) Kyle Robarts (McMurry University), Craig Sachson (Princeton), Scott Selheimer (Delaware), Tim Tessalone (USC), Don Tomkalski (Tulsa), Tom Schott (Purdue) and Shelley Poe (at Ohio State).

NFL help was provided by Jack Brennan (Bengals), Zack Bolno (Redskins), Derek Boyko (Eagles), Jim Christman (Bears), Rich Dalrymple (Cowboys), Mark Dalton (Cardinals), Harvey Greene (Dolphins), Stacey James and Berj Najarian (Patriots), Bill Johnston (Chargers), Jeff Kamis (Buccaneers), Craig Kelley (Colts), Burt Lauten and Dave Lockett (Steelers), Pete Moris (Chiefs), Rick Smith (Rams), Chad Steele and Patrick Gleason (Ravens), Bruce Speight (Jets) and Dave Pearson (Seahawks).

Early on, Greg Cosell of NFL Films sat down and took me through film of the Cover Two. Bill Hofheimer of ESPN helped get me together with Jon Gruden, who can also sling some serious football knowledge in a short time and leave any civilian struggling to keep up.

The list of players and coaches interviewed is a long one, and I found that almost all of them embraced the opportunity to talk about what they actually do for a living. I called on the following, some for lengthy interviews, some for quick thoughts along the way and still others long before the book began but whose insight was included in some way:

Ken Anderson, Bill Arnsparger, Zack Asack, Deron Bayer, Emory Bellard, Bill Belichick, Brian Billick, Mark Bliss, Robbie Bosco, Bill Bradley, Drew Brees, Kurt Bryan, Bobby Bowden, Joe Bugel, Jermon Bushrod, Cam Cameron, Dom Capers, Pete Carroll, Virgil Carter, Bruce Coslet, David Cutcliffe, Greg Davis, Greg Darlington, Fisher DeBerry, Paul Dietzel, Jed Drenning, Tony Dungy, Joe Lee Dunn, Dennis Erickson, Boomer Esiason, Jim Fassel, Gary Fencik, Dan Fouts, Chan Gailey, Jeremy Gallon, Rich Gannon, Jason Garrett, Joe Gibbs, Todd Graham, Trent Green, Rex Grossman, Jim Hanifan, Dan Henning, Mike Holmgren, Lou Holtz, Paul Hornung, Steve Humphries, Cosmo Iacovazzi, Paul Johnson, Charlie Joiner, Jim Kelly, Will Kennedy, Monte Kiffin, Shaun King, Ron Kramer, Mike Leach, Ryan Leaf, Dick LeBeau, Thaddeus Lewis, Scott Linehan, Mike Lude, John Lynch, Gus Malzahn, Archie Manning and Peyton Manning.

Also: Mike Martz, Jim McNally, Urban Meyer, Quintin Mikell, Rick

Minter, Howard Mudd, Hal Mumme, Will Muschamp, Jerious Norwood, Tom Osborne, Gary Patterson, Chad Pennington, Doug Plank, Dana Potter, Ed Racely, Tubby Raymond, Andy Reid, John Robinson, Rich Rodriguez, Kurt Roper, Darrell Royal, Buddy Ryan, Doris Ryan, Rex Ryan, George Rykovich, Bart Scott, Lovie Smith, Bill Snyder, Steve Spagnuolo, Steve Spurrier, Jon Stinchcomb, Bob Stoops, James Street, Darrell Stroh, Barry Switzer, Joe Tiller, Charles Tillman, Bill Tobin, Jeremiah Trotter, Justin Tuck, Norv Turner, Brian Urlacher, Mike Wagner, Kurt Warner, Pat White, Woody Widenhofer, Hugh Wyatt, Sam Wyche, Charle Young, Vince Young and Ernie Zampese.

Three of the men who are vital to this book have passed away. I interviewed Jack Neumeier in 1997 about his revolutionary one-back spread offense (designed for John Elway in high school); he died in 2004. I met Max McGee in 2002 while writing about Paul Hornung; Max died five years later. Doug Scovil died in 1989, but his ideas still influence offensive passing systems; his name came up in dozens of my interviews.

My brother, Joe, friend and writer, was just always there.

Most of all, my wife, Janet, tolerated my immersion in this project with uncommon patience, whether by biting her tongue when I shuffled back up the stairs to my office after having already spent the entire day there or by driving on the New York State Thruway to a college cross-country meet while I transcribed notes in the backseat. Our children, Kristen (the other Eph in the family) and Kevin (a Rochester Yellowjacket) kept wondering when the book would be done. Well, it's done now.

Tim Layden
Simsbury, Conn.
May 2010